D0674324

The Rise of Civilization

The Making of the Past

The Rise of Civilization

by David and Joan Oates

Series Editor Graham Speake
Managing Editor Giles Lewis
Picture Editor Andrew Lawson
Design Richard Brookes, Keith Russell
Visual Aids Roger Gorringe, Dick Barnard
Production John Sanders

Frontispiece: human skull with plastered features, the finest example of a group of seven found at Jericho, Pre-Pottery Neolithic B, seventh millennium BC (Amman).

ISBN 0 7290 0015 X

Elsevier–Phaidon, an imprint of Phaidon Press Ltd,
Littlegate House, St Ebbe's Street, Oxford

Planned and produced by Elsevier International Projects Ltd, Oxford,

Origination by Art Color Offset, Rome, Italy
Filmset by Keyspools Limited, Golborne, Lancs.
Printed and bound by Brepols, Turnhout - Belgium

Contents

Preface to the series

This book is a volume in the Making of the Past, a series describing the early history of the world as revealed by archaeology and related disciplines. The series is written by experts under the guidance of a distinguished panel of advisers and is designed for the layman, for young people, the student, the armchair traveler and the tourist. Its subject is a new history – the making of a new past, uncovered and reconstructed in recent years by skilled specialists. Since many of the authors of these volumes are themselves practicing archaeologists, leaders in a rapidly changing field, the series is completely authoritative and up-to-date. Each volume covers a specific period and region of the world and combines a detailed survey of the modern archaeology and sites of the area with an account of the early explorers, travelers, and archaeologists concerned with it. Later chapters of each book are devoted to a reconstruction in text and pictures of the newly revealed cultures and civilizations that make up the new history of the area.

Titles already published

The Egyptian Kingdoms
The Aegean Civilizations
The Spread of Islam
The Emergence of Greece
Biblical Lands
The New World
Man before History
The Greek World
Barbarian Europe

Future titles

The First Empires
The Roman World
Ancient Japan
The Iranian Revival
Ancient China
The Kingdoms of Africa
Rome and Byzantium
Prehistoric Europe
India and Southeast Asia
Archaeology Today

Introduction

The Near East has sometimes been described as the cradle of civilization. Civilizations have been born, and died, at different times in many parts of the world, springing from diverse origins whose only assessable common factor was a sufficiency of natural resources to support a wealthy economy and the social institutions associated with it. All these developments cannot be discussed within the compass of a single book or the competence of any two professional archaeologists, and this volume concentrates on the Near East for two main reasons. It affords the earliest and probably the best-known example of the process that led from the first agricultural settlements to literate, city-dwelling communities. Secondly, those communities were the foundation of Mesopotamian culture, which in turn had a profound influence on later societies both in its own region and in the Mediterranean lands from which our civilization sprang.

The region is one of wide contrasts both in geography and in climate. It is bordered on the north and east by the mountains and high plateaus of Anatolia and Iran, on the west by the coastal ranges of the Levant and on the south by the Arabian massif. Much of the central basin, through which the Tigris and Euphrates flow to the Arabian Gulf, is barren steppe habitable only by nomads, and rainfall sufficient for cultivation is now available only in the highlands and in a strip of land – the so-called Fertile Crescent – that runs from the Levant around the northern and northeastern rim of the plain. There have been minor fluctuations of climate, but the pattern of ancient settlement suggests that the overall picture has not greatly changed in the last 10,000 years. But in various parts of the Fertile Crescent and in the mountain ranges on its borders there lived, after the end of the Last Ice Age, wild species of the animals and plants that were the first to be domesticated, and formed the basis of the earliest farming economies throughout western Asia and Europe.

The Near East in the last 200 years has often been the scene of intense political rivalries between European powers because it lay astride one of their principal routes of communication with India and the Far East. Among the first to take an interest in its antiquities were their diplomatic representatives and travelers, but they were long concerned only with the spectacular remains of early civilizations, partly because these illustrate the background of the Biblical world, and partly because the idea of the great antiquity of man, and hence the study of prehistory, did not take shape even in Europe until little more than 100 years ago. We trace the development of this idea, and the mounting tide of research into the earliest settled Near Eastern societies that has resulted from it in the last two generations. Much of the evidence with which we have to deal has been produced in the last 30 years, partly through a concentration of archaeological interest, partly by the development of new techniques that enable us to recover much more information about the economy and way of life of the first farmers.

Our account of the evidence deals first with the origins of farming throughout the region and the earliest, isolated settlements of a size and complexity that entitle them to be called towns. We then narrow the field to Mesopotamia, considering the spread of rain-fed agriculture in the northern plain and the earliest appearance of irrigation techniques that made possible the exploitation of land outside the rainfall zone. Finally we consider the extension of settlement, dependent on widespread irrigation, in the rich alluvium of southern Mesopotamia, the urban society that grew up there and the progressive extension of its influence over large areas of the Fertile Crescent. Our story ends with the invention of writing when this society emerges into history as the Sumerian civilization.

Chronological Table

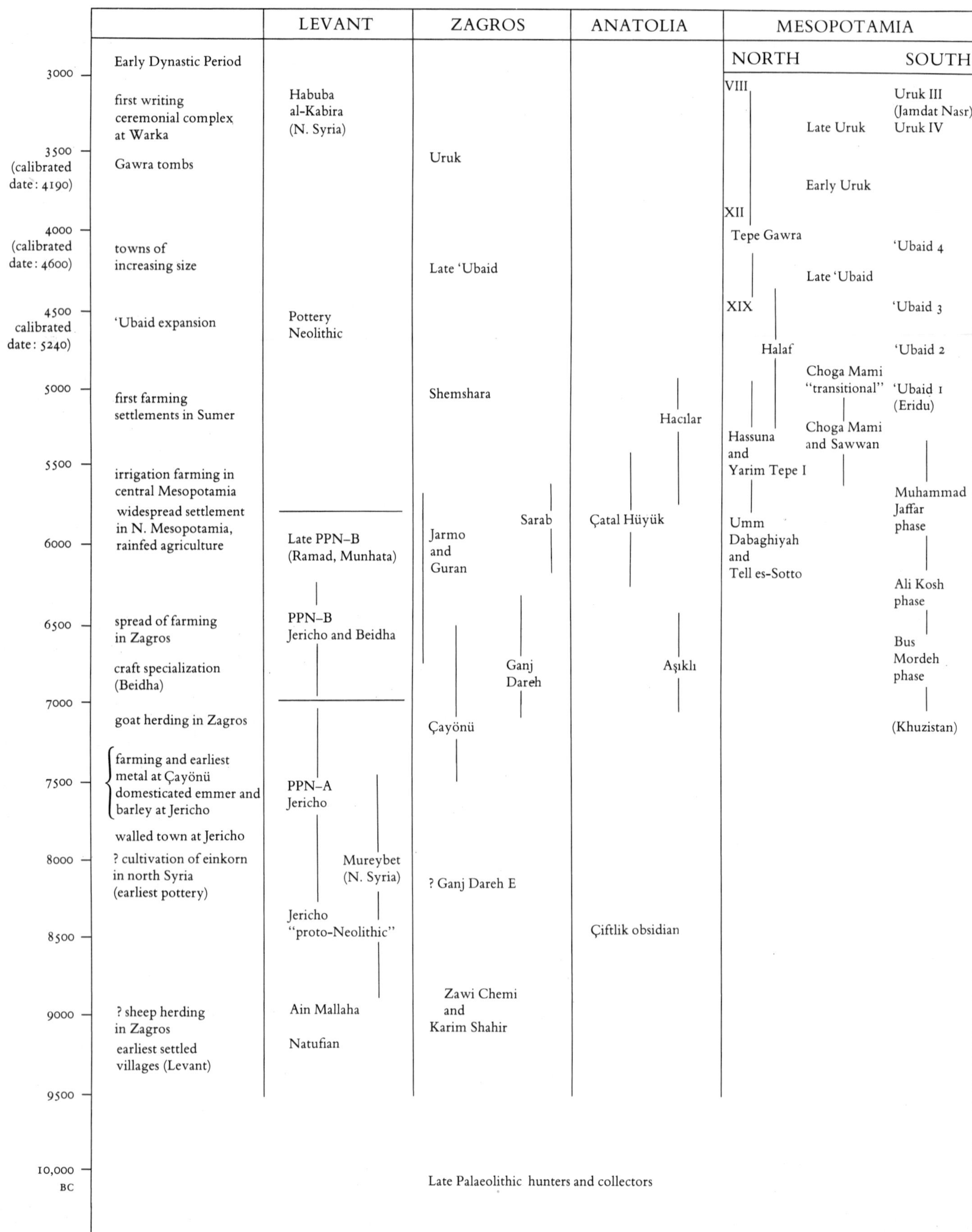

		LEVANT	ZAGROS	ANATOLIA	MESOPOTAMIA NORTH		MESOPOTAMIA SOUTH
3000	Early Dynastic Period				VIII		
	first writing ceremonial complex at Warka	Habuba al-Kabira (N. Syria)				Late Uruk	Uruk III (Jamdat Nasr) Uruk IV
3500 (calibrated date: 4190)	Gawra tombs		Uruk			Early Uruk	
					XII Tepe Gawra		
4000 (calibrated date: 4600)	towns of increasing size		Late 'Ubaid			Late 'Ubaid	'Ubaid 4
4500 calibrated date: 5240)	'Ubaid expansion	Pottery Neolithic			XIX		'Ubaid 3
					Halaf		'Ubaid 2
5000	first farming settlements in Sumer		Shemshara	Hacılar		Choga Mami "transitional"	'Ubaid 1 (Eridu)
					Hassuna and Yarim Tepe I	Choga Mami and Sawwan	
5500	irrigation farming in central Mesopotamia						
	widespread settlement in N. Mesopotamia, rainfed agriculture		Sarab	Çatal Hüyük			Muhammad Jaffar phase
6000		Late PPN–B (Ramad, Munhata)	Jarmo and Guran		Umm Dabaghiyah and Tell es-Sotto		
							Ali Kosh phase
6500	spread of farming in Zagros	PPN–B Jericho and Beidha					Bus Mordeh phase
	craft specialization (Beidha)		Ganj Dareh	Aşıklı			
7000	goat herding in Zagros		Çayönü				(Khuzistan)
7500	farming and earliest metal at Çayönü; domesticated emmer and barley at Jericho	PPN–A Jericho					
	walled town at Jericho						
8000	? cultivation of einkorn in north Syria (earliest pottery)	Mureybet (N. Syria)	? Ganj Dareh E				
8500		Jericho "proto-Neolithic"		Çiftlik obsidian			
9000	? sheep herding in Zagros	Ain Mallaha	Zawi Chemi and Karim Shahir				
	earliest settled villages (Levant)	Natufian					
9500							
10,000 BC			Late Palaeolithic hunters and collectors				

1. The Theme and its Setting

Towards civilization. About 18,000 BC the Last Ice Age reached its peak. Much of Europe was tundra, stretching away from the great Scandinavian ice cap. In Mediterranean latitudes the climate was considerably colder than it is today, and both Spain and the Near East were drier, although parts of North Africa and possibly Arabia appear sporadically to have received more rainfall. At this time there were very small populations in all these regions who lived by hunting and food-gathering and were often, particularly in the harsher lands of the north, very highly specialized in gaining a livelihood from the plants and animals available to them.

Over the next 10,000 years there was a progressive, though probably fluctuating, rise in temperatures. And in the Near East, the region with which we shall be principally concerned, the little evidence we have suggests an increase in rainfall from about 9000 BC onwards, although it may not have reached even its present level until as late as 3500 BC. The distribution of plant and animal species altered with the climate, and this change in food supplies upset the balance of the old hunting and gathering economies in many regions. Although our evidence for this transitional period is very sparse, particularly in the Near East, we may assume that many of the people involved simply adapted their hunting and gathering techniques to new sources of food, or moved to other areas where their traditional supplies could be found. Hunting has remained until this century an important supplement to the diet of many Near Eastern communities, and in the Zagros mountains between Iraq and Iran modern hunters pursue some of the same species of large animals as their predecessors of the Last Ice Age.

Other groups, however, took what is probably the most decisive step in human history. They began deliberately to sow certain plants and to breed in captivity some of the animals that were a staple part of their food supply. How this came about we do not know. It is easy to guess that seeds that had been collected might have sprouted in storage or been thrown out on a rubbish heap, to produce an accidental crop in the next growing season. The domestication of sheep or goat needs no more elaborate explanation than the appeal of an abandoned lamb or kid to a child, followed by accidental or deliberate breeding. But this must remain speculation. The differences in the form of cereals or in the bones of animals that now distinguish domesticated from wild species took many generations of breeding to develop, and obviously cannot be identified in the very earliest stages of the process. What is certain is that we have evidence for domesticated varieties of plants, mainly cereals, and animals well before 7000 BC in many places from the Aegean eastwards to Iran, and there is every reason to believe that the domestication of particular species took place at much the same time in different areas.

The special problems involved in the study of this development are discussed in more detail in Chapter 4, where we deal with the earliest known settlements of herdsmen and farmers. But for the purpose of this chapter, a summary of our subject and its background, we must emphasize the phrase that we have just used, "the earliest known settlements of herdsmen and farmers." Although it was long believed that the hunter-gatherers even of the most recent Ice Age lived in camps, caves or rock shelters that were at most temporary homes during certain seasons of the year, there is growing evidence in some regions that more permanent settlements existed. But very rarely do we find an uninterrupted occupation of such a site through the period of climatic and economic change that has just been described. On the other hand, some of the earliest farmers chose the sites of their villages for reasons that have remained valid to the present day. Their vital needs were water, fertile land and good grazing and, with the increase of populations and the exchange of goods between them, good communications. Thus a site well chosen for an early village might, and often did, prove suitable for a town or city that was to be continuously occupied for thousands of years. Such continuity of settlement is the main factor that gives this book a coherent theme. We begin with the earliest farming villages because, although the evidence before 7000 BC is still tenuous, they represent the origins of the economy on which the earliest civilizations were based.

Unfortunately continuous occupation of many of the best-favored sites in the most fertile areas has also created a major problem for the archaeologist, since their earliest levels are buried under a vast accumulation of later buildings that excavators can neither afford nor often be permitted to remove. This obstacle to the recovery of evidence is most apparent in Near Eastern sites where the use of mud and later unbaked brick as a building material encouraged the construction of a new building on the leveled debris of its predecessor, and led to the formation of the characteristic mounds (*tells*) that sometimes rise to more than 40 meters above the plain. As a result, much of our knowledge of the earliest periods comes either from very small soundings on the largest mounds or from sites that for one reason or another could not be continuously occupied and are therefore unlikely to represent the most successful communities of their time. In either case the evidence is obviously far from complete. It is worth observing that the difficulty of extensive excavation on important sites with a long history is by no means unknown outside the Near East. The Romans founded London on a hitherto unregarded site because it satisfied two requirements for a working city in their new province, a good port and good communications. These twin advantages have ensured its subsequent growth, with the result that Roman London is, for archaeologists, one of the most inaccessible sites in Britain.

Previous page: the snow-covered Taurus mountains in southern Turkey.

Mount Ararat, an extinct volcano in eastern Turkey, 16,950 feet high.

Returning to our theme, we must now explain the choice of the Near East as its setting. On present evidence, this region saw the appearance not only of the first agricultural settlements but also of the oldest cities in the world. Historical priority alone would not excuse us from taking account of other regions, such as eastern Asia and Central America, where plants and animals have been domesticated at different times and local civilizations have arisen without any apparent external stimulus. But, with the conspicuous exception of China, none of these other centers has preserved its own native civilization intact into modern times. Indeed, the principal reason that directs our attention to the Near East is that the classic civilizations of Mesopotamia and Egypt, which were the twin peaks of its cultural development, also exerted an important influence on later civilizations from the Mediterranean to India. The story we are telling is, in fact, an early but vital episode in a history that culminates in the achievements of Europe on the one hand and the world of Islam on the other.

Time scale. We are not, however, concerned in this volume with even the earliest civilizations, only with the developments that led up to them. These we have for convenience divided into three stages. The first stage, down to about 6000 BC, comprises the earliest agricultural settlements and the first larger and more highly organized communities, deserving the name of town, that grew up in rare and obviously special circumstances, such as Jericho in the Jordan Valley or Çatal Hüyük in the Konya Plain of western Anatolia. Our second stage, *c.* 6000–5000 BC, saw the expansion of rain-fed agriculture over the Near Eastern plains and the beginnings in Mesopotamia of irrigation farming, the technique that was to provide the increase of wealth on which the earliest cities of southern Mesopotamia were founded. In the third stage we trace the rise of these cities and their increasing influence on other areas down to the late fourth millennium BC when the first written documents appear. Each of these stages forms the subject of a detailed chapter in the second part of this book, but we should emphasize here that the divisions between them are only an aid to description and have no historical significance. Man's history is not a ladder of progress with regularly ascending steps.

The unreality of such distinctions is perhaps best illustrated by examining briefly what we mean when we say that our story ends, as its title implies, with the advent of civilization. The criteria by which archaeologists commonly define the beginning of civilization are the existence of cities and the use of writing, but the definition is an arbitrary one and can be misleading. Large urban communities with monumental public buildings that suggest a high degree of social organization certainly existed before the first known use of writing, so the two criteria cannot represent a single moment in time. And just as men's other skills such as agriculture or architecture developed gradually and often unevenly, so writing evolved from simple pictographic notation, as an aid to the keeping of accounts, into elaborate systems that could record every inflection of the spoken language and even the most abstract ideas. For several centuries after the first appearance of written records in southern Mesopotamia (Sumer) in the late fourth millennium BC, the texts do not tell us very much about the history of the cities in which they were written, and throughout Mesopotamian history

The earliest known pictographic writing is illustrated on this limestone tablet from Kish, to be dated sometime after 3500 BC. Among the signs are those for head, hand, foot, numerals and a threshing sledge (Iraq Museum).

– except in private letters which were dictated to an official scribe – they tell us very little about the personal opinions of the author. Moreover, less than 400 miles away in northern Mesopotamia we have at present no evidence for the use of writing at all before about 2400 BC. Yet the discovery of statues in characteristically Sumerian style on some northern sites, and even of much earlier temples whose distinctive plan is almost identical with that of temples in the south, shows that the two areas were in close contact long before 2400 BC. It may be that earlier written documents remain to be discovered in the north, and we are looking for them. But to say on the existing evidence that one society was "civilized" and the other was not, except by the arbitrary standards that we have adopted, clearly has little meaning.

It is more relevant that the introduction of advanced writing systems capable of recording the niceties of language marks an immense change in the nature of our evidence, and the final comment in this introduction to our subject is a warning to the reader who is unfamiliar with the ways of archaeologists. In all the 5,000 years spanned by our theme we rely solely on material evidence, the remains of flora and fauna and of man's own products, whether they are tools and pottery or buildings and works of art. Recent improvements in the techniques of excavation and in the recovery and study of evidence have greatly enhanced our ability to reconstruct the habitat, economy and way of life of prehistoric man. But no technical advance can enable us to recreate from material evidence ideas and motives, or the effect of individual personality in a particular situation. It is, for instance, tempting to suggest that changes in the environment at the end of the Last Ice Age forced man to domesticate plants and animals, or that the exceptional resources of a particular area caused a growth in population, and hence an advanced economic and social system. We prefer to regard these undoubtedly important factors as the background which made such developments possible, but not inevitable. It is conceivable, although we can never prove or disprove the proposition, that some communities adopted domestication or developed a civilization through their more ready acceptance of new ideas as much as the superior opportunities that their environment offered.

The geographical setting. The physical geography of the Near East was an important factor in its history long before the age of oil although, unfortunately, it is only in the last two generations that the demand for oil has encouraged any detailed study of its geological structure. The great upheavals that formed its mountain ranges, plateaus and basins took place, of course, long before the appearance of man, but the last, almost imperceptible spasms of this process still continue and have affected its topography to the present day. The region lies at the junction between the continents of Asia and Africa, which incorporate the two great masses of very ancient rocks known to geologists as the Siberian and African Shields. Lateral movement between the two masses has produced, in the Near East, cracks around the edge of the African Shield, parts of which have been forced upward while others have dropped, forming the long depressions known as rift valleys. One famous rift is the Jordan Valley running down to the Dead Sea. Another, open to the Indian Ocean and so completely drowned, is the Red Sea that divides northwest Africa from the Arabian massif which is, geologically, a detached part of the African Shield.

A second effect of the lateral movement of the shields has been the crumpling of the later sedimentary rocks that overlie them, leading to the formation of long chains of "folded mountains." Two of these chains, the Pontine and Zagros ranges, bound the Anatolian plateau on the north and south, converging in the east around Mount Ararat, and then separating once more into the Elburz and Zagros mountains along the northern and southwestern borders of the Iranian plateau. Between the folded mountains of Anatolia and Iran and the Arabian massif the underlying rock structure was depressed, forming a long trough, the Mesopotamian basin, that is cut off from the Mediterranean by the coastal ranges of Palestine and Lebanon and slopes southeastwards to the Arabian Gulf. The northwestern part of this basin, down to a line that extends approximately from Hit on the Euphrates to Samarra on the Tigris, is filled with relatively ancient deposits, forming an undulating plain interrupted by broken hill chains that are the last outliers of the Taurus and Zagros ranges. Southeast of the Hit-Samarra line the land in the basin is recent alluvium, brought down by the Euphrates, Tigris and their tributaries from their catchment areas in Anatolia and western Iran.

Gulf coastline. At the peak of the Last Ice Age, when a substantial part of the water in the oceans of the world was taken up into the great ice caps and the sea was more than 100 meters below its present level, large areas of the Gulf were dry land. The melting of the ice brought sea level to, and even slightly above, its present height by 3000 BC. Archaeologists long believed that in the later stages of this incursion the head of the Gulf reached the Hit-Samarra line, and that the recent alluvium to the southeast of this line – that is, the whole of southern Mesopotamia – was a delta formed since about 4000 BC by the deposition of riverborne silt. This theory is reflected in maps of the prehistoric Near East published before 1950 and, more importantly, it led to the belief that there could have been no early prehistoric population in the southern alluvium because the land did not exist. But in 1952 two oil company geologists, Lees and Falcon, pointed out that as a residual effect of the folding process which formed the mountain ranges and the Mesopotamian basin, the rock structure underlying the southeastern end of the basin was still being spasmodically depressed, thus compensating from time to time for the continuous deposition of silt. They concluded that there had been approximate equilibrium between land and sea levels during the past 6,000 years, and that any advances or recessions in the shoreline at the head of the Gulf had been relatively local.

The argument is a complicated one, and it is sufficient to say here that their general conclusion is now widely accepted. But it is important to remember that it does not preclude the possibility of local inundations, which could have occurred for a number of reasons. Southern Mesopotamia is very flat, with a drop of only some 35 meters from Baghdad to the Gulf, a distance of over 300 miles. Basra, 70 miles upriver, stands only 2 meters above sea level. Effective drainage is exceptionally difficult, and large areas of lake and marsh have existed throughout historic and probably also in prehistoric times. Over much of their course the rivers have built levees so that their beds are actually above plain level. From late February to April they are swollen by the spring rains and melting snows in their upper catchment areas and widespread flooding has often resulted, particularly before the construction of modern barrages. Obviously any change in the delicate relationship between land and sea levels, whether caused by tectonic movement in the structure of the basin or by a rise in sea level, could encourage inundations of even more dramatic effect. We know, in fact, that the rivers have changed their courses on many occasions since the fourth millennium BC, and that the Hor al-Hammar, one of the largest existing lakes, came into being after serious floods about 600 AD. Similar events may explain the Flood legends, and the flood deposits found on a number of ancient sites in the south. But our later discussion of prehistoric developments in this area is based on the belief that, although the position of rivers, lakes and even the coastline has changed from time to time, the overall character of the country has altered little during the period with which we are concerned and certainly since the date of the earliest settlements so far discovered.

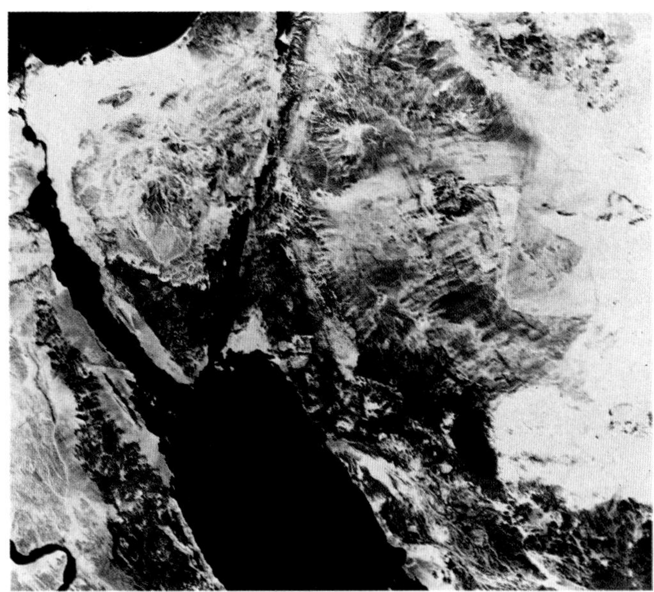

The northern end of the Red Sea photographed from a satellite. This is the largest of the rift valleys formed by the interaction of the African and Siberian Shields.

Climatic changes. On the western side of the Gulf, in eastern Arabia, recent research has revealed dramatic changes during the early part of this period, before about 3000 BC. It is now a barren country, relieved only by a few oases whose wells are supplied by water-bearing strata that were charged, like a reservoir, by the rains of remote pluvial periods, and this supply is progressively being depleted. Modern rainfall is negligible, except in the mountains of Oman in the extreme southeast of the peninsula, and to the northwest of Oman lies the Rub‘ al-Khali, or "Empty Quarter," one of the most fearsome deserts in the world. As we have already mentioned, there is evidence of more rainfall in Arabia during the Last Ice Age, and recent discoveries suggest that the ensuing progressive desiccation was interrupted by wetter phases. Sea level in the Gulf was at least a meter higher than at present during the fourth millennium BC, and this would have meant that the salt flats (*sabkha*) which are found in many places along the east coast would then have been lagoons or inlets. More startling, however, is the conclusion reached by geologists that even inland *sabkha* were open water until at least 4000 BC, and that the Rub‘ al-Khali before that time was largely occupied by a chain of lakes or marshes, fed by rainfall from the mountains of Oman and discharging through perennial streams into the southern end of the Gulf. Unfortunately precise dates for the stages of a gradual process such as desiccation are hard to obtain, but it certainly seems that climatic conditions in some parts of eastern Arabia down to the fourth millen-

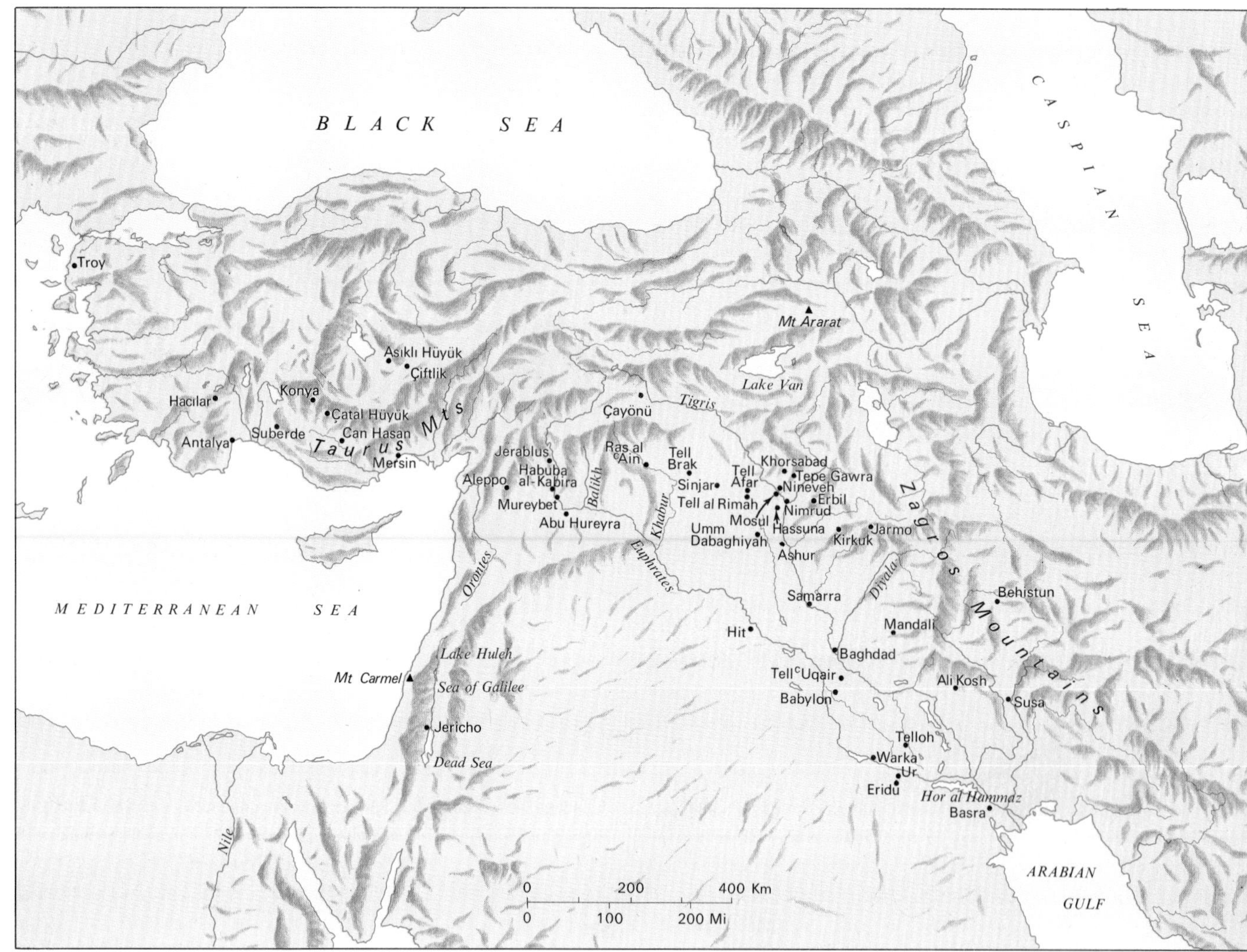

The Middle East.

nium had more in common with those prevailing in southern Mesopotamia than with the harsh landscape of today.

Elsewhere in the Near East the character of the different areas has changed far less, except for the deforestation of the mountain and hill ranges that has resulted from the need of man for fuel and timber and the appetite of his goats for anything that grows. By far the most important single factor that controls land use throughout the region is climate, and especially rainfall. Almost everywhere the climate is of "continental" type, with hot summers and relatively cold winters. Except in the mountains of southwestern Arabia, which are watered by summer monsoons from the Indian Ocean, and on the south coasts of the Black Sea and the Caspian where there is no consistently dry season, rainfall is almost entirely confined to the winter and spring months and tends to be concentrated into periods of a few days within these seasons. Its geographical distribution varies greatly, as can be seen from the map. It derives in the main from rain-bearing depressions moving eastwards from the Mediterranean, but the effect of these depressions is by no means uniform in different areas.

Over the Anatolian and Iranian plateaus their passage is blocked during much of the winter by high atmospheric pressure systems that form because the land masses are relatively colder than the seas around them. As a result much of their rain falls at the beginning and end of winter, and the spring rains of Anatolia combine with melting snows to increase the annual floods in the Euphrates and Tigris river systems. Annual totals are highest in the mountains, where they may reach as much as 1,000 millimeters, but differ considerably between the two plateaus. The Anatolian plateau nowhere receives less than an average of 200 mm per annum and in many parts more than 300 mm, whereas in Iran only the mountains exceed 300 mm and most of the plateau receives less than 200 mm. These figures are of especial significance to us because a *reliable* annual aggregate of 200 mm is the minimum necessary for agriculture without irrigation, and the boundary of this reliable rainfall corresponds approximately with the line, or "isohyet," that denotes an overall average of 300 mm. So only a small area of central Anatolia is not potentially cultivable by rainfall alone, whereas cultivation in central Iran is confined to oases, fed by springs or perennial streams, that are dotted along the flanks of the mountains from which their water comes, and even in the oases it is almost entirely dependent on irrigation.

The situation in the Mesopotamian basin is different. Here the winters are less cold, and there are no long-lasting high-pressure systems to inhibit the passage of the Mediterranean depressions. But they are intercepted along much of the Levant coast by the hills of Palestine and the higher ranges of Lebanon and Anti-Lebanon, which attract the greater part of their rainfall. There is, however, a gap between the north end of the Lebanese mountains and the Amanus range that thrusts southwards from the Taurus. Through this gap the depressions pass eastwards to water the northern part of the Syrian and Mesopotamian plains and eventually the Zagros mountains. Consequently, much of the northern plain is good rain-fed farming land, while the central and southern sectors lie in the "rain-shadow" of the Levantine ranges and receive little, and very unreliable, rainfall. Here agriculture is possible only by irrigation and in the central sector, from the border of the rainfall zone down to the Hit-Samarra line, the opportunities for irrigation are severely limited by its topography.

The central plain is an undulating steppe through which the rivers, the only major source of water, have at some very early epoch cut deep trough valleys that are at most three or four miles wide. The present courses of the rivers thus lie well below the level of the surrounding countryside, and the only land that can be irrigated from them without the use of large dams, long canals or elaborate lifting systems is the bottom of the trough valleys. Other small irrigation systems could and do exist on the eastern rim of the plain where, just as on the further side of the Zagros in Iran perennial streams issue from the mountains and water a line of oases. One of these oases, Mandali, which lies about 75 miles northeast of Baghdad, has indeed yielded the earliest direct evidence for irrigation in Mesopotamia, dating from the latter half of the sixth millennium BC. Finally, the alluvial plain of southern Mesopotamia is, as we have said, flat land where the riverbeds are often raised above the level of the countryside and irrigation is theoretically possible almost anywhere, although it presents special problems that we discuss later.

Natural resources. Up to this point we have spoken only of the possibilities of agriculture as the basis of local economies in the plains and on the plateaus, and in these areas the staple crops are barley and less often wheat, which has a lower resistance to drought and salty soils. The mountain zones, with their well-watered but comparatively small parcels of land in the valley bottoms and on the lower hillsides, favor the cultivation of fruit as well as cereals. Apples, grapes and figs are widespread, while olives are extensively grown on the Aegean and Levantine coasts. Dates are a major crop in the oases and along the rivers in the south, but they will not ripen in the northern plain and the palms are sometimes killed by winter frost.

But agriculture is only one facet of the economy even in many areas where it is most prosperous. Most villages have their flocks and herds of sheep, goats and sometimes cattle. Pigs were common in antiquity, but are now rare because they are regarded as unclean by both Muslims and Jews. Sheep and goats are sometimes in the care of specialist herdsmen, either members of the village community or of some neighboring nomadic tribe, and are often driven for very long distances between winter and summer pastures. There are still professional hunters in the Zagros, and in the plains gazelle provided an additional source of meat until the coming of the motorcar and the machine gun almost annihilated their herds. Wild boar are still common, though now prohibited as food, in the river valleys and in the marshes of southern Mesopotamia, where fishing and fowling are also widely practiced. Even food-gathering has a minor place in the economy. Certain wild plants are cooked or eaten raw, while in the spring one may often see dignified figures of almost Biblical aspect pacing with their eyes bent on the ground. Apparently deep in meditation, they are in fact searching for the cracks that betray the presence of *kīma*, a local and highly prized version of the truffle.

Outside the cultivable zones and oases the population is nomadic and almost wholly dependent on herding, of sheep on the borders of the settled land or of camels on the steppe where water and forage are more difficult to find. These are the people known in Arab countries as the Bedouin. Their annual migrations extend over many hundreds of miles and follow set patterns, for tribal grazing and water rights are well defined and jealously

The trough valley of the Euphrates east of Aleppo in Syria showing cultivation in the flood plain and mud-brick houses in the foreground.

The Euphrates River at Babylon.

guarded. Traditionally they despise sedentary cultivators, and at most they may sow a little barley in the bed of a dry watercourse, hoping that on their return months later they may find a small crop germinated by one of the rare and unpredictable rainstorms of the steppe. But it is a great mistake to regard them as a permanently separate element in the population of the Near East. A few years of drought, a lack of grazing or of water in the wells, can force them to encroach on the settled land, and we know from the historical records of the past 5,000 years of many occasions when these incursions have been successful. Many of the villages and towns of Mesopotamia and Syria are inhabited by people whose ancestors were Bedouin, and both Turks and Iranians came at different times from the steppes of Central Asia. Nor is the nomadic, herding way of life confined to the steppes outside the rainfall zone. In southern Anatolia and western Iran there are some tribes who adhere strictly to it, although they move through territory inhabited by cultivators.

The relationships between these various communities are complicated but only hostile in moments of crisis. The nomads exchange the products of their flocks and herds – including, in Anatolia and Iran, woven or knotted carpets – for the simple necessities of their life, grain, pottery or metal vessels, cloth, tools and the like. A Bedu may now carry an old British rifle and offer coffee in a cup of traditional Arab shape that was made in Czechoslovakia, but the beaked coffee pot and the brazier on which it stands will have been bought in the metalworkers' street of some local bazaar. Different towns and villages have their own special products, jars for various purposes, woven baskets, particular patterns of cloth and so on. Even the marsh dwellers of southern Iraq have a valuable export in the form of reed matting which, overlaid with mud, covers the roofs of traditional village houses.

A few examples from our own experience in Iraq may bring this commerce more vividly to the reader's eye. For many years we excavated a site not far inside the boundary of the settled land on the northeast rim of the steppe. We built a house of sun-dried bricks made on the site from local clay and straw, with a roof of reed matting and mud supported on poplars from the Tigris valley. Our drinking water was stored in huge jars from a village 70 miles away on the east of the Tigris, and placed on the table in smaller vessels with a slightly permeable body that cooled it by evaporation. The best of these can be bought only in one town in the mountains near the Turkish frontier. Much of our furniture and many of our tools were made and maintained by craftsmen in the local town, which was also particularly famous as the Savile Row of sheepskin coats and waistcoats. We even had our own small seasonal industry. In the early summer Bedouin regularly camped around us, grazing their sheep on the stubble of the harvest before moving on to pastures in the nearby hills. For some time before their coming the wife of our camp guard would fashion, from the clay of a nearby watercourse, small domed ovens of a type that has been used for at least 8,000 years for the baking of unleavened bread. These were allowed to dry in the sun until they were hard enough to be portable, and were then sold to the Bedouin.

A local shepherd in southern Iraq. The potsherds at his feet show that he is standing on an ancient mound.

A copper-worker's shop in Kadhimain bazaar near Baghdad.

Environmental change. Up to this point we have discussed only the resources, vegetable or animal, that depend directly or indirectly on the soil and are restricted by the climate. It is indeed a very conspicuous fact that in much of Mesopotamia, and particularly in the alluvial plain, these are the only resources available, and it is true in more senses than one to say that Sumerian civilization was founded on mud. But the examples we have cited reflect recent conditions, and we must ask whether the environment has altered substantially since prehistoric times. Two main factors could have affected the situation, a change in climate and the activity of man himself.

Man has certainly contributed to, if not entirely caused, the disappearance of some species of game from areas where we know that they once lived. We have evidence for the hunting of onager on the central Mesopotamian plain about 6000 BC, and Assyrian kings of the 9th to the 7th centuries BC record their exploits in the killing of wild oxen on the border of the steppe west of the Tigris, ostriches in Arabia and even elephants in Syria. The Arabian oryx is extinct in its native country, gazelle have been decimated within our memory, and larger species of deer have vanished from many places where their bones are found on ancient sites, partly no doubt through hunting but more significantly through the deforestation of the hills to satisfy an ever increasing human demand for timber and fuel.

The cutting of trees and shrubs, and even the extraction of their roots by charcoal-burners, have destroyed the stability of the soil and laid it open to erosion by wind and water. In the open plains potentially fertile topsoil is often blown away, while much of the rain that falls, even in the hills, is not absorbed but rushes in destructive spates through deep-cut gullies. Lack of foliage itself affects the exchange of water between the ground and the atmosphere that can be particularly important in areas of marginal rainfall, for in country with good vegetation cover the leaves give off moisture by day that returns as dew by night. We have often passed in the early morning from a barren valley in harsh sunlight to the next, planted with olive groves, that was covered by a blanket of mist. Agriculture, too, can have detrimental effects. Deep plowing that disturbs the cohesion of the subsoil is a modern innovation but, as we have mentioned above, even the very ancient practice of irrigation presents considerable problems. The water of the rivers that descend from Anatolia and the Zagros contains a very high proportion of dissolved salts which are then deposited in the alluvium. The difficulty of drainage in this very flat land and the intense summer heat lead to high evaporation which in turn brings the salts to the surface of the fields, where they can sometimes even be seen as a white crust. No cereals will tolerate such salinity, and we know that salination had already damaged the fertility of some parts of southern Mesopotamia by the third millennium BC.

The history of the post-glacial climate is a complex problem, and our present evidence is too meager to justify more than a few observations that are only isolated pieces in a very elaborate puzzle. A reliable reconstruction requires detailed local studies, especially of plant remains and fossil pollen which are the best indicators of change because plants react more directly than animals to variations in temperature and rainfall. Such precise information now exists only for a few places, principally in the mountains north and east of Mesopotamia, which do not necessarily reflect conditions in the basin itself or in Arabia. But it is our general impression that, as in other parts of the world, there have been many minor fluctuations of temperature and rainfall for which we have occasional clues in historical and archaeological evidence, although such evidence is sometimes open to more than one interpretation. An apparently unequivocal instance can be cited from the medieval period. In the 10th century AD an Arab geographer states that the date palm flourished abundantly around the town of Sinjar, which lies at the foot of the hills of the same name which intersect the north Mesopotamian plain. At present, dates will not ripen north of Samarra, almost 200 miles to the southeast, and we must conclude that a thousand years ago both summer and winter temperatures were marginally higher than they are now.

Settlement patterns. But such definite and well-dated evidence is very rare. The distribution of agricultural settlements in marginal areas may reflect slight changes in the reliability of rainfall, although it must be said that the overall limits of farming have altered little in the past 8,000 years, and at least some of the recessions have taken place for political rather than climatic reasons. Indeed on the steppe and its borders climatic and political factors are very difficult to distinguish. For instance, a drought in central Arabia may trigger tribal movements that end in incursions into the settled lands of Palestine, Syria and Mesopotamia unless the inhabitants of these areas are strong enough to resist them. Two examples of apparent changes in the limits of settlement may help to illustrate the use of this type of evidence, which comes largely from surface survey and the collection of potsherds of known and approximately datable types.

On the northeastern edge of the Mesopotamian steppe there is a scatter of small mounds which have produce pottery of the sixth millennium BC. The land around the is potentially very fertile, but the rainfall is highly u certain. In our memory, covering the last 20 years, t land has not always been sown, but on average the cro has failed completely through drought in at least two, an has attained its maximum and very profitable yield in on one out of every five years. These are conditions u acceptable to a farmer unless he is backed by more reliab resources elsewhere. In fact the sowing of this land i recent years has been underwritten by absentee landow ers or merchants with other sources of income, wh made a very substantial profit if the crop succeeded an could afford to accept the loss if it failed. Compariso with the modern situation suggests two possible expla nations for the apparent extension of settlement beyon the normal modern limits of cultivation in the sixt millennium. We may infer either that there was mor reliable rainfall at that time or that, as much as 8,000 yea ago, the existence of these villages was insured in som way by the resources of larger centers of population. It interesting that the only excavated site in this grou apparently housed, about 6000 BC, a community of onage hunters who could have exchanged hides or meat fo grain and other staples from areas with higher rainfal This site, Umm Dabaghiyah, is discussed in more detail i Chapter 5, but we must observe here that its apparentl specialized economy is not necessarily typical of othe unexcavated villages in the same marginal zone, and th question of a slight extension of reliable rainfall at this tim remains open.

Our second example comes from the Khabur basin o northeastern Syria, some 130 miles northwest of the grou of sixth-millennium sites we have just mentioned. Th Khabur river is a northern tributary of the Euphrates, fe largely by streams that rise in the Anatolian foothills an partly by the rainfall of the north Mesopotamian plain Like the middle Euphrates, the Khabur and its perennia tributaries run in trough valleys below the level of th surrounding countryside and cannot be used for irrigatio outside the valley bottoms without artificial devices t create a head of water. In fact all cultivation outside th valleys is and, as far as we know, always has been dependent on rainfall, although the second problem o settlement – an assured supply of water for people an animals – is greatly relieved by the perennial streams. I the northern part of the basin crops are now reliable, but i its center there is an area about 30 miles across wher rainfall is at present uncertain.

Archaeological surveys of the basin have shown a very interesting pattern of settlement at different periods Occupation before about 3500 BC was apparently confined to sites that lay either inside the modern zone of wholly reliable rainfall or on the watercourses that are now perennial. But from c. 3500 to 3000 BC we find a sudden expansion of settlement in the marginal zone. Many ıounds with pottery of this period stand in open country ·etween the perennial watercourses, and nearly all the ıame sites were occupied between 2300 and 2000 BC. We o not know whether some of them were abandoned in he interval. When we collect sherds on a mound we annot be sure of finding a selection that fully represents all he periods of occupation, nor of identifying correctly all he sherds that we do find. We can, of course, only date articular shapes or types of decoration if they have been ound in stratified levels on excavated sites, and too few ites have so far been excavated to give us a complete ecord of the designs and decorations used by potters in ny area or period in the Near East. Nonetheless, we can e sure that in the late fourth and the late third millennia C – and perhaps in the intervening period – there were nany more villages in the middle Khabur basin than there ad been before, and that the yield of the land on which hey presumably depended is not entirely reliable at the resent day. We also know that in the late third millen-ium, if not earlier, the area was under the direct control nd presumably the protection of south Mesopotamian ulers. This would have been a factor in maintaining the prosperity of settlements, but could not have affected the climate on which their original existence depended. There does, in this case, seem to be good reason to suggest a somewhat higher rainfall in the northern plain during these two phases, although we cannot yet say whether it declined in the intervening period.

We believe that such minor fluctuations were a regular feature of the climatic pattern throughout our period, but this alone does not imply any great variation in the availability of plant and animal resources, except perhaps in the sort of marginal area from which our last two examples have been drawn. But taken in conjunction with the overall climatic changes that mark the end of the Last Ice Age, these fluctuations might have had a significant effect on, for instance, the distribution of wild species of plants and animals in the period between 9000 and 7000 BC when we have the first evidence for their domestication. We cannot assume that the present occurrences of

A nomadic encampment in western Iran. The black tents are used by Bedouin throughout the Middle East and are made of strips of cloth woven from goat hair.

wild barley and wheat, still less of wild sheep and goats which have been hunted by man, accurately represent their distribution during this very important phase. But in general it seems that there has been no dramatic change in Near Eastern conditions since the period covered by this book, except in parts of the Arabian peninsula, and that in most areas information about the present environment and traditional ways of exploiting it can help in the reconstruction of ancient situations.

Raw materials and trade. We have dealt at some length with the basic economies of different communities, both farmers and pastoralists, and the factors of topography and climate that influenced their development. But we have made only passing reference to their material equipment and the resources necessary to provide it. In this respect the modern situation is much less relevant because of the great advances in technology that have taken place, although it is interesting that in more remote areas we can still see farmers tilling their land with the light wooden plow – more correctly called an ard – that is depicted on Sumerian seals, or threshing their grain with sleds shod with chipped flints. On the other hand the possible sources of different varieties of stone and, later, metals that were needed to produce such things as tools, weapons and ornaments are still the same as they were 10,000 years ago, although our information about them is still far from complete because detailed geological surveys of some areas have not yet been published.

Apart from this uncertainty we often cannot be sure which sources were actually exploited in antiquity. Archaeological evidence for quarrying and mining is rare and difficult to date, and many types of stone could, in any case, be collected on the surface. To prove that a particular piece came from a certain place it must have distinctive characteristics that are found only in material from that source. Many varieties of stone were employed in our period for the manufacture of tools and weapons. Flint, chert and obsidian were used to make cutting tools, limestone and quartzite for heavier implements such as hammers, mace-heads and pounders that did not need a sharp edge, and basalt especially for querns, mortars and pestles. Almost all of these materials are found in many places in the mountains, on the plateaus and in the northern and western parts of the Mesopotamian plain. As an extreme example, to pinpoint the origin of a piece of limestone is obviously a hopeless task because it is the commonest rock in all the folded mountains.

Obsidian, however, is found only in the volcanic areas of central and eastern Anatolia, and specimens from the two areas differ in the chemical impurities they contain. Modern techniques of examination and analysis have enabled us to identify these trace elements in tools and fragments of obsidian not only from Anatolia, where it was naturally in very wide use at an early date, but from sites as far away as Palestine and the Zagros. On these sites it is rare before 7000 BC but increases considerably i proportion to flint and chert during the next tw millennia. Thus we can detect patterns of long-distanc trade that began at least 9,000 years ago. We cannot o course reconstruct its organization without written docu ments, and we should not necessarily assume that it wa conducted by individual traders who traveled the whol length of the routes. It is perhaps more likely at first t have involved a series of relatively short-distance ex changes between neighboring communities, in whic pastoral groups may well have played a part. Unfortunately the remains of their encampments are among th most difficult for archaeologists to recognize.

With the growth in the number and prosperity o settlements that took place during and after the sixt millennium, we find increasing evidence of trade in rav materials as the demand for manufactured goods grew and many of these products were not purely functional Personal ornaments are a good example. They are no functional in the basic sense, although they may serv some purpose beyond simple adornment, such as th investment of wealth or the display of prestige as the commonly do nowadays, and their prehistoric owner

Opposite: an Iranian farmer plowing with a wooden plow of a type known at least as early as the fourth millennium BC.

Below: a Late Uruk seal impression depicting man leading an ox and holding a primitive form of plow (Ashmolean Museum, Oxford).

may have attached to them religious or magical significance at which we can only guess. At the time when the obsidian trade was in its infancy, cowries and dentalium shells were being brought from the Mediterranean or the Arabian Gulf to inland sites to be worn as beads and pendants. Of course local materials were also used. The earliest known settlers in the Zagros area showed great proficiency in the making of polished stone bracelets, and at Çatal Hüyük, some 125 miles southwest of the central Anatolian sources of obsidian, even that intractable material was being fashioned into necklaces and mirrors before 5500 BC. But in later periods we find an ever-increasing variety of ornamental and semi-precious stones, as well as precious metals, that must have traveled over long distances from their place of origin. Graves of the mid-fourth millennium BC at Tepe Gawra in northern Mesopotamia, a prosperous but by no means a large settlement by the standards of its time, have produced great quantities of beads of obsidian, carnelian, quartz, turquoise, jadeite, haematite, diorite and lapis lazuli, as well as cowries and objects of gold, silver and their alloy electrum. Most of these materials are available in Anatolia or western Iran, but the cowries probably came from the Gulf and the only known source of lapis lazuli, of which 450 beads were found in one tomb alone, is in the Badakshan area of northern Afghanistan more than 1,300 miles to the east.

Metalworking. This section is not intended to be more than a selective commentary on the supply and distribution of geological resources in the prehistoric Near East, and we shall revert to some of these topics in more detail, but it may be surprising to a reader accustomed to the products of modern technology that we have not yet discussed the use of metal in the manufacture of implements and weapons. In fact the only metal that was at all frequently employed for this purpose before 3000 BC was copper. It is one of the few metals that occur, even rarely, in their native state rather than in the form of ores, and this apparently led to the discovery that it could be shaped by cold hammering. Small objects of hammered native copper and a bead of malachite, one of its ores, were found in early seventh-millennium levels on the site of Çayönü near Ergani in southern Anatolia and only 12 miles from an important source of copper ores that are still mined today, and the same technique was being employed at Ali Kosh in southwestern Iran before 6000 BC. Since copper ores are available in a number of places in the Near East, including the Sinai peninsula as well as parts of Anatolia and Iran, it seems likely that cold hammering and the later processes of smelting and casting were independently invented in the neighborhood of different sources. Smelting, which permitted the exploitation of the much larger resources of ore, was apparently known before the middle of the sixth millennium BC even in the north Mesopotamian plain, for a cylindrical copper bead and several pieces of ore have been discovered in buildings of this date at Yarim Tepe, south of the Sinjar hills.

A collection of necklaces found at Çatal Hüyük in central Anatolia.

We do not know when casting began, but it does not seem to have progressed beyond the use of an open or a two-piece closed mold, suitable only for the production of objects with a simple profile, until towards the end of our period. The step that made more complex castings possible was the invention of the *cire perdue* or lost wax process, in which a wax model of the desired object was built up on a clay core and then encased in clay. The whole was then heated until the wax ran out, metal was poured into the space which it had occupied, and after cooling the mold was broken and the object removed. The introduction of this technique in fact marks the first occasion

Painted jar of the latest 'Ubaid phase (late fifth millennium BC) from Arpachiyah, northern Iraq (British Museum).

when the range of shapes that could be produced in metal notably exceeded the possibilities of stone, or at least of the harder stones that are most suitable for implements and weapons. Unfortunately we again do not know when or where it was first used in the Near East. The evidence from southern Mesopotamia suggests that it was not adopted there until the early third millennium BC, although it may have originated elsewhere at an earlier date.

Despite this advance, however, metal was evidently not regarded as superior to stone for some purposes even in the third millennium. Some of the finest flint points ever made in Mesopotamia were produced around 2700 BC, and at Tell Brak in the Khabur basin, which between 2300 and 2000 BC housed the provincial headquarters of the south Mesopotamian rulers referred to above, all the arrowheads of this period that have been found are of stone. In this particular instance the cost of copper, which might have been high enough to discourage ordinary villagers from using it, is hardly an explanation since Brak controlled one of the main roads from the south to the mines near Ergani. A more probable reason is the relatively late discovery that the hardness of copper was greatly improved by alloying it with about a tenth of its own volume of another metal to produce bronze. The second metal that has been almost universally employed in Europe for this purpose is tin, but so far we have been unable to find any definitely attested source of tin in the Near East. This is still a mystery, for tin was certainly available in considerable quantities from some source after 2000 BC. But tin bronzes are very rare before that date. Other alloys such as arsenic or lead were sometimes used, but the great majority of Near Eastern metal objects older than 2000 BC that have been described by excavators or museum curators in the past as bronze have, on analysis, proved to be copper with only such impurities as might have been present in the original ore. Nonetheless, the quantity of copper objects found on sites throughout the Near East rises steadily, with a very marked increase in the fourth millennium BC, and the amount actually recovered probably gives us a minimal estimate of the proportion of objects that were made of metal rather than stone, because metal was commonly reused.

The increased use of metal in the fourth millennium BC is only part of a general expansion of trade that coincided with the emergence in southern Mesopotamia of the first towns which grew into cities during this time. Southern Mesopotamia, as we have observed, has no native resources other than the products of its very fertile soil, and we may well imagine that the increasing demand of its inhabitants for metals and for other essential and luxury materials would have stimulated the economies of the areas where they were produced, and of the lands through which the trade routes passed. This is not to say that trade was the only factor in the development of these areas, some of which were already creating their own forms of urban life. Another motive which appears to have encouraged people to live together in large communities, particularly where the growth of population created competition for available resources, was self-defense. But the spread of south Mesopotamian influence can be seen in the archaeological record.

Pottery styles. From the early fifth millennium BC we find a particular type of painted pottery, 'Ubaid ware, which up to that time had been made only in the southern alluvium, spreading towards the Zagros and southwards into eastern Arabia, then progressively north and northwestwards and into western Iran where it is found side by side with, and often replacing, the earlier local wares. Some of this material may actually have been made in the alluvium; a great deal of it consists of local imitations of the southern pottery. It is clear evidence of increasingly close contacts, but what the nature of these contacts was we cannot say on the evidence of pottery alone, for decorated pottery is very much a matter of fashion and fashions can be transmitted in different ways. But about 4000 BC, at the north Mesopotamian site of Tepe Gawra, elaborate temples were built which in their plan and decoration closely resemble southern temples of the same date. The design of formal religious buildings of all ages tends to reflect the ceremonies that are performed in them, and in this case it is hard to believe that north and south did not share some common religious observances, although the divinities worshiped were not necessarily the same. Such a community of ceremonial must surely imply that people from one area were actually resident in the other, if only in small numbers as traders or the like.

Shortly after this time there was a great change in pottery styles, marked by the introduction of the plainer "Uruk" wares that are named after one of the great southern cities, and have in turn given the name to the period that covers most of the fourth millennium. These again are very widespread throughout the Mesopotamian basin and into southwestern Iran. In the later Uruk period there were even contacts with Egypt, and seal impressions in the Mesopotamian style have been found as far away as Seistan on the eastern borders of Iran. The tradition of temple building continued at Tepe Gawra, and at Tell Brak in the Khabur basin a whole series of temples of Late Uruk date, endowed with rich offerings, again suggest direct connections with the south, where Uruk itself now had a religious precinct of vast extent. At Brak, as at Gawra, we cannot yet interpret these connections historically, although we may recall that a thousand years later Brak was an outpost of southern political power. But the most startling discovery of all has very recently been made on the bend of the Euphrates in Syria, where it approaches most closely to the Mediterranean and where the very ancient route up the valley from southern Mesopotamia branches either northwest to the Taurus or westwards to Aleppo and the sea. Here, at a site called Habuba al-Kabira overlooking the west bank of the river, German archaeologists have found a settlement over 1,000 meters long with a massive fortification wall, projecting towers and a heavily defended gateway, in which not only is the pottery wholly of Late Uruk type but even the bricks are of a distinctive shape that is characteristic of Uruk itself at this time. No documents have yet been found, although the first known pictographic script was now being used in the southern cities, but Habuba al-Kabira must surely be a town deliberately founded from southern Mesopotamia to control the trade route, perhaps even to administer the surrounding countryside.

Here, in fact, we get our first authentic whiff of the political control which, partly for economic reasons, the Mesopotamian empires of the third and later millennia exercised over their neighbors. The achievements of these empires are the subject of another volume in this series. But the discovery of Habuba al-Kabira emphasizes another point that is of the greatest importance to our theme. Ten years ago no one had guessed that such a site existed. In the next ten years other sites of different periods will have been discovered which in turn will alter our whole knowledge of Near Eastern prehistory, and scholars will propose different interpretations which will affect our understanding of it. In a subject as young as ours we must realize that the often unexpected revelation of new facts and the ideas and prejudices of those who interpret them are an integral part of the study. It is the progress of research, often controlled by changing mental attitudes, that forms the subject of our next two chapters.

2. The Pioneers of Near Eastern Archaeology

Censuyt la table du mireur du monde.
Comment nostre seigneur crea adam et eue. Et de leur gene
ration jusques a larche que noe fist au deluge. De noe et de ses
enfans. et de leurs generations. jusques abraham. De abraha
ysaac iacob et de leur lignie. Du comencement des regnes et
dominit seigneurie temporelle. Du regne des assiriens. et des fondations
de plusieurs cites. Des roys degypte. de moyse. et de plusieurs prophetes.
Du preux josue. de saint samuel. Du roy saul. de david. de salmon et des
aultres roys de judee. De hercules. theseus. jason. Du siege de troie la grant
et la destruction dicelle troye. de la fondation de romme. de sicambrie. et de
lutesse. et daultres cites. Dalexandre. Des roys de surie. Des romains qui
conquesterent la seigneurie temporelle de tout le monde. Du preux judas
machabeus et des machabees. Des batailles de lucius silla. et de gayus marius
deux consulles de romme. De pompee le grant et du preux julius cesar. Coe
julius cesar fut premier empereur de romme. De lempereur octovien auguste. et
de la bataille dycelluy octovien. et de anthoine. Du regne octovien jusques

The idea of prehistory. The study of Near Eastern prehistory is less than a century old and the existence of many of the earlier communities described in this book was hardly suspected even 50 years ago. To a large extent its development reflects the motives, ideas and prejudices of archaeologists and, equally if not more important, the sponsors who gave them money. Until the last generation most of the archaeologists and their funds came from Europe or America, and we must look briefly at the changing attitudes to the origins of human society that were current in these countries when archaeological exploration in the Near East began.

In Europe an interest in the material remains of the past had long been among the more scholarly pursuits of educated people. In Britain published surveys of the countryside from the 16th century onwards often included some description of its ancient monuments, and indeed one of the earliest collectors of such information, John Leland, was appointed King's Antiquary in 1533, the first and until now the only holder of this title. The fashion for collecting antiquities that began at about the same time in Italy quickly spread through Europe and these collections form the nuclei of many of our modern museums. In them the art of Rome and, in the 18th century, of Greece took pride of place, for these were the civilizations whose inheritance European gentlemen of taste regarded as their own. Prehistoric objects were sometimes included in cabinets of curiosities, but like the more substantial stone monuments and earthworks that attested the activity of early man, they were often interpreted in ways that seem to us bizarre. In the mid-17th century some writers believed that flint implements were produced by the action of lightning on metallic matter in thunder-clouds, although the more rational explanation that they were the tools or weapons of people who had no knowledge of metal had already been put forward before 1600. Inigo Jones, who made the first survey of Stonehenge for King James I, described it as a Roman temple. A later antiquary, John Aubrey, who worked under the patronage of Charles II, attributed it to the Druids, which was one step nearer to the truth.

We must remember that when the early antiquaries were dealing either with monuments or with smaller antiquities they relied on written evidence for the interpretation of their material, and their two main sources were the Bible, whose authority was virtually unquestioned, and the Greek and Latin historians. The beginning of history in France and Britain was the Roman conquest, and any finds that were too primitive to be Roman were vaguely attributed to the Ancient Britons or the Gauls. Moreover the account of the Creation in Genesis, when taken literally, could be used as proof that the world came into existence not more than six or seven thousand years ago. Archbishop Ussher in his study o Biblical chronology published about 1650 assigned th event to the year 4004 BC and this date was long printed i the margin of the Authorized Version of the Bible. I acceptance implied that less than 4,000 years had elapse between the time when Adam lived in the Garden of Ede and Julius Caesar's conquest of Gaul. The Garden of Ede was of course in the Near East, and there the tradition chronology was even more compressed for the Ol Testament recorded the existence of pre-Greek civiliz ations in Mesopotamia – the Assyrian and Babylonia empires – and in Egypt. When 18th-century schola turned to the Greek historians they found that Herodotu writing in the mid-5th century BC, had questione Egyptian priests whose records showed that the pharaoh had already ruled Egypt for 10,000 years. Their calcula tions were exaggerated, but by any interpretation th accepted Ussher's chronology, there was even less time fo prehistory in the Near East than in Europe.

In fact, even educated people before 1800 had n conception of the vast span of human history th preceded the first known civilizations, but in the 19t century new ideas began to emerge. Western Europe w already producing evidence that made it more and mor difficult to maintain the comfortable ascription of ever pre-Roman antiquity to a few millennia since the Crea tion. Stone implements and parts of human skeletons ha from time to time been discovered, together with th bones of extinct animals, deeply buried in gravel deposi or in caves where they were sometimes sealed by layers o stalagmite, and the fossil remains of earlier forms of li were found incorporated in sedimentary rocks. More over, geologists such as Sir Charles Lyell, who publishe his *Principles of Geology* between 1830 and 1833, believe that the formation of geological sediments must hav taken place at a uniform rate throughout the world' history, and would therefore have required a vastly longe span of time than the literal interpretation of Ol Testament chronology allowed. This argument, the found ation of modern geology, was countered by the "Di uvial" theory whose proponents maintained that ther had been a series of universal floods of which the Biblic Flood was merely the last, and explained the geologic evidence on which Lyell relied as the result of thes catastrophic inundations. Serious opposition to Lye continued until the middle of the century, but more an more scholars were coming to accept both the authenticit and the great antiquity of many relics of man's past and, a least implicitly, to reject the literal interpretation of th Bible. We should not forget how difficult this was. Th fashion of agnosticism led many people to reject revolu tionary ideas without considering them.

The other great innovation in the study of prehistor during the first half of the 19th century took place i Denmark. A mass of objects had accumulated in th National Museum in Copenhagen and, since the countr

Previous page: Adam and Eve in the Garden of Eden, from a 15th-century manuscript in the Bodleian Library, Oxford.

The Flood by Francis Danby (1793–1861). The Biblical Flood story not only caught the imagination of painters, but was long regarded as an established event that changed the history of the world.

had never even been on the borders of the Roman Empire, there was no written record of ancient tribes to whom they could be attributed. The first Curator, C. J. Thomsen, who was appointed in 1816, conceived the system of classifying the collections according to the material of which the objects were made, stone, bronze or iron, which in his view represented successive stages in the development of technology. The germ of this idea can be found in the writings of antiquaries as early as the end of the 16th century, but it was Thomsen who demonstrated its practical application and, by his example and his teaching, brought about its widespread acceptance in Western Europe. In his book *A Hundred Years of Archaeology* Glyn Daniel rightly observes that this was "the first step in dispersing the thick fog, the first step from the ignorance of antiquarianism to the knowledge of archaeology."

The Near East - travelers and diplomats. It was against the background of these developments and controversies that the serious examination of Near Eastern antiquities began. In the late 18th and early 19th centuries the imperial rivalries of European countries, particularly France and Britain, were focused on India. Although the Great East Indiamen that carried its trade were forced to make the long sea voyage around the Cape of Good Hope, the fastest route between Europe and India for the administrators and the mails on which their business depended lay overland from the east Mediterranean ports to the Red Sea or the Arabian Gulf. All the territory through which the overland routes passed was part of the decaying Turkish Empire, but Ottoman authority in Egypt was nominal from the end of the 18th century and Mesopotamia was virtually independent from 1704 to 1831. Britain and France both strove by various means to establish their influence in the area. Napoleon attempted the conquest of Egypt and was frustrated by Nelson's destruction of his fleet at the Battle of the Nile in 1798, but his expedition was accompanied by scientists and draughtsmen whose task was to record the geography and antiquities of Egypt and who remained to form the staff of the French Egyptian Institute, the first of many foreign research institutes that have been established in Near Eastern countries and have made a considerable contribution to knowledge of their history. It is ironical, though not surprising to an archaeologist, that the most important discovery made during the brief French military occupation of Egypt was made by Napoleon's sappers rather than his scholars, but the presence of the scholars ensured that the significance of the find was recognized. This was the Rosetta Stone, uncovered during the building of a fort near Alexandria, and it bore the same inscription in Greek and in two versions of the ancient

Egyptian script, thus providing the key for the decipherment of the Egyptian language.

Elsewhere the two countries sought to protect their interests by the more peaceful method of appointing diplomatic representatives. These were naturally drawn from the same educated class that produced, in their home countries, the scientists and antiquaries of the period, and the particular interest that led them to follow a career in the still mysterious East inspired some to become great pioneers of archaeology. The British East India Company had maintained a Resident at Basra since 1798, and in 1807 the first Resident arrived in Baghdad. He was a young man of 21 named Claudius James Rich, who had been appointed to a military cadetship in the Company's service four years earlier. Rich possessed to an extraordinary degree the intellectual curiosity of his time. When he visited the Company's offices in London to take up his appointment, it was suddenly discovered that he had a competent knowledge of Arabic, Persian and Turkish which he had gained by private study and by contact with Charles Fox, a Quaker merchant of Bristol, and an acquaintance with Hebrew, Syriac and even Chinese imparted to him by his mathematics master. Such was the versatility of the age. His linguistic ability ensured his immediate transfer to the civilian branch of the service as a "writer" destined for Bombay, but since there was no immediate vacancy there he spent some time in the Mediterranean and Turkey before reaching India by way of Baghdad. A few months later he returned to Baghdad as Resident, a post which he held until shortly before his death of cholera in Iran in 1821.

Despite the problems of maintaining the Company's interests and prestige in the face of sometimes hostile Turkish officials, Rich found time to pursue his linguistic interests, to study the history and antiquities of the country and to keep open house for other travelers of like mind. One of these, W. S. Buckingham, has left an account of his visit to the Residency in 1816 when he was on his way to India. He pays glowing tribute to the Riches' hospitality and, referring to the illness that prolonged his stay, says "the tedium of my confinement was considerably relieved by the number and variety of excellent books which Mr. Rich's library contained, and which were accompanied also by the most unreserved communication from the gentleman himself of everything calculated to increase the interest of my journey eastward." But the most significant assessment of Rich's work, not only in his library but in the field, came from Austen Henry Layard, who was born in the year after Buckingham passed through Baghdad and, 30 years later, was to prove himself the greatest of the British pioneers of Mesopotamian archaeology in the 19th century. Layard's remarks are worth quoting at length.

"The first to engage in a serious examination of the ruins within the limits of ancient Assyria was Mr. Rich, many years the political Resident of the East India Company at Baghdad, – a man, whom enterprise, industry, extensive and varied learning, and rare influence over the inhabitants of the country, acquired as much by character as by position, eminently qualified for such a task. The remains near Hillah, being in the immediate vicinity of Baghdad, first attracted his attention; and he commenced his labours by carefully examining the nature and extent of the site they occupied, and by opening trenches into the various mounds. It is unnecessary here to enter into a detailed account of Mr. Rich's discoveries among the ruins of Babylon. They were of considerable interest, though, of course, in results far behind what accident has recently furnished. They consisted chiefly of fragments of inscriptions, bricks, engraved stones, and a coffin of wood; but the careful account which he drew up of the site of the ruins was of greater value, and has formed the groundwork of all subsequent inquiries into the topography of Babylon. In the year 1820 Mr. Rich, having been induced to visit Kurdistan for the benefit of his health, returned to Baghdad by way of Mosul. Remaining some days in this city, his curiosity was naturally excited by the great mounds on the opposite bank of the river, and he entered upon an examination of them. He learnt from the inhabitants of Mosul that, some time previous to his visit, a sculpture, representing various forms of men and animals, had been dug up in a mound forming part of the great enclosure. This strange object had been the cause of general wonder, and the whole population had issued from the walls to gaze upon it. The ulema having at length pronounced that these figures were the idols of the infidels, the Mohammedans, like obedient disciples, so completely destroyed them that Mr. Rich was unable to obtain even a fragment. With the exception of a small stone chair, and a few remains of inscriptions, Mr. Rich obtained no other Assyrian relics from the ruins on the site of Nineveh; and he left Mosul, little suspecting that in these mounds were buried the palaces of the Assyrian Kings. The fragments collected by Mr. Rich were subsequently placed in the British Museum, and formed the principal, and indeed almost only, collection of Assyrian antiquities in Europe. A case scarcely three feet square enclosed all that remained, not only of the great city Nineveh, but of Babylon itself!"

The decipherment of cuneiform. If that was true of the relics of Mesopotamian civilization it is small wonder that prehistory passed unnoticed. Rich's collection, which included coins and Syriac manuscripts as well as objects from Babylonian and Assyrian sites, was bought for £8,000 by the British Museum after his death, but the earlier material was at first little regarded because the cuneiform writing employed in ancient Mesopotamia could not yet be read. It required a key such as had been provided in Egypt by the Rosetta Stone. The key existed in the trilingual inscriptions in cuneiform script and in the Persian, Elamite and Babylonian languages that had been cut on the spectacular monuments of Persepolis, one of the capitals of the Achaemenid dynasty (6th to 4th century BC), and on the rock reliefs of the Achaemenid kings in western Iran which had attracted the attention of many European travelers. They had been partly copied by a great Danish explorer, Karsten Niebuhr, in the late 18th century, and by 1802 a German scholar, Grotefend, had made some progress in picking out the kings' names and titles and in recognizing the letters that were represented by different cuneiform signs in the Persian text. But in the Elamite and Babylonian versions the signs represented syllables, not letters of the alphabet. This made the task of decipherment vastly more difficult, and it was not in any case until 1847 that a full copy of all three texts of the most important inscription, that of Darius I at Behistun near Hamadan, became available.

A young Indian Army officer, H. C. Rawlinson, had begun the task ten years earlier when he was stationed in Hamadan as a member of a military mission. It was only completed after he had been appointed at his own request, in 1843, to Rich's old post as Resident in Baghdad so that he might pursue his cuneiform studies in his leisure time. His final achievement was a copy of the Babylonian text on an almost inaccessible rock face, and this was in fact executed by "a wild Kurdish boy who had come from a distance," who ascended the face of the rock by a chimney, traversed it by toe and finger holds and finally suspended himself on a cradle to take molds of the inscription under Rawlinson's directions. From this moment the decipherment of cuneiform was virtually assured and Rawlinson was one of its leading scholars. As Resident in Baghdad he was also in a position to influence the course of archaeological exploration in the field, and this was particularly important at the moment when major excavations were about to begin. But excavation in the Near East, where a single mound representing the citadel of an important ancient city may be 100 acres in extent and up to 40 meters high, was far more expensive than the investigations of local archaeologists in Europe and could be financed on a large scale only by the support of wealthy individuals or governments. It was not just the concern of scholars that counted, but the enthusiasm of men of influence and of the increasingly wealthy – though not necessarily educated – middle class.

The years since Rich's death had seen in Europe a growing interest in the monuments of Near Eastern civilization, stimulated by the accounts of Rich himself, of Buckingham and other travelers of different nationalities. One of these who had also been Rich's guest in Baghdad and had traveled widely in Iran was Sir Robert Ker Porter. Of him the German-American Assyriologist H. V. Hilprecht wrote in 1903: "He had become a famous painter of international reputation, whose eminent talents, striking personality, and final marriage with a Russian princess had secured for him a social standing which enabled him, by his pen and brush, to reach circles but little influenced by the books of ordinary travelers and the scientific and often dry investigations of men of the type of Otter, Niebuhr, Beauchamp and Rich. In his popularisation of a subject which had so far stirred the minds of only a limited class of people, and in appealing by his religious sentiment, the manner of his style, and the accurate representation of what he had observed, not less to the men of science and religion than to the aristocratic circles of Europe, on whose interest and financial support the resurrection of Assyria and Babylonia chiefly depended, lies the significance of Ker Porter as a Babylonian explorer."

Hilprecht had reservations about Ker Porter's standing as a scholar, for he goes on to say: "Compared with the clear statements and sober facts presented by his predecessors, Porter's book is sometimes deficient in definite information, – pious meditations and personal speculations occasionally becoming the undesirable substitute for an intelligent description, judicial discrimination, and logical reasoning." We have quoted Hilprecht at length because he made a number of important points, and he made them with feeling because he too was a 19th-century archaeologist who had to raise money for his excavations. The Russian princess is a nebulous figure in the history of Near Eastern archaeology but she, and Ker Porter's standing as a fashionable painter, gave him a hearing in influential circles. His "religious sentiment" was an obvious recommendation to a wider audience, and it is interesting to notice that Hilprecht's own book, which is a straightforward study of 19th-century archaeology in the Near East, is entitled *Exploration in Bible Lands*. But Porter's "accurate representation of what he had observed" must have had an even greater appeal. In the present century two of the most important media that have brought archaeology to the attention of the public are illustrated books and magazines and television because, for most people, to read about something is no substitute for seeing it.

Unfortunately the appearance of Porter's volumes on the coffee tables of the great did not in fact produce, at least in Britain, any sustained financial support for Near Eastern research. Indeed the only major project that was undertaken was the Expedition for the Survey of the Rivers Euphrates and Tigris, which was mounted between 1835 and 1837 under the personal patronage of William IV and the command of Col. F. R. Chesney. The prime object of the expedition was to test the navigability of the Euphrates as part of the route to India and to explore the possibilities of Mesopotamian markets. It was indeed an unparalleled enterprise, involving the transportation of two iron paddle-steamers in parts to the mouth of the Orontes in Syria and thence by camel to the bend of the Euphrates, where they were reassembled and proceeded downstream. Although its main purpose was commercial, the expedition accumulated a vast amount of information about the topography, history and antiquities of the lands through which it passed, and it is characteristic of the time that its surgeon, W. F. Ainsworth, was also the official geologist and an enthusiastic antiquary. It is no less to be expected that he interpreted his archaeological observations in the light of his extensive knowledge of the Bible and of Greek, Roman and Arab writers. Prehistory simply did not occur to him.

Flandin's view of Kuyunjik, citadel of Nineveh, with the outer city wall in the foreground and on the skyline the city of Mosul, Nineveh's modern successor.

The first excavators. Such was the situation when the great era of Assyrian and Babylonian excavation began. Both scientific and popular interest was focused on the material remains of the ancient civilizations as illustrations of Biblical and Classical history, and scholars were also largely concerned with the decipherment of their language. Money for research that offered no immediate diplomatic or commercial return was – as ever – short, and it is important to remember that the first excavators, like the explorers who preceded them, were amateurs who came to the Near East at their own expense or in some other employment. They had received no archaeological training, for there was none to receive, and it is surprising not that they made mistakes but that they made so few.

The first of them to arrive in Mesopotamia was P. E. Botta, a professional member of the French consular service who had served for some years in Egypt and was appointed in 1842 as the first French vice-consul in Mosul. He was immediately urged by the Société Asiatique in Paris to search for Assyrian remains in Kuyunjik, the citadel of Nineveh which faces Mosul across the Tigris. He did so for some time at his own expense with little result, probably because Kuyunjik, lying at the most important crossing of the Tigris in the northern plain, had been occupied for more than 1,000 years after the fall of Assyria in 612 BC and the remains of its Assyrian palaces and temples were overlaid by a mass of later debris. But while he was working at Nineveh Botta received reports of sculptures found at another site, Khorsabad, some ten miles to the northeast. At first he was skeptical. Stories of carved stones are all too familiar to Near Eastern archaeologists and to investigate them usually means a considerable waste of time and effort. We have vivid personal memories of leaving one of our party behind with a high fever in a small Turkish town and jolting in a cart over the southern Taurus mountains to visit an alleged Roman city which proved to be a basalt quarry. But Botta was more lucky, for Khorsabad was an exceptional site, a capital of the Assyrian Empire created by one of its greatest kings, Sargon, whose palace was lined with magnificent stone reliefs and lay close to the surface of the mound. After a few days' work with a small gang Botta wrote on 5 April 1853 to the Société Asiatique, "I believe myself to be the first who has discovered sculptures which with some reason can be referred to the period when Nineveh was flourishing."

He was also fortunate that the tradition of support for scientific investigation so lavishly inaugurated by Napoleon on his Egyptian expedition was still alive in Paris. He was immediately given a government grant to continue the work and an experienced artist, E. Flandin, was dispatched to assist him in recording his discoveries. Flandin returned to France in 1845, and was followed in 1846 by the first consignment of sculptures, which were floated on rafts down the Tigris and shipped from Basra aboard a French warship to find a permanent home in the Louvre. Botta's work was continued from 1851 to 1855 by his successor as vice-consul, Victor Place, who was a professional architect, the first of many whose rigorous training has enabled them to make a special contribution to Near Eastern excavation. The result was an almost complete plan of the vast palace as well as many new reliefs and inscriptions. Botta and Place published their discoveries with commendable speed and on a generous scale made possible by further government subsidies, and Hilprecht's assessment of their impact is worth repeating. "With great astonishment, artists and scholars began to realise how high a standard this people in the East had reached at a time when Europe as a whole was still in a state of barbarism. With extraordinary enthusiasm, students of philology and history welcomed the enormous mass of authentic material which, by its constant references to names and events mentioned in the Bible, was eagerly called upon as an unexpected witness to test the truthfulness of the Holy Scriptures. There has never been aroused again such a deep and general interest in the excavation of distant Oriental sites as towards the middle of the last century, when Sargon's palace rose suddenly out of the ground."

Flandin's drawing of the citadel mound of Khorsabad, scene of the pioneer French excavations in the mid-19th century. In the background is the first outlying ridge of the Zagros mountains.

Layard. The achievements of Botta and Place in the revelation of Assyria were matched on the British side by Austen Henry Layard, whose tribute to Rich we have already quoted. As a young man his boredom with the law to which he was apprenticed was matched by a great enthusiasm for the Orient, fired by early reading of the Arabian Nights and later the accounts of European travelers with one or two of whom he was acquainted. When he could stand a solicitor's office no longer he accepted the offer of a post with an uncle in Ceylon and set out to ride overland through Turkey and Iran with one companion who, like himself, had no money for the more luxurious forms of transport. Layard later became a member of parliament and minister at the Ottoman and Spanish courts, but he always looked back "with feelings of grateful delight to those happy days when, free and unheeded, we left the humble cottage or cheerful tent, and lingering as we listed, unconscious of distance or the hour, found ourselves as the sun went down under some hoary ruin tenanted by the wandering Arab, or in some crumbling village bearing a well-known name." In the spring of 1840, when he was just 23, he arrived in Mosul where he met W. F. Ainsworth, the surgeon and archaeologist of the Euphrates Expedition, and Christian Rassam, a native of Mosul and the British vice-consul whose brother Hormuzd was to become Layard's assistant and successor. In their company he visited the sites of the great Assyrian cities, and then continued to Baghdad where he was entertained at the Residency and made good use of the library. After a period of often dangerous travel among the tribes of western Iran he returned penniless and in rags to Baghdad, whence he was sent with dispatches to Istanbul. Stopping for three days in Mosul, he met Botta who had just arrived, and discussed with him the prospects of excavation in the great mounds they had observed. In Istanbul his intimate knowledge of the tribes and personalities on what was then the Turkish-Iranian frontier commended him to the British Ambassador, Sir Stratford Canning, who employed him as his personal secretary. During this time he was privileged by Botta's friendship to read the reports of his discoveries on their way to Paris, to write summary reports on them for the *Malta Times*, and to see Flandin's drawings as the artist passed through Istanbul early in 1845. In the spring of that year Botta wrote to Layard "Come, I pray you, and have a little archaeological fun at Khorsabad."

There was nothing Layard would have liked better, but Canning had failed to get him an established diplomatic post and he had no money of his own. Layard finally left Istanbul in October 1845, when Botta had already returned to France, with a personal advance from Canning of £60 for the journey and £20 a month for a two-month season of excavation on the site of an earlier Assyrian capital, Nimrud, some 30 miles south of Mosul. The work at Nimrud was immediately successful in uncovering sculptures but Layard's reports and appeals for money, although enthusiastically supported by Canning, were at first coldly received in London and when grants were

Above: Layard saved money by digging perilous tunnels at Nimrud. But the notebook under his arm was filled with admirable records, and his illustrations are works of art.

Below: Layard's interest was Mesopotamian civilization, but his sponsors demanded works of art for the British Museum. Their transport was not the least of his problems.

finally made by the British Museum and later the Treasury, they were niggardly by comparison with the support accorded to Botta and Place by the French government. Moreover the publication of Layard's discoveries was not financed as in France by public money but by a private publisher, John Murray. Murray had no reason to regret his investment, for Layard had employed the intervals between his early seasons of excavation from 1845 to 1847 – periods of leisure that were largely imposed by the delay in obtaining funds – in travels through northern Mesopotamia and eastern Turkey. His first two volumes, *Nineveh and its Remains* (1849), not only give an entertaining and scholarly account of the excavations at Nimrud, which he then believed to be part of ancient Nineveh, but also include descriptions of his journeys that compare easily with the best travel books ever written. The *Times* review called it "the most extraordinary work of the present age" and Layard's uncle Benjamin Austen wrote "Half the noblemen in the country are calling on Murray." Layard reported in a letter to Mitford, his earliest Near Eastern traveling companion, that 8,000 copies had sold in one year, "which will place it side by side with *Mrs. Rundell's Cookery*." Indeed an abridged version of the book was published in 1851 especially for sale on railway bookstalls, the first ancestor of the popular books on archaeology that have done so much to stimulate public interest in man's past.

We cannot dwell on the achievements of Layard and his French colleagues or their successors, which were in detail more relevant to the discovery of the ancient Near Eastern civilizations than to the development of prehistory. But this great period of pioneer excavation cannot be ignored because its dramatic discoveries once again blocked the idea of prehistory in the minds of scholars and of the educated public on whom they relied for money. Even Layard, who was a brilliant observer both in his excavations and on his travels, never asked himself what lay in the thick deposits of stratified material beneath his Assyrian palaces. On his excavation budget he could hardly afford to do so, but on his journeys he also assumed that any site he saw must be attributed to the ancient civilizations he knew. When he passed across the northern edge of the Mesopotamian plain he spent the night in Tell Afar, about 50 miles west of Mosul. "From the walls I had an uninterrupted view over a vast plain, stretching westwards towards the Euphrates, and losing itself in the hazy distance. The ruins of ancient towns and villages rose on all sides; and, as the sun went down, I counted above one hundred mounds, throwing their dark and lengthening shadows across the plain. These were the remains of Assyrian civilisation and prosperity." We have had the good fortune to follow in Layard's footsteps among those very mounds during the last 20 years. Judging by the pottery that we found on the surface, some were indeed reoccupied in the Late Assyrian period, but the great majority are settlements that were originally founded in prehistoric times and at least one fifth of them were inhabited villages before 5000 BC. Even the greatest of archaeologists sees what experience has taught him to expect.

Layard left Mesopotamia in 1851 after a second campaign of two years financed – inadequately in his opinion – by the British Museum. This work was focused on Kuyunjik, which he now recognized as the citadel of Nineveh, and was also increasingly directed under Rawlinson's influence to the recovery of texts, for Rawlinson and other scholars were rapidly approaching a real understanding of the language. The proof of their success came in 1857, when a baked clay cylinder bearing a historical inscription was independently submitted to three other experts who agreed so closely with Rawlinson's translation that there could be no further question of its essential correctness. There followed a period of intensive translation and publication of the texts which yielded two discoveries of particular interest. The first was the identification of Sumerian as an independent language. As early as 1869 the French scholar Jules Oppert suggested that it had been spoken by a pre-Babylonian people, although it was not until French excavations at the south Mesopotamian site of Telloh in 1877 revealed a number of their characteristic statues that the civilization of the Sumerians began to assume a visible form. But the recognition of their existence pushed back the boundaries of history and led scholars to wonder who they were and where they had come from. The second discovery appealed to more popular and traditional interests. In 1872 George Smith announced that he had found a Babylonian account of the Flood among the tablets from Nineveh in the British Museum, and this gave dramatic support to those who regarded the Old Testament as a precise historical source for which archaeologists merely provided the illustrations.

Unfortunately archaeology did not make comparable progress. The Crimean War diverted public attention and money in Britain and France, and the excavators who followed Layard, Botta and Place were not men of the same caliber. Layard had ruefully admitted that the parsimony of his sponsors had forced him "to obtain the largest possible number of well-preserved objects of art at the least possible outlay of time and money," yet his reports and plans and those of his French colleagues are still consulted by their successors today. But many of those who came after them in the next 30 years had neither their competence nor their conscience, and the sites they dug still present formidable problems to modern archaeologists. It is small wonder that although buildings and cone mosaics of the late fourth millennium BC, contemporary with the earliest pictographic writing, were uncovered at the great Sumerian site of Warka (ancient Uruk, Biblical Erech) in 1854 they could not be dated and attracted little attention. From 1877 to 1882 Layard's assistant Hormuzd Rassam, working for the British Museum, was in nominal charge of many simultaneous digs throughout the province of Baghdad, some of which he visited only at intervals of several months. As Hilprecht remarks, "It was the old system of pillage in a new and

From the citadel of Tell Afar (seen here) Layard counted more than 100 ancient mounds, "throwing their dark and lengthening shadows across the plain"; but the plain in his day was inhabited only by Bedouin.

enlarged edition." Moreover, to legalized looting on behalf of the great museums, whose agents had at least the duty to report the provenance of their finds, there was now added the scourge of illicit digging by dealers who kept no records at all and were interested only in the prices they could obtain. Nowadays such abuses are regulated by departments of antiquities administering strict antiquities laws. But a hundred years ago, although official excavations required a permit or *firman* from the Ottoman government, local supervision was in the hands of officials who were ignorant of archaeology, often antagonistic and sometimes corrupt.

The dawn of the new order. The beginning of the end of this free-for-all came with the foundation of the Imperial Ottoman Museum in Istanbul and the appointment of its first director in 1877. He was Hamdi Bey, a young man of 34 and son of a former grand vizier, who had studied painting and sculpture in Paris and then served briefly and unwillingly in the Diplomatic Service. Starting with one small building in the gardens of the sultan's palace, a miscellaneous collection of antiquities of all ages and sizes and not even a crowbar to move his packing cases, he labored for 25 years to create the great museum that is now one of the most important in Europe. His energetic devotion to archaeology and in particular to the enlargement of the national collections led him to seek more effective control over excavations throughout the Turkish dominions, and his personal influence ensured that the necessary regulations were made. To put them into effect was another matter. Wallis Budge, who represented the British Museum in Egypt and Mesopotamia in the latter years of the 19th century, referring to the antiquities trade in Baghdad, remarks "It was quite easy for Hamdi Bey and the Ministers in Stambul to frame laws and draft regulations, but it was a wholly different thing to enforce them in a region which was some fifteen hundred miles distant, and was controlled chiefly by telegrams from the Porte." In fact Budge himself was a great buyer and proudly recounts the devices by which he outwitted the local authorities. But the long and distinguished rule of Hamdi Bey inaugurated a new attitude to antiquities in the Ottoman Empire and the separate Turkish and Arab states that are its descendants.

At the same time excavators and their methods were changing. The change came earliest in the lands outside Mesopotamia where written documents of the pre-Classical periods were rare or as yet undiscovered, and there was no vast booty of *objets d'art* to divert the archaeologist's attention from the more mundane evidence for the history of his site as a place where generations of people had lived, buildings had risen and decayed, tools and pots had been made and broken. This often dull material was the stuff of prehistory in Western Europe, but in that temperate climate the choice of a place to live had never been as restricted as it was in the Near East

Above: a reconstructed section of Late Uruk cone mosaic from Warka, similar to that found by Loftus in 1854.

Opposite: Sir Flinders Petrie (1853–1942), one of the great pioneers of systematic excavation in Egypt and Palestine.

Below: a second-millennium city in the plain below Tell Afar, founded on the site of a prehistoric village.

where the need for water dictated the choice of sites and one settlement was commonly founded on the ruins of its predecessor. What was needed here was a technique for the excavation of stratified mounds, and one of its pioneers was Heinrich Schliemann. Schliemann's career was the epitome of the 19th-century tradition of self-help. Born the son of a clergyman, he rose from grocer's assistant to millionaire merchant by the age of 40, and in 1863 decided to retire from business and pursue an interest in archaeology inspired by his boyhood reading of Classical literature. Like his predecessors he was an amateur, unlike them a wealthy one, and the book that inspired him was not the Bible but Homer's account of the Trojan War, which many then regarded as pure legend. He had in his private studies, and in opposition to scholarly opinion, determined that the site of Troy was the mound of Hissarlik overlooking the mouth of the Dardanelles and after some years of exploration among the Homeric sites of Greece he began to dig at Hissarlik in 1870. Seton Lloyd, one of the pioneers of the modern school of Near Eastern excavation, says in his *Early Anatolia* (1956) "Schliemann's excavations at Troy brought him at once in contact with a civilisation at whose prodigious antiquity he could only guess," and his guesses were wildly inaccurate. In the sequence of seven cities that he recognized, he claimed the third and later the second as the site of Homeric Troy, but later research has shown that they must both be dated more

than 1,000 years earlier. The methods of excavation too left much to be desired, although they were somewhat improved by the arrival of W. Dörpfeld, first as his collaborator and then his successor. Dörpfeld increased the number of cities to nine and this remains the basis of the modern classification. But to unravel the stratigraphy of this very complex site and to turn it into history without the assistance of inscriptions required five years of patient work in the 1930s by an American expedition with professional training and a vastly increased knowledge of the material, produced by two intervening generations of research and excavation on other sites. The achievement of Schliemann and Dörpfeld was to expose the problems of digging a stratified site, and it is no discredit that they failed to solve them.

Petrie. The greatest contribution to method in Near Eastern excavation in the last quarter of the 19th century was made by W. M. Flinders Petrie. In his autobiography, *Seventy Years in Archaeology* (1931), Petrie says that even as a child he was "in archaeology by nature" and claims that at the age of eight he had been horrified at hearing of the excavation of a Roman villa in the Isle of Wight "by the rough shovelling out of the contents, and protested that the earth ought to be pared away inch by inch to see all that was in it and how it lay." As a young man he tramped through southern England making precise surveys of prehistoric monuments, and one of his earliest works was a study of Stonehenge, published in 1880 when he was 27. At the end of the same year he arrived in Egypt for the first time. "The state of affairs into which I emerged was in great transition. The recognition of flint implements had been the great battle during my boyhood, and they were at last accepted. Layard and Newton and Schliemann had begun to dig up great things, but the observation of the small things, universal at present, had never been attempted. The science of observation, of registration, of recording, was yet unthought of; nothing had a meaning unless it were an inscription or a sculpture."

Petrie's efforts to resolve this confusion and to introduce what he called "Systematic Archaeology" were embodied in his book *Methods and Aims in Archaeology* (1904) which was the first manual of technique for the Near Eastern excavator and can still be read with profit. One problem which he faced for the first time was the relative dating of Egyptian prehistory. This was especially difficult because the evidence, which was just beginning to emerge, came from cemeteries and not stratified settlements, which are still almost unknown in Egypt today. Petrie devised a system which he called "Sequence Dating," whose principle is best given in his own words. "Let us suppose some old country mansion, where it has been the habit to close permanently any room in which an owner had died, and leave everything in it undisturbed. If we went through such a series of rooms we could not doubt their order of date if we looked at their contents. The William IV room could not be put to the middle of George III's reign; the George II room could not be supposed to go between those of James II and Anne. Each room full of furniture would have some links of style with that of the generation before, and of the generation after it, and no real doubt could exist as to the sequence of the whole series. What is true of a room full of furniture is equally true of a grave full of pottery." The simplicity of the statement conceals the vast and patient labor of classification, of recording the progressive changes in form and fashion that the contents of the cemeteries revealed, but in the end Petrie was able to assign each grave to a chronological group represented by a number in the sequence from 30 to 80, 1 to 29 being reserved for older periods as yet undiscovered. Although Sequence Dating was never adopted outside Egypt, this was a most significant advance in archaeological thinking, for it recognized the need for a chronological system that did not depend on absolute dates, and it also marked the beginning of statistical analysis of archaeological material. Petrie may be said to have anticipated the computer prehistorians of today by three-quarters of a century, and it was particularly appropriate that he should be elected a Fellow of the Royal Society in 1901.

In the meantime, however, he made a more immediate impact on methods of excavation outside Egypt when he was invited in 1890 to excavate on behalf of the Palestine Excavation Fund. Most earlier exploration in Palestine had been directed to the topography of the Holy Land, in particular of Jerusalem, and based on surface survey. Petrie's first season there lasted only three months, and a mere six weeks were spent excavating at Tell el Hesy, which he believed to be the site of Biblical Lachish. He did not dig in Palestine again until 1926, but his work at Tell el Hesy made a profound impression on his successor at the site, F. H. Bliss, who wrote in *The Development of Palestine Exploration* (1906) "Tell el Hesy to the eye of most travellers counterfeited a natural hill, but to his trained vision promised rich results even before systematic excavations were begun. Pocket-knife in hand, he climbed the steep slope to the east, where, owing to the encroachment of the stream during the course of ages, a section of the artificial mound had been practically laid bare. The story of the site was suggested in outline by fragments of pottery of various ages, as well as by the indication of strong walls of mud-brick not easily to be distinguished by the ordinary observer from natural unworked soil, but clear enough to Petrie's eye, and clearer still after a little scraping with the pocket-knife." When the season was brought to a close by the departure of his laborers to the harvest, Petrie used the sequence of pottery that had been obtained to date the archaeological sites he found during a month's survey of southern Judaea. Here in a nutshell we have examples of the two basic techniques that have contributed most to the study of Near Eastern prehistory, the stratified excavation of a tell, including the examination of a section through its successive occupation levels, and the use of the information thus gained to identify other sites by surface survey. It is worth recalling that the "trained vision" owed nothing to outside help, for only five years previously Petrie had complained that he received neither training nor criticism from his sponsors in London, and indeed when he offered a collection of pottery from his Egyptian cemetery to the British Museum it was rejected as "unhistoric rather than prehistoric."

The great expeditions. The great European museums and the American institutions that were now entering the field were still concerned mainly with the sculptures and inscriptions that were the products of civilization, whether in Egypt or Mesopotamia, and the priority of the Aegean, Anatolia and Palestine in the effective study of prehistory was largely due to the fact that in these areas history began so late. But in the 30 years before World War I put a stop to archaeological activity there were discoveries and developments in Mesopotamia and Iran that began to focus attention on the existence of a remote pre-Sumerian antiquity, and to lay the foundations of technique by which it would eventually be explored. The age of the digging consuls and the amateurs was at last coming to an end, and they were replaced by expeditions staffed by men whose immediate competence was not necessarily superior, but whose aims and methods were increasingly judged by an international standard of excavation.

The first of the new-style expeditions resulted from a visit by the French archaeologist, Jacques de Morgan, in 1891 to the vast mounds in the southwest Iranian province of Khuzistan that mark the site of Susa, one of the capitals of the Achaemenid Empire from the 6th to the 4th centuries BC. Material of the Achaemenid period had already been found there, but de Morgan collected sherds of painted pottery and flint implements around the base of the mounds and correctly deduced that they contained the debris of an immensely long period of pre-Achaemenid occupation. The French government was persuaded of the importance of the site and purchased from the Shah not only the concession for excavation at Susa but the exclusive right to dig on any ancient site in Iran. Thus was born the Délégation Française en Perse, probably the most important and widest-ranging European expedition ever mounted in a Near Eastern country. De Morgan dug at Susa from 1897 until World War I and his successors are there to this day. He had been Director of Antiquities in Egypt and was unfamiliar with the problems of such a site, nor did he have Petrie's flair for excavation, and his interpretation of the sequence of prehistoric cultures has subsequently been amended and expanded. But his work had two important effects. The very elegant painted pottery that he sent back to the Louvre made educated society aware for the first time that Near Eastern prehistory had something to offer to their cultured taste. Secondly, the massive financial support accorded to the Délégation by the French government – an initial estab-

A painted beaker of the Susa A phase (early fourth millennium). The early discovery of prehistoric painted pottery at Susa encouraged the long-held belief that the 'Ubaid peoples came from Iran.

ishment grant of £4,000 and an annual subsidy for working expenses of over £5,000, worth almost ten times as much today – ensured the continuity of work at Susa and other sites without the necessity that plagues so many expeditions to justify their continuance from year to year by spectacular discoveries. On these terms the study of prehistory was a practical proposition, and indeed the work of the Délégation so dominated the scene that until World War II any new discovery of prehistoric pottery in Mesopotamia that showed a degree of artistic refinement was almost automatically explained in terms of "Iranian influence."

Discoveries of prehistoric pottery were in fact made in Mesopotamia during the years before World War I although their significance could not be fully appreciated at the time. Baron Max von Oppenheim, a German diplomat who had traveled widely in the Arab countries and acquired an intimate knowledge of the Bedouin, was commissioned in 1899 to reconnoiter the line of a projected railroad to be built by German engineers from Istanbul to Baghdad. It is interesting to observe that the purpose of his mission reflects the international rivalry for influence and the control of communications in Turkish Arabia that had led to the pioneer archaeological exploration of the previous century, although it was now Germany and not France that was Britain's competitor in the political field. Near Ras al 'Ain in northern Syria Oppenheim heard reports of the discovery of sculptures on a nearby mound, Tell Halaf, but he was unable at the time to do more than confirm their existence. It was not until 1911 that he returned to excavate the site, where he worked until 1913 and again after the war in 1927 and 1929. The sculptures formed the decoration of a 9th-century palace belonging to a local ruler, but their primitive aspect at first led some scholars to suppose that they were reused and had originally been carved at a much earlier period, the early third or even the fourth millennium BC. In fact they are contemporary with the palace, and the most striking relic of the earlier occupation was a collection of finely made pottery, brightly painted with intricate designs in red, brown or black over a light slip. Now known as Halaf ware, this is technically the finest product of prehistoric Mesopotamian potters and actually dates from the first half of the fifth millennium, although its true position in the sequence of prehistoric cultures was not recognized until the excavations at Nineveh and Arpachiyah in the early 1930s which are described in the next chapter. Indeed the origin and character of the people who produced and used it are still something of an enigma.

While Oppenheim was engaged on his first season at Tell Halaf, another German traveler and scholar, E. Herzfeld, was excavating the site of Samarra, on the Tigris 75 miles north of Baghdad, which it replaced briefly as the capital of the Abbasid Empire in the 9th century AD. Beneath the Islamic city Herzfeld happened on a group of much earlier graves containing handmade pottery painted with elaborate geometric designs and some stylized animal and plant motifs which again is known by the name of the site as Samarra ware. Once more it was impossible to date at the time and its stratigraphic position was first established at Nineveh, but it is only in the last 15 years that it has certainly been recognized as characteristic of the first known communities who practiced irrigation farming in central Mesopotamia in the second half of the sixth millennium BC. But although neither Oppenheim nor Herzfeld was able to anticipate later knowledge in the interpretation of their material, the importance of their discoveries should not be underrated because they excited interest in prehistory and posed questions that their successors are still trying to answer.

New standards. The most valuable achievement of German archaeologists at this time, however, was not the fortuitous discovery of new types of prehistoric pottery but the introduction of new standards into Mesopotamian excavation. A new German Oriental Society, the Deutsche Orient-Gesellschaft, was founded in 1898 under the patronage of Kaiser Wilhelm II and at once mounted an expedition to Babylon under the direction of R. Koldewey. In his history of Mesopotamian excavation, *Foundations in the Dust* (1947), Seton Lloyd has admirably summarized its purpose. "Like their colleagues of other nationalities these newcomers were by no means averse to the discovery of removable antiquities for their museums or the acquisition of texts for the benefit of the many German scholars who had followed Grotefend in the realm of Assyriology. Yet their main purpose was a new one, namely, the careful examination of the architectural and social setting from which such antiquities had hitherto been so heedlessly removed. Their second aim was to elucidate for the first time the historical significance of stratification in Mesopotamian mounds." From the latter point of view Babylon presented unexpected problems, for although it had been an important town as early as the 18th century BC when it was Hammurapi's capital, the monuments that the expedition actually exposed were nearly all of the Neo-Babylonian Empire in the 6th century when the city was largely rebuilt by Nebuchadrezzar, and the earlier levels proved inaccessible because they were below the water table. But digging and recording were meticulous, and for the first time in Mesopotamia an effective technique was developed for the excavation of the unbaked mud-brick which is by far the commonest ancient building material in the country. It is a mark of changing attitudes that epigraphists were not full-time members of the German team, which included – as subsequent German expeditions have traditionally done – a high proportion of architects. Among Koldewey's chief assistants were three who were to continue and improve on his methods, Walter Andrae at the Assyrian capital of Ashur from 1903 to 1914, and J. Jordan and A. Nöldeke at the southern site of Warka from 1929 onwards.

As we shall see in the next chapter, Warka was to prove a revelation in Mesopotamian prehistory, but it was Andrae at Ashur who, in addition to excavating the major buildings and sampling the upper levels by a series of trenches set out on a grid pattern, executed a deep sounding to examine the stratigraphy of the site. The earliest levels he reached were of the first half of the third millennium BC and in them he found a temple containing statues of Sumerian type, the first evidence of the expansion of Sumerian influence outside the southern alluvium. Ashur is an important road station and may have been one of their trading colonies. Andrae found no earlier material and it is possible that the site was not occupied in the prehistoric period, for it lies on the very edge of the zone of reliable rainfall. But it was the technique of the deep sounding first carried out at Ashur that was perhaps the most important of his many contributions to archaeological method in Mesopotamia, for it was subsequently copied on other great city sites such as Nineveh, Warka and Eridu where it produced essential evidence for the sequence of prehistoric cultures and for their relationship to the earliest historical periods.

The era of the great expeditions had begun and fortunately there had been time, before they were interrupted by World War I, to establish the new pattern of meticulous long-term excavation and the professional code that it embodied. When work was resumed after the war, not only were the new standards widely accepted by expeditions of many nationalities, but the local workmen whom Andrae had trained at Ashur – known as Sharqati after the modern name of the site – brought their skills to the excavation of many sites throughout the country that was now independent Iraq. Working at the second-millennium site of Tell al Rimah in the northern plain west of Mosul between 1964 and 1971 we employed many of their sons and grandsons, and in 1971 actually received a visit from one of the original generation who had worked with us at Nimrud 14 years before and had started his archaeological career as Andrae's surveying assistant at Ashur in 1903.

Above: a Samarran bowl from Hassuna, with a centrifugal design of stylized ibexes. This pottery was first found in sixth-millennium graves below the Abbasid capital at Samarra.

Below: a Halaf bowl from Arpachiyah. Probably the finest prehistoric ware in Mesopotamia, it was first identified by Baron von Oppenheim at Tell Halaf in northeast Syria.

The Art and Craft of Prehistoric Pottery

VISUAL STORY

Pottery is one of the most useful types of object found by archaeologists. Not only does it reveal something of the activities and technology of the people who made it but potsherds are virtually indestructible and their presence littering the surface of a Mesopotamian site often gives the archaeologist his first clue to its date. Ceramic styles change relatively rapidly, and it is for this reason that pottery is a useful criterion for distinguishing one archaeological period from another.

The first known pottery comes from Mureybet in Syria and is dated c. 8000 BC. It is crudely made and not highly fired. This means that it remained porous and was therefore not useful as a container for liquids. Coarse lightly fired pottery is also found at Ganj Dareh in Iran (late eighth millennium). In the latter part of the seventh millennium BC pottery came into widespread use in the Zagros, but other types of container were still preferred in the Levant and Anatolia. The first pottery from lowland areas of Mesopotamia is that of the Hassuna period, the earliest phase of which is represented at Umm Dabaghiyah and Tell es-Sotto. The jar illustrated *below* comes from an early level at Hassuna (Ic).

The earliest pottery was handmade, the clay being crudely shaped into some form of container. Firing increases the hardness of pottery and decreases its porosity, but some simple handmade containers, still common in the Near East today, are merely sun-dried. After an initial period when crude pottery is found, and then only rarely, techniques of pottery manufacture improved rapidly; by the sixth millennium BC "professional" potters were turning out pottery of a high quality, though it was still only handmade. By the late fifth millennium a slow wheel was in use, probably turned by hand, but on which the potter was able to achieve more regular, thinner-walled vessels. By the beginning of the Uruk period a fast-spinning potter's wheel had been invented, and it is at this time that the first mass-produced pottery appears. Both potters illustrated here are using a foot-operated wheel on which the pot is "thrown." The Turkish potter on the far left (*opposite*) is shaping a large vessel from a long roll of clay held over his shoulder. The vessel rests on a tall stand on the wheel which he rotates with his foot. A pile of carefully prepared raw clay can be seen in the background. The Afghan potter shown on this page (*above*) is piling coils of clay, a technique well attested in antiquity, preparatory to throwing a pot. In the foreground a jar is drying before being fired. In the lower photograph (*left*) the same potter is shown throwing a jar like the one illustrated above.

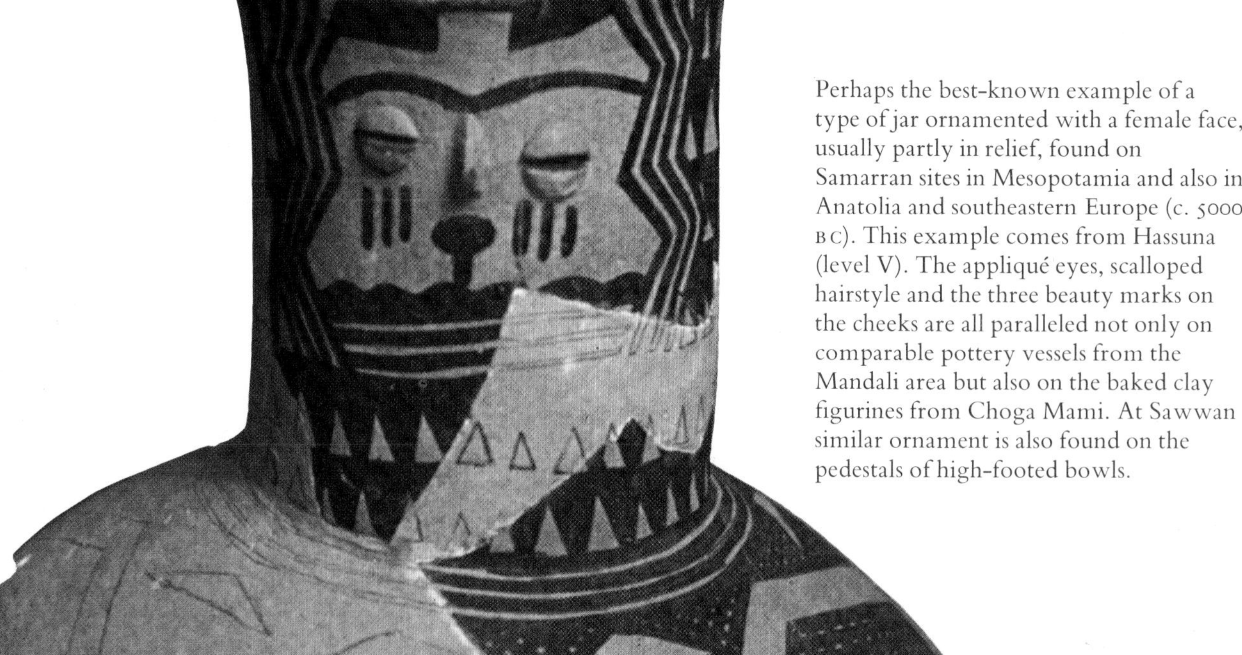

Perhaps the best-known example of a type of jar ornamented with a female face, usually partly in relief, found on Samarran sites in Mesopotamia and also in Anatolia and southeastern Europe (c. 5000 BC). This example comes from Hassuna (level V). The appliqué eyes, scalloped hairstyle and the three beauty marks on the cheeks are all paralleled not only on comparable pottery vessels from the Mandali area but also on the baked clay figurines from Choga Mami. At Sawwan similar ornament is also found on the pedestals of high-footed bowls.

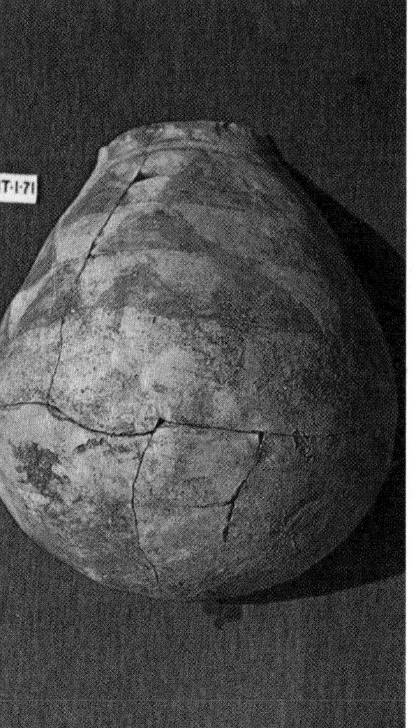

A two-chambered pottery kiln is first found at Yarim Tepe I in the sixth millennium BC. This technological advance coincides with an increased professionalism and the occurrence of clearly demarcated "industrial" areas on the site. The Yarim Tepe kiln (illustrated *opposite*) shows clearly the lower firing chamber, in which traces of burning can be seen, and the remains of the upper, originally domed part, with heat vents in the floor, in which the pottery was placed for firing. The large painted jar from Yarim Tepe (*far left*) is an example of one type of Hassuna pottery manufactured at the site, when these kilns were in use.

Left: the first extensive use of animal ornament on prehistoric pottery is found in the Samarra period. One of the most amusing examples from Choga Mami is this large pot (ht. 28 cm) ornamented with three panels of defecating ibexes with a background of centipedes and swastikas, the latter a very common Samarran motif.

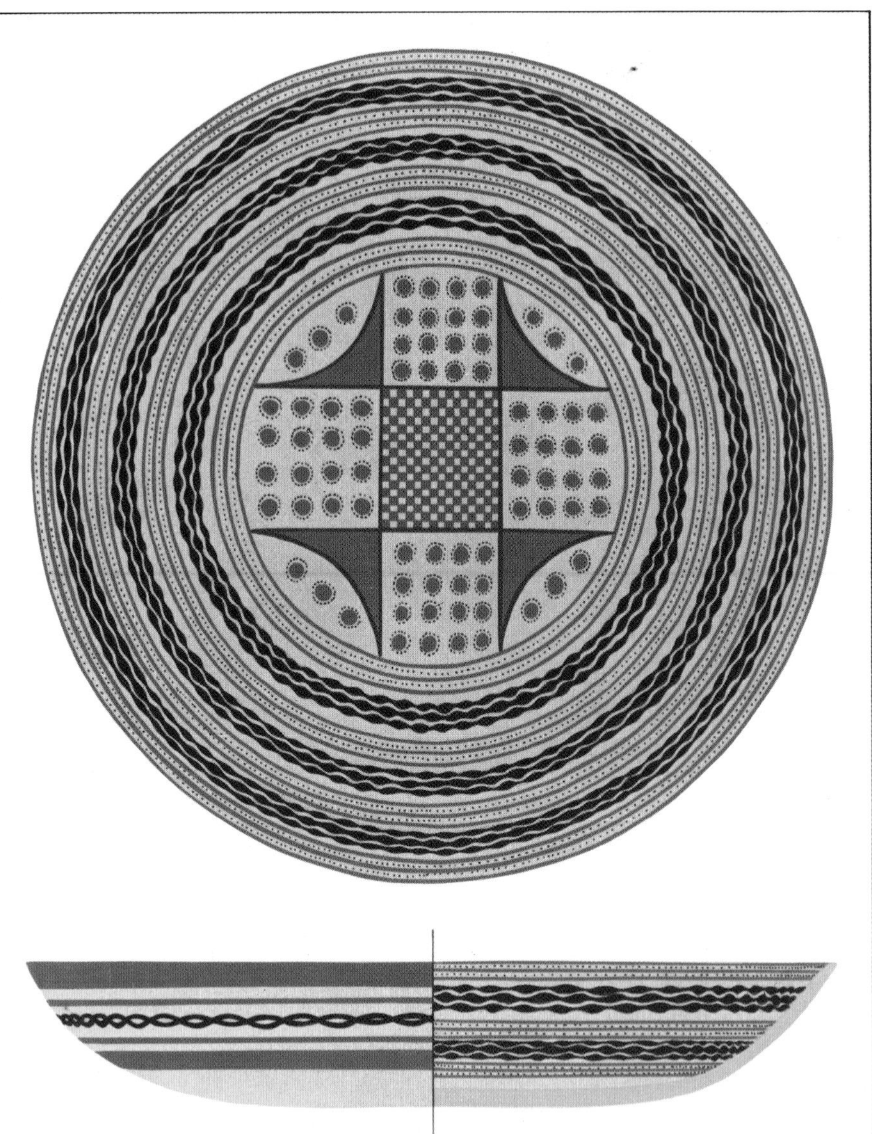

Right: the extraordinary competence of Halaf potters is perhaps best illustrated by this elaborately ornamented polychrome plate (diam. 24 cm), one of a group found at Arpachiyah in what is thought to have been a potter's workshop (TT 6). The house had been burned and the pottery deliberately smashed. Arpachiyah is thought to have been an artisans' village, serving what was almost certainly a more important Halaf settlement at the nearby mound of Kuyunjik (Nineveh), situated at the major northern crossing of the Tigris.

Below: pottery decorated with human figures appears for the first time in the Samarra period. These "dancing figures," male and female, ornamented a bowl of the slightly later "Transitional" style (c. 5000 BC). A similar motif, the so-called "dancing ladies," appears in a highly conventionalized form on the inner rim of vessels at a number of Samarran sites.

Left: one of the finest examples of early animal design on painted pottery is this handsome cobra with its double fangs. This is a very early Halaf piece from Arpachiyah, late sixth millennium BC.

Below: these early Halaf sherds come from a small unexcavated site not far from Tell Afar. They are ornamented with bulls' heads or bukrania, a motif common on Halaf pottery. In later Halaf levels this motif becomes highly stylized, developing finally into a horizontal figure-of-eight-shaped pattern. The method by which Halaf potters obtained their splendid lustrous effects is not entirely understood but is now being studied. What *is* clear is that they did not use special clays, as has often been suggested, but employed the same raw materials used to make the superficially very different Samarra and 'Ubaid ceramics.

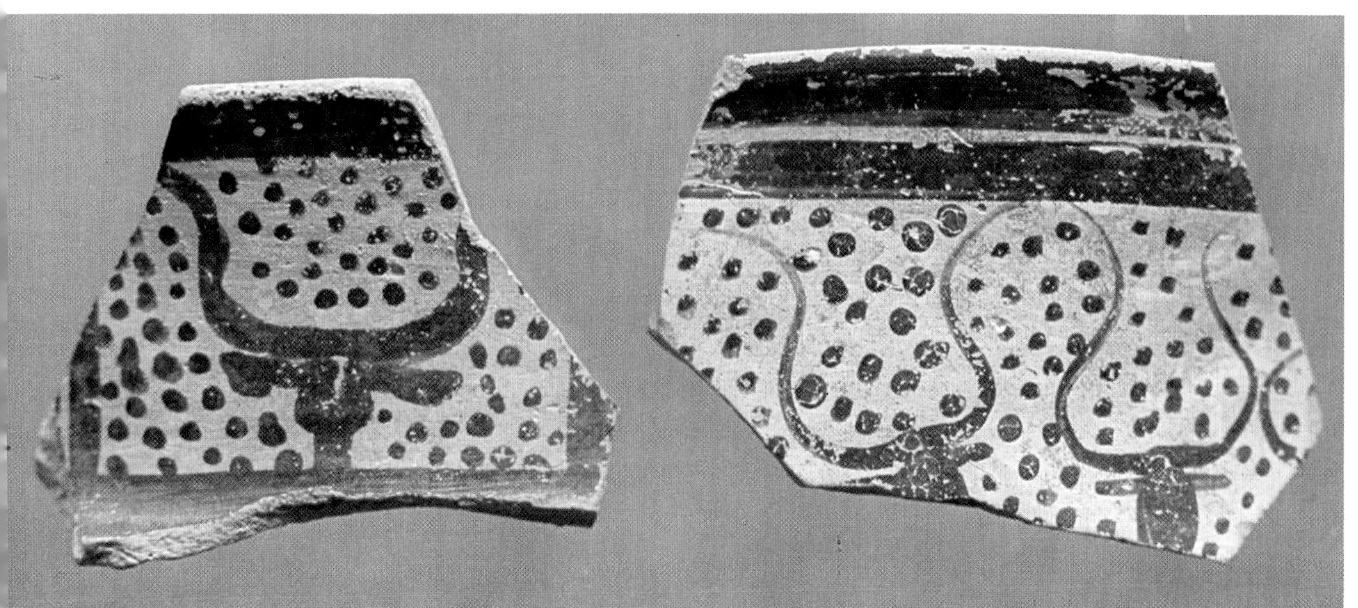

)pposite: a spouted jar from the site of ımdat Nasr, an example of a type of heel-made painted ware that is to be ated to the very end of the Uruk period, : a time when most Mesopotamian ottery was no longer decorated.

Right: a painted plate from the latest hase of the al 'Ubaid period ('Ubaid 4) diam. 23 cm). It was found at Ur in a rave dug into the so-called "Flood" eposit in Pit F. The simple boldly ainted design is characteristic of pottery rom this latest 'Ubaid phase (Woolley's Jr-'Ubaid II).

Below: a large painted bowl from level I t Hacılar (c. 5000 BC). This red-on-cream vare, decorated predominantly in a linear tyle, is characteristic of Hacılar I. This is n contrast with the less common but nore attractive painted ware of levels V-I, on which highly complex geometric atterns, often reminiscent of textiles, are ound.

Painted ware of a very high quality continued in use far longer in Iran than in the urban centers of neighboring Mesopotamia. *Above* is an example of the elaborately ornamented pottery found at the site of Susa in Khuzistan, dated to the early fourth millennium BC (Susa A). This pottery shows a very high degree of technical competence and great variety in decoration. It represents without doubt one of the most beautiful and sophisticated of ancient pottery styles. The beaker (*left*) is from western Iran and illustrates a very attractive type known from the site of Sialk (level III, fourth millennium BC). Animals, often ibexes or goats, with elaborately drawn horns, form a common decorative element, while the "skidding" posture is particularly characteristic.

3. The Birth of Near Eastern Prehistory

The 20th century. World War I not only interrupted archaeological exploration; it changed the political face of the Near East. What had been the Arabian provinces of Turkey were carved up into separate states, which in the Levant and Mesopotamia were placed by League of Nations mandate under the tutelage of the victorious powers whose traditional interests had lain there. Until World War II Lebanon and Syria were effectively administered by France and Palestine by Britain, while Iraq remained under British mandate until 1932. One benefit of these arrangements was that European advisers regulated archaeological activities in the mandated countries by the establishment of antiquities departments and the promulgation of antiquities laws covering the proper conduct of excavation and the ownership and disposal of antiquities, of which the more important now found a home in national museums. A second and not unnatural consequence was that British and French archaeologists were the first to resume work in their respective mandates.

The Antiquities Service of Iraq and the first Iraq Museum were organized almost single-handed by the dominant figure of Gertrude Bell, then Oriental Secretary at the new British Embassy, whose accounts of Near Eastern journeys and records of ancient monuments from 1892 onwards rank her among the greatest of British travelers, and who had served during the 1914–18 war in the Arab Bureau in Cairo. On 23 August 1921 the Emir Faisal, who had been head of the short-lived Arab Government in Damascus until the previous year, was crowned as the first king of Iraq. On 17 September Gertrude Bell wrote to her family, "It's not at all true that I have determined the fortunes of Iraq, but it is true that with an Arab government I have come into my own."

Both her energy and her influence were most effectively devoted to the cause of antiquities, for on 17 July 1922 she was able to say "Today the King ordered me to tea and we had two hours' most excellent talk. First of all I got his assistance for my Law of Excavations which I've compiled with the utmost care in consultation with the legal authorities. He has undertaken to push it through Council – he's perfectly sound about archaeology, having been trained by T. E. Lawrence – and has agreed to my suggestion that he should appoint me provisional Director of Archaeology to his government, in addition to my other duties. I should then be able to run the whole thing in direct agreement with him, which would be excellent." From then until her death in 1926 her letters are full of references to her museum, which was gradually being filled with objects from the excavations conducted under the new Law, and to the "divisions" in which she, representing the Government, drove a hard bargain with the excavators at the end of each season.

Previous page: the city of Erbil in northern Iraq, inhabited continuously for at least 8,000 years, provides one of the finest examples of the formation of Mesopotamian mounds or "tells."

The first excavators to resume work after the war also included many men who had been employed in the Near East as political or intelligence officers. T. E. Lawrence who is most famous as a leader of irregular troops and adviser to the Emir Faisal during the Arab revolt, never returned to archaeology, although it had been the occasion of his early Near Eastern experience, when he worked at Carchemish (modern Jerablus) on the Turkish-Syrian frontier. The first director of that expedition in 1910 was D. G. Hogarth, head of the Arab Bureau during the war and so Gertrude Bell's and Lawrence's immediate superior and its other members at different times were R. Campbell Thompson, whom we have already encountered digging at Nineveh, and Leonard Woolley.

The first of them to start excavating was Campbell Thompson, who found himself in 1918 as a captain in the Intelligence Corps in Mesopotamia, and even before the armistice was making soundings at Ur and Eridu on behalf of the British Museum, though to no great effect, for he was himself more Assyriologist than excavator and used

bove: Sir Leonard Woolley, famous as the excavator of Ur of the haldees and the first great British pioneer in Mesopotamian ·ehistory.

pposite: Gertrude Bell, founder of the Iraq Antiquities Department, ·ith T. E. Lawrence who excavated at Carchemish before his more ›ectacular career in World War I.

ıdian troops to do the digging. His immediate successor s the Museum's representative, H. R. Hall, who was sent ut from England in 1919, had little more success at Ur – e used Turkish prisoners of war – but he did discover a umerian temple at the nearby mound of al-'Ubaid, a site whose name is one of the most famous in Mesopotamian rehistory because it yielded to Woolley the first known ettlement of the "'Ubaid" people whom we regard as the rehistoric ancestors of the Sumerians. Woolley himself ecame a major in the intelligence service, was captured nd spent two years as a prisoner of war in Turkey. On his elease in 1918 he was sent as political officer to the Jerablus rea, and briefly reopened the excavations in 1920, but was ummoned in 1922 to direct the expedition at Ur. One of Gertrude Bell's letters records his arrival (1 November 922). "I've been figuring in my capacity as Director of Archaeology. Mr. Woolley arrived on Sunday. He is a irst-class digger and an archaeologist after my own heart – .e., he entirely backs me up in the way I'm conducting the Department. He has come out as head of a joint expedition ›rganised by the British Museum and Pennsylvania Jniversity and they are going to dig Ur, no less, and are ›repared to put in two years' work."

Leonard Woolley. Woolley's Anglo-American sponorship did not relieve him of the familiar problem of noney, for on at least one occasion he was obliged to pass he hat around the British community in Baghdad in order o meet the expenses of a season. But despite his financial worries he dug at Ur for 12 seasons, and in that time he nade an outstanding contribution, not only to the collections of the new museum in Baghdad and of the nuseums in London and Philadelphia to whom the Iraq Antiquities Department assigned a share of the finds, but o standards of excavation and publication. Realizing the impossibility of excavating such a vast and complex site with the untrained labor that was locally available, he brought his highly skilled foreman, Hammoudi, and his two sons from Jerablus and set about training a competent team of workmen on the less demanding tasks. His forebearance in this respect, when spectacular discoveries in the early seasons might have brought him greatly increased financial support, is illustrated by the fact that, although he knew in the first season that there was rich material to be found on the spot where he later discovered the Early Dynastic Royal Cemetery, he deliberately postponed its excavation until 1926 when he felt that his workmen were equal to the undertaking. His meticulous recording of everything he found is evident from the annual reports presented in the *Antiquaries Journal* and the series of massive volumes, all drafted by him, that are still appearing 16 years after his death. Nor was he a dry-as-dust excavator. To him all that he found was the stuff of history, and although we may disagree in detail with his interpretations, they remain both valuable and readable.

The second of his famous discoveries was the so-called Flood Deposit, one of a number of such deposits that have been observed on sites in Sumer. They do not all date to the same period and their precise significance is still a matter for argument, but it seems that at least some of them represent local inundations of considerable severity that might have coalesced in folk memory into the Flood legend. For our own purpose the Flood Deposit has another interest, for it overlay the remains of mud-brick houses and reed huts, part of a settlement that Woolley thought had been built on an island in the marshes. These settlers used a distinctive type of painted pottery that also reappeared in somewhat different form in graves sunk into the upper levels of the deposit itself. Sherds of this ware had been found by Campbell Thompson at Eridu and by Hall at al-'Ubaid. Woolley himself dug at al-'Ubaid in 1923–24 and found a similar settlement of flimsy houses, considerably earlier than the Early Dynastic temple discovered by Hall, and a cemetery containing the same painted pottery as at Ur, which was known henceforward as "'Ubaid" ware. For the first time stratified evidence of prehistoric Sumer was coming to light.

It is interesting to notice that, although the main and natural preoccupation of excavators in southern Mesopotamia at this time was the civilization of Sumer, the best of them were looking further back to the question of Sumerian origins, and in doing so they adopted the method pioneered by Andrae at Ashur of making a deep sounding beneath the historical buildings that they had exposed. A sounding at Kish near Babylon by another Anglo-American expedition in 1926–28 produced in its lowest levels some puzzling microlithic flint implements, followed by polychrome painted pottery. Again the excavators turned to a nearby mound where the same material was found on the surface and the polychrome ware, which we now know to be characteristic of the latest prehistoric phase, was named after the site, Jamdat Nasr.

Warka. The most important event of these years, however, was the reopening in 1928 of the German excavations at Warka (ancient Uruk) where work begun in 1912 had been cut short by the war. Andrae played a considerable part in the arrangements for the expedition but was never its director. Nonetheless, the directors of the Warka expedition have always maintained the exact standard of excavation established by him and by Koldewey at Babylon, and the only criticism we might make is that they have not presented, as Andrae, Koldewey and Woolley did, a readable summary of their results for the general public. Although Warka was a large city as late as the Parthian period it happens that, presumably as a result of erosion, the late prehistoric levels are close to the surface on some parts of the site. W. K. Loftus had discovered the remains of colored cone mosaics there in 1854 without having the least idea of their date. Now the German expedition was to reveal, by meticulous brick-by-brick excavation, an astonishing range of great monumental temples and other buildings, originally two separate complexes that had been the focuses of different settlements and had apparently merged to form the religious and ceremonial center of the unified city of Uruk towards the end of the prehistoric period. The center of one of these complexes (Kullaba) before the unification was the "White Temple," a building of the so-called tripartite plan, with a long central chamber and symmetrically disposed side rooms. It is thought to have been dedicated to Anu, the god of the heavens, whose sanctuary was close by in later times, though in the absence of documents this cannot be proved. But of more immediate interest to us is the fact that it stood on a high terrace, commonly known as the Anu ziggurrat, within which were incorporated the remains of earlier sanctuaries, obviously in observance of a religious convention that forbade their complete demolition when they had to be replaced.

General view of the site of Warka.

Apparently in the other complex (Eanna) this convention did not apply, for here a succession of vast buildings, some also tripartite in plan, had been erected and then razed almost to the ground to make way for new layouts. There was evidently no high terrace like that on which the White Temple stood until after the unification when the White Temple had gone out of use. The level (Eanna III) in which it first appeared was dated to the period of the polychrome Jamdat Nasr pottery, while the preceding levels yielded a plain, largely wheel-made pottery style to which the name "Uruk ware" was given. A deep sounding in 1930–31 revealed 'Ubaid pottery below the Uruk levels, and thus established a sequence of prehistoric "cultures" in Sumer for which the names 'Ubaid, Uruk and Jamdat Nasr were formally adopted by a congress at Leiden in 1931.

Nineveh. Meanwhile in northern Iraq Campbell Thompson had resumed the excavations at Nineveh in 1927, and was joined there in 1931 by M. E. L. Mallowan who had served on Woolley's staff at Ur. The work was concentrated largely on the buildings of the Late Assyrian capital, but here too a deep sounding was carried out by Mallowan in 1931–32 which penetrated more than 2[illegible] meters to virgin soil. As in all deep soundings stairways had to be left to give access to the lower levels and as these spiraled downwards the excavated area, 20 by 14 meters at the top, contracted to about 2 meters wide at the base. But no less than 22 meters of the deposit proved to be prehistoric in terms of northern Mesopotamia, where writing is not yet known to have been used until the second half of the third millennium BC. The fifth level – at Nineveh they were numbered from the bottom – produced evidence of an obviously prosperous settlement contemporary with some phase of the Early Dynastic period in the south. Its distinctive painted and incised pottery has since been found on a number of mounds in the northern plain as far west as the Khabur, though the precise dating and significance of this widespread culture, known as Ninevite V, remains one of the major puzzles in third-millennium history. In level IV, about 5 meters thick and so denoting a lengthy occupation, were found the characteristic unpainted Uruk wares, while level III, represented by another 8 meters of deposit, again contained largely Uruk materials. Finally the last two levels yielded Halaf and then Samarra painted wares and, at the very bottom, sherds decorated with painted or incised patterns or a combination of the two. This material, then described as Ninevite I, was not to be put in any larger context until the excavation of Hassuna during World War II, but its relative date, like that of Samarra ware, was first established at Nineveh.

After work ceased at Nineveh in 1932 Mallowan turned his attention to the problem of the Halaf pottery which

Above: polychrome Halaf plate from the potter's workshop in level TT 6 at Arpachiyah, to be dated in the early fifth millennium. Diameter 32 centimeters.

Below: the mound of Tepe Gawra during excavation. The expedition has already been forced to abandon its intention of clearing the whole site level by level.

although long known from the site of Tell Halaf itself and from surface collections on northern mounds, still remained only a ceramic style. Of its makers and their way of life nothing was known. The opportunity lay close at hand in the small mound of Arpachiyah, only four miles east of Nineveh, where sherds of Halaf ware were abundant on the surface. In a single season of excavation during the winter of 1932–33 Mallowan produced the first, and still the only published, information about the houses, material equipment and way of life of the Halaf people, whose traces have since been found from Syria to the Caucasus. We shall speak again of the details of his discoveries in Chapter 5, but it is worth mentioning here that this was the first expedition supported by the British School of Archaeology in Iraq, founded in 1932 as a memorial to Gertrude Bell and partly endowed by a legacy from her estate, and the first of many expeditions that Mallowan himself directed. With Seton Lloyd, a trained architect who was then working with a Chicago expedition in the Diyala basin east of Baghdad and later became adviser to the Iraq Antiquities Department, he must rank in the company of Layard and Woolley among the greatest of British Near Eastern archaeologists.

Expansion of prehistoric investigation in the Near East. While the excavations at Nineveh and Arpachiyah were in progress another major contribution to north Mesopotamian prehistory was being made by an American expedition under the leadership of E. A. Speiser at the mound of Tepe Gawra ten miles northeast of Nineveh and close to Jebel Bashiqa, the first outlying range of the Zagros foothills. Layard had made a very brief sounding here in 1849 but had abandoned the site on finding only potsherds, although he noted that it deserved a more complete examination. Eighty years later it was the potsherds that were its main attraction, and the Americans

indeed proposed a complete examination, for it was their original ambition to excavate the whole of the mound to virgin soil. Despite its relatively small size, however – it measures only 130 meters across at the base – the project proved beyond their resources and the area of excavation had to be progressively reduced. Nevertheless, Gawra's 22 meters of stratified deposits gave a unique picture of the sequence of occupation of a small country town from the middle of the second back to the late sixth millennium, and produced startling evidence of its prosperity and wide contacts in the form of a series of elaborately planned and decorated tripartite temples closely resembling those of southern Mesopotamia. Twenty levels were identified in the main area of excavation. The first identifiable material was of the Halaf period, and this was succeeded by 'Ubaid and then Uruk phases to which the sequence of temples belonged. Another exceptional building in an early Uruk level was a large house surrounded by a massive circular wall, evidently the residence of a person of importance, and perhaps reflecting the need for defense against unruly neighbors in the nearby mountains – the preceding level had apparently been destroyed by fire.

That this period, the fourth millennium BC, was one of widespread prosperity in the northern plain was further demonstrated by Mallowan's next undertaking, a survey of sites combined with excavations in the Khabur basin and the Balikh valley in northern Syria. The survey revealed a great extension of settlement in the Uruk period, with occupation continuing on most sites through the third millennium. The principal excavations were carried out on two mounds, Chagar Bazar, where most of the finds were of the historical period but a deep sounding revealed a Halaf settlement, and Tell Brak. Brak is a vast site, over 80 acres in extent and 40 meters high, which overlooks an important crossing of the Wadi Jaghjagh, an eastern tributary of the Khabur, and must have controlled one of the principal routes from the Tigris valley across Jebel Sinjar to the Diyarbakir region of Anatolia. We have observed in Chapter I that it was in the third millennium BC a provincial capital of the rulers of Agade in southern Mesopotamia, and it may well have served a similar function in the fourth millennium, for beneath the ruins of the Agade "palace" Mallowan found a tripartite temple. This building was apparently dedicated to some cult of which the eye was the principal symbol and it is known as the Eye Temple. It had been decorated with stone rosettes very like those found at Warka in the Jamdat Nasr phase and other finds date it securely to that time, but it was only the last of a series of prehistoric shrines whose remains were embedded in the underlying platform, as in the so-called Anu ziggurrat at Warka. The ruins of the early temples had been plundered in ancient times by robbers who sank shafts and drove tunnels through the platform, but even what they had left behind provided Mallowan with a rich collection of amulets, beads and seals that had evidently been deposited as offerings in the shrines and sometimes even incorporated in the brickwork as foundation deposits.

The implications of all these discoveries will be discussed when we come to deal with the cultures concerned but we must observe here what a flood of new information was being produced by the deliberate concentration on prehistory that is perhaps the most important development of the 1920s and 1930s. The deep soundings on major sites, accompanied by the more extensive excavation of smaller mounds where the prehistoric material was not overlaid by the massive remains of later periods, had produced an outline of the relative chronology of Mesopotamian prehistory and begun to illustrate the economy and way of life of the population at different times and places. Moreover, field survey was being increasingly used, not merely as a means of finding sites for excavation, but to assess the distribution and density of settlement in different periods.

These developments were not, of course, confined to Mesopotamia. A major project including both survey and the excavation of three sites was carried out by an expedition from the Oriental Institute, Chicago, from 1933 to 1937 in the 'Amuq plain between Antakya and Aleppo in Syria, and not only provided much information about the sequence of prehistoric cultures there, but also proved that of 178 sites recorded more than a third had been occupied before 3000 BC. And in four seasons immediately before and after World War II an expedition led by John Garstang of Liverpool University excavated the mound of Yümük Tepe, on the outskirts of the modern port of Mersin in southern Turkey, revealing no less than ten meters of Neolithic deposits, followed by Chalcolithic and later occupations.

Garstang had been the first Director of the new Department of Antiquities set up in Palestine by the British Mandatory Government in 1920, an event that effectively regulated archaeology there for the first time and proved a great stimulus to research. We have already mentioned Petrie's contribution to method in Palestinian excavation in the late 19th century, and the Germans too, in their work at Jericho in 1909, had introduced their own meticulous standards of investigation, as they were doing at Ashur at the same time. W. F. Albright, the great American Biblical scholar and archaeologist, indeed observes in his *Archaeology of Palestine* (1949), "For the first time in our story we meet with a properly staffed excavation." But the work before the war had been almost entirely on historical sites or at least in their historical levels. Albright goes on to say, "The most extraordinary advance in Palestinian archaeology has certainly been in the field of prehistory. In 1920 this branch of our science was wholly undeveloped." The digging of cave sites from 1925 onwards, in particular by the English prehistorian Dorothy Garrod and Renée Neuville, a French consular official, led to the identification of Palaeolithic and Mesolithic cultures, the latter including the Natufian which

The mound of Jericho, showing the great trench that revealed levels of occupation going back to the ninth millennium BC.

appears to have been the precursor of the first Neolithic settlements. And in 1929 Garstang resumed the excavation of Jericho, where he penetrated for the first time to the levels at the base of the mound and revealed the existence of a Neolithic settlement in which the use of pottery was not yet known.

This period also saw the first attempts at a synthesis of the prehistoric Near Eastern evidence, notably by the great Australian prehistorian Gordon Childe, who performed the same service for European prehistory in his *Dawn of European Civilisation* (1925). The speed with which the subject was moving is demonstrated by the fact that Childe's first survey, *The Most Ancient East*, published in 1928, had by 1934 to be completely rewritten and reappeared under the title *New Light on the Most Ancient East*, and despite the interruption of almost all archaeological work during the war years, another new edition was required in 1952. Childe was a Marxist, and his acceptance of the Marxist approach to history sometimes colored his interpretation of prehistory. On the other hand his knowledge of the evidence was vast and he thought and wrote with exceptional clarity about its value. Moreover, his insistence on the importance of economic and social factors was a vital reminder that prehistory, like history, is an attempt to reconstruct the behavior of people. Unlike history, prehistory has no means even of guessing at their motives, and rigid theories of social evolution are a dangerous substitute for the documents that we shall never have. But there were in the 1930s too many archaeologists who regarded the study of flints, pottery or even art and architecture as ends in themselves, and the fact that this purely technical expertise has given way to a much broader view of what we are trying to do is largely due to Childe. He may not have converted many people to his own views, but he forced them to think.

Developments in Iraq. World War II interrupted archaeological activity nearly everywhere in the Near East with the exception of Iraq, where the Antiquities Department, with Seton Lloyd as adviser and two very able Iraqi archaeologists, Fuad Safar and Mohammed Ali Mustafa, as his colleagues, made fundamental discoveries on two prehistoric sites. These are best summarized in Seton Lloyd's own words (*Foundations in the Dust*, 1947). "Early in 1940 the first full-scale government excavation was undertaken on a prehistoric site called Tell 'Uqair, fifty miles south of Baghdad. A sensational discovery was made. This mound represented the well-preserved remains of a temple dating from the proto-Sumerian period and its walls were covered with painted frescoes. Its publication two years later in Chicago was the first intimation to archaeologists in their wartime *diaspora* that in Iraq at least excavations were still in progress. In the years that followed, other sites were selected for excavation in such a way that the periods which they represented should fall into sequence and eventually cover the whole panorama of Mesopotamian history. The training of staff was thus greatly facilitated, and by 1943 their standard of competence could be considered equal to that of most Western expeditions. It was under these circumstances that the site called Hassuna was discovered.

"As early as 1928 D. Garrod had found in the Kurdish mountains traces of Palaeolithic man. But a prodigious gap existed between these cave-dwellers and the settled agricultural communities of Tell Halaf and Samarra, with

Above: the site of Tell 'Uqair during the excavations of the Iraq Antiquities Department that revealed a Late Uruk temple with painted friezes, standing on a high terrace.

Below: drawing of an 'Ubaid 2 ("Hajji Muhammad") pot (after Ziegler).

their evidence of copper-smelting and other advanced processes. Working at Nineveh in 1931 Mallowan found indications of a culture preceding Samarra, but at such a depth beneath the surface that little evidence of its character could be recovered. Twenty miles south of Nineveh, at Hassuna, the Department now discovered a little mound whose surface, amid the grass and flowers, was littered with broken fragments of this pre-Samarra pottery. Its seven meters of super-imposed settlements in fact ended on the surface at almost the exact point beyond which the great pit at Nineveh had been unable to penetrate. During the months that the mound was under excavation the horizon of prehistory once more receded several centuries. Revealed in the simplest terms of archaeological evidence was a new and earliest chapter in the history of what may reasonably be called civilised man."

As part of this continuing program of research the Iraqi Department returned during the years 1947–49 to the site of Eridu, where there had previously been only a few desultory soundings. Excavating beneath the corner of the third-millennium ziggurrat they exposed a long series of prehistoric temples, all except the earliest tripartite in plan, and a sequence of 18 levels of occupation that went back to the beginning of the 'Ubaid period about 5000 BC, considerably earlier than anything that had been found in the deep sounding at Warka. In the lowest levels they found what was then regarded as a new variety of painted pottery which they termed Eridu ware, and above that sherds painted in a style known as Hajji Muhammad which had been identified on a site of that name near Warka just before the war, but not – until now – placed in its correct stratigraphic position. Most archaeologists now agree that Eridu and Hajji Muhammad are simply early forms of 'Ubaid pottery and they are commonly referred to as 'Ubaid 1 and 'Ubaid 2 respectively. This was a most important addition to knowledge of Mesopotamian prehistory, for it greatly extended the time range of occupation in the south, and most appropriately so at the moment when Lees and Falcon, as we have seen in Chapter 1, were working to disprove the traditional assumption that the area was beneath the waters of the Gulf until the fifth millennium. The second significant fact that emerged from the Eridu excavations was that throughout this long period of prehistory temple after temple attested the continuity of religious observance on the same spot where the precinct of Enki, the Sumerian god of water and one of the chief deities in the pantheon, later stood. This was a strong indication, if short of absolute proof, that the prehistoric inhabitants of the site were the ancestors of the Sumerians themselves. Moreover it suggested that the changes in pottery and material equipment – always gradual rather than abrupt – that had taken place through the 'Ubaid and Uruk periods reflected changes in style and technology rather than the "invasions," from Iran or elsewhere, to which archaeologists had been wont to ascribe them.

Lake Zeribar in the Zagros mountains in western Iran (c. 4000 feet high). Pollen cores taken from this lake provide one of our few sources of climatic evidence.

The aftermath of World War II. Foreign expeditions gradually returned to the Near East, some to continue the traditional work of long-term excavation which remains the fundamental source of archaeological information. New ideas and approaches were however emerging, and new techniques were being evolved for the recovery and study of evidence that had simply been irrecoverable ten years before. Improvements in the process of digging and recording can be traced in part to the influence of excavators trained in Europe, where the comparative flimsiness of many prehistoric sites had produced refinements of technique whose relevance to the excavation of Near Eastern mounds was not apparent until they were applied there. The best example of this development is the reexcavation of the site of Jericho to which Kathleen Kenyon returned in 1951. We shall have much to say about the results of her exploration of the early levels in the next chapter, and it is sufficient here to note that her meticulous methods, applied by a large staff many of whom had been trained on British sites, produced one of the most spectacular discoveries of this generation, a stone-walled town of the early eighth millennium BC with earlier occupation going back to the Mesolithic Natufian culture. Another feature of these latest campaigns at Jericho was the attention paid to the recovery of organic remains, animal bones and seed samples, though in the latter case the finds were disappointingly few.

The concern for faunal and floral material, as evidence both for the diet and economy of prehistoric peoples and for climatic conditions at different periods, became increasingly important in many prehistoric investigations at this time, particularly those relating to the earlier periods of settlement whose existence was only now being brought to light. Purely climatic studies of the post-glacial period in the Near East still lag far behind those in Europe, largely because Near Eastern conditions are much less favorable to the preservation of the husks of plant and tree pollen which have provided such useful indicators of climatic conditions in European prehistory – animal bones are less relevant in this respect because animals react less immediately to climatic variations than plants. Where pollen samples have been obtained, as for instance at Lake Zeribar in the Zagros, they indicate a climatic pattern that is at variance with other evidence elsewhere in the region, and this is not a problem that archaeologists alone can resolve. Indeed as archaeologists have come, in the last 25 years, to take more and more account of evidence that they are not personally trained to interpret, they have increasingly called on the services of specialists in scientific disciplines to deal with their material, not only in the laboratory but in the field. It is – or should be – as natural now for a prehistoric expedition to include a palaeobotanist or climatologist as it is for the excavator of a historical site to have a trained epigraphist on his staff.

In this respect American expeditions took the lead after the last war, partly because they had more money available, but also because they undoubtedly contributed a

Above: view of the site of Çayönü in southeast Turkey.

Opposite: alabaster human head from the Late Uruk "Eye Temple" at Tell Brak, 17 centimeters high. It is the earliest example of sculpture yet found in northern Mesopotamia.

new approach to prehistory which in their universities is a branch of anthropology and, commonly, concerned much more with social and economic interpretations than was the case in most European universities 25 years ago. The doyen of this movement is Robert J. Braidwood of the Oriental Institute, Chicago, who served on the American expedition in the 'Amuq plain before the war. Presented with the new evidence for early farming settlement at Hassuna in the north Mesopotamian plain, he applied himself to the problem of the origins of farming in the Fertile Crescent. Reasoning that the first domestication of plants and animals was unlikely to have taken place in areas where they were not, at least on modern evidence, to be found in the wild state, he decided to combine excavation and survey of sites in the hilly flanks of the Zagros where the wild species now exist and from whence the practices of herding and agriculture might have spread into the plain. The results of this initial project, begun in 1948 and published in 1960 as *Investigations in Iraqi Kurdistan,* embodied the work not only of archaeologists but of specialists in geology, zoology, botany and other fields of natural science. Hans Helbaek of the National Museum in Copenhagen was a notable member of the expedition, for he was the principal pioneer of the study of plant domestication from the changes that it produced in the form of the plants themselves, and also devised the first effective method of recovering minute remains of plants and seeds from archaeological deposits, the so-called "flotation" process.

The main site excavated by Braidwood during this operation was Qal'at Jarmo, on a hilltop not far north of the modern town of Chemchemal, which proved to be a settlement of the seventh and early sixth millennia BC with evidence for the domestication of both cereals and animals but, in its early stages, no pottery. We refer to Jarmo in more detail in the next chapter, but it is important here to reemphasize a point that Braidwood himself made, that Jarmo is but one of a number of small settlements that correspond roughly in density with modern villages in the area. It was certainly not a community on the scale of pre-pottery Jericho, and is unlikely to have been a pioneer center in the development of farming or any other techniques – it is quite clear for instance that pottery, already competent in manufacture, was introduced there from some other more important center. It is probable, in fact, that the remains of more advanced settlements of the same period lie irretrievably buried under the great tells piled up by millennia of continuous occupation at more naturally favored sites in the area such as Chemchemal, Kirkuk and Erbil.

Modern techniques. Later consideration led Braidwood to extend the zone where he would expect to find evidence of primary domestication to include the southern and southeastern flanks of the Anatolian plateau as well as the hill country of Lebanon and Palestine, and in 1969 he commented "our original 'hilly flanks of the crescent' was rather too restrictive (although the phrase still tends to hang about our necks like a dead albatross)." He and his colleagues undertook further surveys in western Iran and, in collaboration with Istanbul University, in southern

Turkey where they excavated the site of Çayönü and found a settlement with evidence of cereal cultivation going back possibly to 7500 BC. But one of Braidwood's main contributions to research has recently been well expressed by one of his assistants on the Turkish project; "his stimulation of a whole generation of archaeologists to undertake intensive fieldwork, with natural scientists included as a matter of course, on the problem of the origin of food production." Surveys and excavations designed to throw light on this large question have indeed been carried out in many parts of the Near East during the last quarter of a century, not only in what Braidwood called the "Nuclear" or "Natural Habitat" zone, but in areas such as Khuzistan in southwest Iran where it seems unlikely that all of the early domesticated plants and animals found there had ever lived in the wild state. The investigators have included scholars of many nationalities – Americans, British, Canadians, Danes, Dutch and French have all played a prominent part – but there is no space to enumerate them here. We attempt to summarize their results in the next chapter, but even that must be to some extent a catalog of incomplete evidence from which no firm general conclusions can be drawn. The issues involved are central to the development of settled life and hence of civilization, but it may be another 20 years before anyone can write a history of early farming societies.

We must not give the impression, however, that investigations devoted to the elucidation of individual problems were focused entirely on the very early phases of human settlement, or that they were the only form of logically planned operation during this time. We ourselves were especially interested in two cognate questions concerning a somewhat later period, the nature of the earliest settlement – apparently associated with Samarra pottery – in central Mesopotamia, and the origins of the irrigation techniques that must have been necessary for successful agriculture there and were certainly fundamental to the development of towns and cities in the south Mesopotamian alluvium. The excavation by the Iraq Antiquities Department of Tell es-Sawwan, which lies on a bluff overlooking the flood plain of the Tigris some 70 miles north of Baghdad, had already revealed a settlement with pottery almost exclusively of Samarra type in an area where rain-fed agriculture would have been quite impossible without a major change of climate, and for this there was no evidence. Survey in the Diyala basin east of Baghdad had revealed no sites of this period (sixth millennium BC), but the rate of deposition of alluvium in this area has been very high and has even effaced the traces of canals earlier than the first millennium BC. We therefore determined in 1966–68 to investigate the eastern rim of the plain where silt deposits become progressively thinner as one approaches the Zagros, and here we found a number of mounds with Samarra and 'Ubaid as well as later material. A season of excavation on one of these sites, Choga Mami, gave us not only specimens of seeds which, according to Helbaek, were almost certainly cultivated by irrigation, but even revealed the cross-sections of canals and smaller watercourses skirting the mound.

The survey of the Diyala basin mentioned above was made in 1957 and was the first of many carried out in central and southern Iraq and Khuzistan by R. McC. Adams and other American scholars which are of special interest because they were designed to identify patterns of

General view of the excavations at Çatal Hüyük.

settlement over many millennia and to relate them to the history and geography of the area. Furthermore, they made use of a tool, aerial photography, which had long been of great assistance to European archaeologists but had not – with the notable exception of Père A. Poidebard's surveys of Roman sites in Syria before the war – been widely employed in the Near East. The photographs, which had been taken for map-making, revealed the ancient courses of rivers and canals which could then be approximately dated by the pottery from sites associated with them. Similar area surveys, though without the benefit of aerial photography, have been made in western Turkey by members of the British Institute of Archaeology in Ankara. In 1950 the prehistory of this large territory was almost entirely unknown, except for sequences on the sites of Troy and Mersin which were hardly likely to be characteristic of the inland areas. Indeed as late as 1956 Seton Lloyd wrote in his *Early Anatolia* "the greater part of modern Turkey, and especially the region more correctly described as Anatolia, shows no sign whatever of habitation during the Neolithic period." Within the next ten years the situation had completely changed. Not only had many Neolithic sites been put on the map but James Mellaart, who played a leading part in the survey, had excavated a village going back to the seventh millennium BC at the site of Hacılar and at Çatal Hüyük, in the Konya Plain, a settlement which in the sixth millennium covered 32 acres and boasted shrines with elaborate wall-paintings and plaster relief sculpture. Yet other discoveries have been made by accident or – as in the case of the very early sites of Abu Hureyra and Mureybet on the Euphrates in northern Syria – as a result of rescue survey and excavation in an area that was to be flooded by a new dam. In such cases as these, although the sites might have been recognized in the ordinary course of archaeological exploration, they would almost certainly not have been found in a deliberate search for early agricultural settlements because they lie well outside the zone in which such settlements were presumed to lie. However apparently logical their approach to a problem may be, archaeologists must always be prepared for surprise discoveries that will radically alter their theories.

Dating. To end this chapter we must at least make mention of the advances in the scientific study of materials that have so greatly increased our ability to interpret archaeological evidence in the last 30 years. New methods of precise analysis that reveal minute differences in the chemical composition of stone and clay have made it possible, for instance, to assign the obsidian often found on sites in the Near East to its exact source, and thus to recognize one of the earliest known patterns of long-distance trade, while work now in progress will, we hope, enable us to reconstruct similar patterns in the production and distribution of pottery. But by far the most important of the new techniques is the "radiocarbon" method of determining the date of organic remains. Arising out of the research in atomic physics carried out during the war, this technique depends on the fact that every living organism contains a proportion of the radioactive isotope of carbon, C-14, which during its lifetime remains constant in relation to the total amount of carbon present, but after its death declines at a uniform rate. All radioactive material decays in this way, being transformed into isotopes of the same element or some other element that are not radioactive. Radioactive carbon decays fast enough to produce measurable changes over periods of a few centuries, and so to permit a calculation of the approximate date when the organism – tree, plant or animal – died. Unfortunately there are a number of doubtful factors in this calculation. The original estimate of the "half-life" of C-14 – that is, the length of time required for half of the original proportion of the radioactive isotope to decay – was approximately 5,570 years. This has later been increased by more accurate observations to c. 5,730 years, but archaeologists conventionally retain the lower half-life because further calculations will almost certainly yield yet another figure and we are, in any case, less concerned with absolute dates than with a technique that can establish the relative chronology of different sites over a wide area. A more serious doubt concerns the original assumption that the proportion of C-14 present in living matter has been constant throughout the ages or – to go a step further – that the intensity of cosmic radiation in the atmosphere that fuels the radioactive isotopes has remained unchanged. This has lately been called into question by a series of dates established by counting the annual growth rings of trees, particularly very long-lived species such as the bristle-cone pine found in the southwestern United States, which do not coincide with C-14 determinations from the same material. The sequence of tree-ring dates can now be carried back with certainty to before 5000 BC, and shows that in terms of calendar years C-14 determinations for the fifth millennium are as much as 700 or 800 years too low. Before that time we are on less certain ground, but it seems that radiocarbon determinations yielding dates in the sixth millennium may have to be increased by perhaps several hundred years, although when we go back to the eighth millennium they may once again be more nearly accurate. In the face of this uncertainty we must still regard radiocarbon as a relative rather than an absolute system of dating, and it is for this reason that we use the somewhat cumbrous word "determination" – meaning a laboratory result – rather than "date" in this context. There are other unexplained anomalies in C-14 results on which we shall comment when they appear to conflict seriously with archaeological evidence. But in general the reader should note that when we give an approximate date without further explanation it is derived from radiocarbon determinations, based on the 5,570-year half-life, and with no attempt to correct it by reference to the tree-ring evidence.

Choga Mami – the choice of a site

Investigation of prehistoric sites in southern Iraq is seriously hindered by heavy deposition of silt over the alluvial plain. Many such sites are thought to lie under thick layers of alluvium or beneath large, long-occupied mounds where their excavation is both financially and technically impossible. For this reason we decided in 1966 to search along the archaeologically unexplored eastern edge of the alluvial plain, hoping to find there early sites still visible above the plain. The area near modern Mandali was specifically chosen because it lay also midway between the southern known limits of the northern Hassuna-Samarra assemblages (Sawwan) and the northern known limits of early 'Ubaid (Ras al 'Amiya). Thus we hoped not only to find prehistoric sites but to investigate the then unestablished relationships between those of the north and south. Our hopes were more than fulfilled by the discovery of a group of prehistoric tells dating back to c. 6000 BC. The largest of these, Choga Mami, a low mound some 200 meters long and 2–5 meters high, is shown *below* (the expedition's camp is situated on the mound). The site proved to be heavily eroded, the latest preserved levels dating to c. 4800 BC. In 1967–68 we excavated four occupation levels of the sixth-millennium BC Samarra culture and succeeding levels attributed to a previously unknown "Transitional Samarra-'Ubaid" phase.

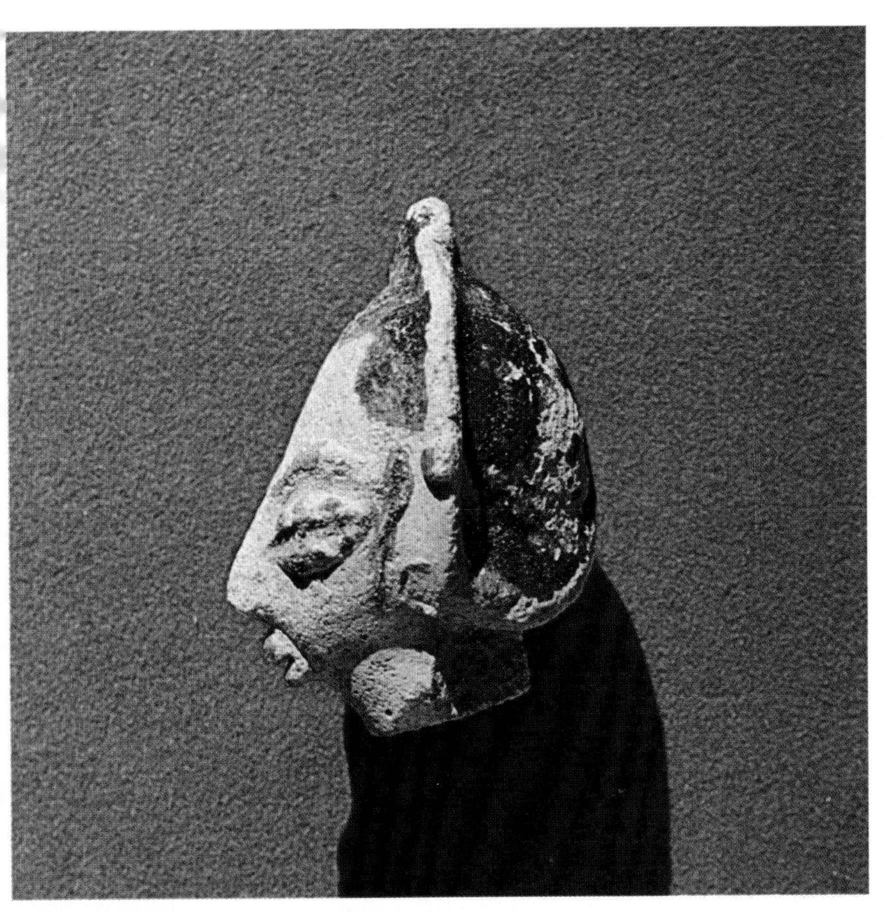

VISUAL STORY

Left: a number of baked clay figurines were found at Choga Mami, unfortunately none complete. This Samarran head (ht. 4·8 cm) is the finest fragment and is unusual among sixth-millennium figurines for its realism. An identical hairstyle can be found on early Sumerian stone statues some 2,000 years later.

Below: these broken fragments of pottery gave the first clue to the importance of Choga Mami. They showed that the site could provide information about all the known prehistoric cultures of Mesopotamia, a situation unique among sites so far discovered. It was for this reason that exacavation was undertaken in 1967. Among the sherds are a weathered example of Zagros "tadpole ware" from a small site 1 kilometer away (*upper left*), and Hassuna, Samarra, Halaf, Eridu, Hajji Muhammad and later 'Ubaid from Choga Mami.

Right: a massive sixth-millennium BC tower built of mud-brick guarded an entrance to the town. A sloping path entered the settlement along two sides of the tower and continued up the stone steps (*foreground*) to an occupational level now eroded.

The most unexpected discovery at Choga Mami was that of a number of small irrigation channels of the sixth millennium BC which ran along the northern side of the mound in a fashion identical with that of the modern channel seen here (*center right*) from the eastern end of the site. Even more surprising was evidence for a canal of substantial size built before the end of the Samarra period. This ran along the southwestern side of the mound on the same line as a number of later canals, including one we excavated dating to c. 4500 BC. The spoil banks of the latest phase of this same canal system, perhaps to be dated only some 1,500 years ago, can be seen in the background of the photograph. The line of this canal, which our excavations show to have originated in the sixth millennium BC, is the westernmost indicated on the map *below*. The spoil banks shown on the map are those visible in the photograph. The modern system of irrigation is a fan of small channels, fed from the Gangir, watering land north and northwest of Mandali, and this was clearly the earliest prehistoric pattern. This system was improved as early as the sixth millennium, and the amount of land brought under cultivation increased by building larger canals running parallel with the line of the hills.

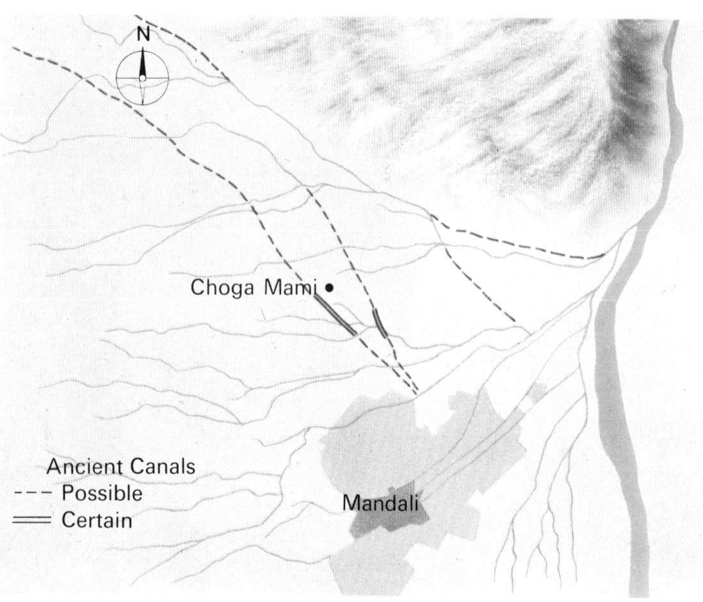

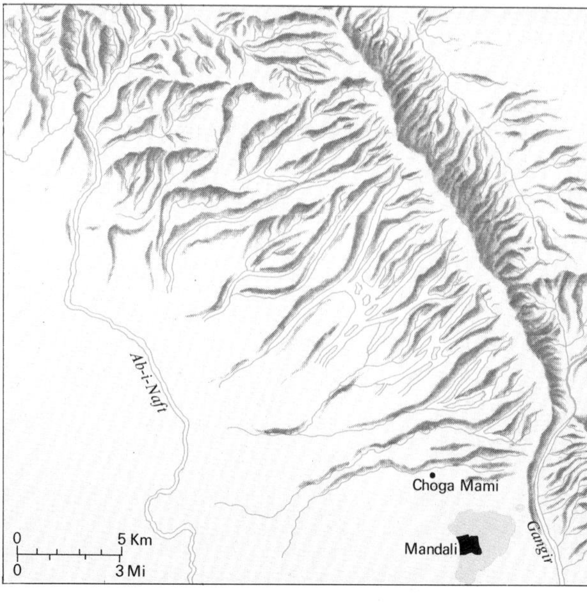

A variety of female figurines made of baked clay were found at Choga Mami; most were decorated with painted ornament, perhaps indicating clothing, although it is possible that the dots or blobs indicate deliberate scarring. Later 'Ubaid figurines from Ur are ornamented with appliqué pellets on the shoulders which closely resemble the deliberate scarring known among some primitive tribes. Standing figures are the most common; the one shown here (*left*) is the only well-preserved seated example (ht. 7 cm). Two types of head have been found, a very naturalistic type, illustrated previously, and a more bird-like variety with an elongated headdress (*below left*), again reminiscent of later 'Ubaid figurines at Ur. The ladies wear a variety of jewelry, examples of which were found on the site. These include necklaces, earrings and studs worn in the nose and cheek. A large number of clay studs were found; three stone examples together with a bead and a shell-shaped pendant are illustrated *below right*. The object in the center is probably a stone labret or lip ornament (3 × 2 cm). A very similar example was found still in position on the lower jaw of a contemporary skeleton at Ali Kosh.

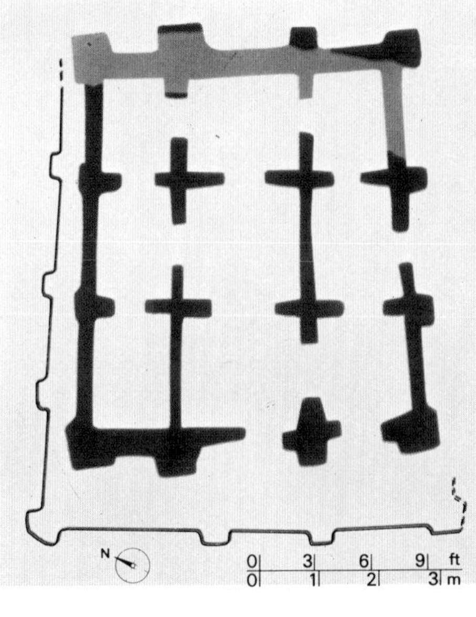
N
0 3 6 9 ft
0 1 2 3 m

Opposite: Samarran houses were very regular in plan. Those at Choga Mami were rectangular, containing either two or three rows of three small rooms. The houses were built of long, cigar-shaped mud-bricks, laid alternately along and across the axis of the wall (*below left*). In one corner of this small room, one of the earliest excavated, was a Samarran painted jar, and in the other, a large undecorated pot containing an infant burial, sealed beneath a later floor. *Below right:* plan of the further house visible in the photograph (*above*). The plan illustrates the practice, at Choga Mami, of building houses on top of, or in this case within, the walls of their predecessors in earlier levels, perhaps evidence for strictly observed property rights already in the sixth millennium BC. The employment of external buttresses on these houses, at the corners and junctions of walls, marks the beginning of a widespread Mesopotamian building technique that was at first functional, to strengthen the structure, but later, in religious architecture, a deliberate decorative convention.

Left: among the discoveries at Choga Mami was a previously unknown type of pottery, found in levels immediately following those in which the classical Samarran types occurred. Some of this pottery, like the two examples illustrated here, closely resembles the earlier Samarran ware, but other types are in style very like the 'Ubaid 1 and 2 ceramic (Eridu and Hajji Muhammad) found in southern Iraq. Some genuinely Hajji Muhammad pottery was found in the latest of these levels at Choga Mami. For these reasons we refer to this new pottery as "Transitional" between the two styles. Examples of this "Transitional" pottery, which clearly originated in central Mesopotamia, have now been found on sites in Khuzistan (Chagha Sefid and Chogha Mish). The fragment (*Above left*) is the upper bowl of a vessel with a pedestal-like foot, a common Samarran type (diam. 26 cm); the complete vessel (*below left*) is one of a group of similarly decorated bowls of different sizes, as it were a prehistoric "dinner service."

Necklaces were a very popular form of personal ornament at Choga Mami. The Samarran clay figurines always wear necklaces, either painted or depicted with small clay pellets to indicate beads. Thousands of clay beads in a variety of shapes and sizes were recovered from the excavations. Two different types are illustrated here. The larger necklace has been strung from half of a single deposit, found on the floor of one of the earliest houses excavated, of over 2,200 of these tiny segmented beads.

4. The Earliest Farming Communities

The origins of agriculture. The period with which this chapter is concerned witnessed the most important single innovation in the evolution of human society before the Industrial Revolution, the seemingly simple change from the acquisition of food solely by hunting and the collecting of wild resources to its deliberate production by stock-breeding and cultivation. Although sometimes referred to as a "revolution" in human behavior, the domestication of plants and animals did not take place as an identifiable event in the past but was the culmination of a long process, in which man came increasingly to rely on certain species and eventually to control their distribution and breeding. The reasons for these very significant changes in man's exploitation of his natural environment, indeed his reasons for selecting certain foods rather than others among the many available to him, cannot be reconstructed from the archaeological record. Nor can the study of food remains from very early sites tell us precisely how much control their inhabitants exercised over individual species at any particular moment. The genetic changes that took place as a direct or indirect result of human intervention enable us to recognize the final "domesticated" varieties, but not the intervening stages of their development from the wild forms. It is as if we had the first and last chapters of a book from which the central pages are missing.

Various plants and animals were domesticated at different times in different places, and the same species were almost certainly domesticated independently in a number of places. Most prehistorians now realize that the search for a single, original center from which the practice of farming was disseminated must prove both pointless and fruitless. Present evidence, however, points beyond doubt to the Near East as one of the first regions in the world where agricultural societies developed. Within the Near East, and more specifically the hills and grassland that flank the arid Syrian steppe and the south Mesopotamian alluvium, there could – and can to this day – be found the wild ancestors of the cereals and animals that were to be the basis of the agricultural economy not only of the Near East but also of Europe. Wild barley, two forms of wild wheat together with other staple plant foods such as legumes and lentils, wild cattle, sheep, goat and pig were all present in a unique association within this nuclear zone. Their precise distribution in prehistoric times cannot be ascertained, for it may have been affected by changes in the early Holocene climate or by the activities of man himself. Nor can we be certain, for example, that the modern strains of wild cereals in the area are genetically similar to their predecessors in 10,000 BC. Nonetheless it is approximately within this zone, where the wild forms now appear to be indigenous, that we find not only the earliest villages but the earliest *farming* villages.

Archaeologists have long been able to study the faunal remains, and thus the meat diet, on most of their sites because Near Eastern conditions are generally favorable to the preservation of animal bones, but botanical remains present a much more difficult problem. Except for infrequent discoveries of recognizable caches of seeds, usually found in clay vessels that had been accidentally subjected to fire or in very dry conditions such as obtain in Egyptian tombs, such evidence was rarely available before the recent development of special field techniques for its recovery. This means that valid information about the total economy of a site may be lacking, either because the site was excavated some years ago or because even the new techniques have failed to provide adequate samples. Where early botanical samples are available, the plants have proved in every case to be morphologically indistinguishable from the wild forms. Unfortunately this does not demonstrate that they were not cultivated but only that, if they were, they had not yet undergone any of the genetic changes that characterize the domestic varieties. Although the very earliest villages have so far yielded no evidence for agriculture, we may infer that the increasing reliance on wild cereals that can be observed on sites of the eighth millennium BC must have implied certain changes in social behavior. For instance, a year's supply of grain – approximately a metric tonne – can even in the wild form be harvested by a single family, but only in the brief period in late spring when the crop ripens, and it then becomes a bulky asset that cannot easily be carried about. This simple fact must be relevant to the increase in the number of permanent settlements that is apparent in the eighth and seventh millennia.

Previous page: a Turkish farmer winnowing with a fork, a technique used since ancient times.

A farmer reaping among the volcanic tufa deposits in Cappadocia.

In the absence of palaeobotanical specimens other clues ay give some indication of the ways in which early pulations exploited plant resources, although none by self constitutes unequivocal evidence for agriculture. A mmunity that utilizes cereals even as a minor element in diet needs storage facilities and tools for grinding the ain into a usable form. Both are known as early as the nd of the Pleistocene, as are sickle blades for reaping. But e discovery of such equipment is not certain proof that reals were being collected. Other foods such as nuts can stored, sickles may be used to cut reeds, and grinding abs were also used for the preparation of red ocher, one f the commonest ancient pigments. Modern archaelogists react with perhaps excessive caution to the facile sumptions of their predecessors. But in this case we can nly say that technology essential to the collection or ultivation of cereals was already available to late Upper alaeolithic communities. We cannot prove that cereals rmed any part of their diet, and we must also remember nat wild cereals as a food source have disadvantages that ave been bred out of their domesticated successors. Bread the staff of life, but primitive forms of grain are nsuitable for bread-making. They have very tough husks r "glumes" that are difficult to remove by conventional nreshing methods, although they can be ground into roats that are then cooked into mush or gruel, and such roats have been found in some of the earliest carbonized rain samples. But men seem to have discovered at a latively early stage that if wild grain was roasted or arched the glumes could be more easily separated when it as ground; and a secondary effect of this treatment was nat it could then be stored without danger of sprouting. ne of the most common features on early village sites, ich as Mureybet on the Euphrates in north Syria (c. 8000 c), are "roasting pits" in which grain may have been arched over heated stones.

Another characteristic of wild cereals is that the axis or rachis" of the spike is usually brittle. On ripening, the ndividual internodes and spikelets detach themselves and ll to the ground separately, whereas in most domesticated cereals the rachis is tough and this disarticulation oes not occur. Clearly the brittle rachis is advantageous to ed dispersal in the wild plant and the tough rachis to seed ollection by man. Both variants exist within the pool of enes that determine the development of the wild varieties, but as long as the grain was only being collected the alance remained essentially unchanged. When deliberate lanting began, however, the farmer unwittingly began shift the balance in favor of the tough and more readily arvested rachis. This morphological change also enabled ne grain to ripen longer, which in turn produced an ncreased yield and better germination. Another genetic hange that occurred very early in the history of cultivaon produced a "naked" kernel that could easily be freed y threshing. When the archaeologist finds cereals that can e shown to possess a tough rachis and a naked grain, he may reasonably assume that they were being deliberately sown. Other mutations took place, for example transforming wild barley (*Hordeum spontaneum*), which has only two fertile rows of kernels and is hence known as "two-row barley," into a six-row variety found at lowland sites by 6000 BC; at about the same time free-threshing hexaploid wheats appeared throughout western Asia.

Mutations and changes in gene frequency also occurred in animal species under human control. These led to forms identified by zoologists as domesticated, although there remain considerable areas of disagreement over the precise criteria to be applied. Among such changes are the economically beneficial development of wool-bearing sheep and a more easily identified but less functional change in the shape of goat horn cores. There is even some evidence to suggest a change in basic bone structure in domesticated animals. The archaeologist may consequently be able to identify specimens of both plants and animals as domestic, but in no case have we any idea of the length of time required to produce the change. Indeed it is more than likely that there was a long phase in the evolution of human society when man was no longer a simple hunter-gatherer, but practiced various forms of control and selection over natural breeding populations before he became a farmer in the true sense of the word. An early example of this type of pre-agricultural "husbandry" can be found in Palestine, where in the Wadi Fellah an unusually high percentage of immature gazelle among the excavated bones in Upper Palaeolithic levels has been interpreted to indicate some human control of the herds already at this early date.

The beginnings of settled life. By the Late Pleistocene (c. 12,000 BC) there is evidence for several types of archaeological site in the Near East. Some of these represent the most transient of occupations, others were clearly inhabited with great regularity by seminomadic hunters and collectors, returning year by year to gather whatever food the local environment had to offer. Archaeologists long believed that at this time people lived predominantly in caves, but it is now clear that extensive use was also made of open-air campsites. In the hilly areas especially, the conditions of life for flora and fauna varied with the elevation and seasonal resources in a wide range of "micro-environments" could be exploited in a restricted territory, not only by the human populations but by the animal herds upon which they were largely dependent. In some areas we can demonstrate a substantial increase in the use of supplementary foods such as fish, snails, water fowl and probably also new varieties of plants. Minute flint blades, known as microliths and often of particular geometric shapes such as lunates or trapezoids, now appear. These were set in bone or wood hafts to form composite tools, reflecting not only a substantial

change in technology but also in methods of food procurement, for they could be used to make extremely effective harpoons and arrows. In Upper Egypt and the Sudan milling stones, querns and sickle blades are found in large numbers, but what – if any – plant foods these were used to prepare remains uncertain, for we believe that barley and the two primitive varieties of wheat, emmer and einkorn, were not native to North Africa. Evidence of permanent dwellings at this time is still rare but at Ain Gev, on the eastern side of the Sea of Galilee, the remains of a circular structure cut into the slope of a hill have been excavated, a Late Palaeolithic precursor of a house type common on all early settlement sites in the Near East.

Thus the stage was set for many of the technological, economic and indeed social developments that were to take place in the period following the Last Ice Age, and by 9000 BC the first archaeological sites that can genuinely be described as villages were in existence. It is doubtful that any of them was occupied throughout the year, at least by all of its inhabitants. As we have already noted, the transition to a more sedentary way of life was a gradual one, and in the Near East it almost certainly preceded the equally gradual shift from a purely hunting and collecting economy to cereal agriculture, which would not have been viable on any scale except for a society that was at least partly sedentary. A number of sites in the Levant and a smaller group in the less well-explored Zagros area can be dated to this earliest phase of settlement. Of these, Ain Mallaha in Palestine, Mureybet on the Euphrates in north Syria, and Karim Shahir and Zawi Chemi Shanidar in Iraqi Kurdistan are the most informative. In the Levant the archaeological material of this phase is known as Natufian, after the cave site in the Wadi al-Natuf in the Judaean hills where it was first identified by Dorothy Garrod in 1928. The Natufian shares with the European Mesolithic cu tures the use of microlithic flints, especially lunates, and rich bone industry including harpoons as evidence c fishing. Some of the most beautiful bone objects ar elaborately carved sickle handles, of which we illustrat one example. Querns, grinding stones and storage pits ar common both in Palestine and the Zagros. Sickle blade identifiable by the sheen that long use in reaping gives t their surface, are more common in the Natufian than o sites further to the east. Natufian burial practices provid the earliest indications of status distinctions in the com munity, for which we have as yet no comparable evidenc even at later Zagros sites.

At Ain Mallaha, a site some 2,000 square meters i extent on the shore of Lake Huleh in the upper Jorda valley, Jean Perrot has excavated three successive villag attributed to an early phase of the Natufian. Thes consisted of perhaps 50 houses arranged around an ope central area in which were a number of bell-shaped storag pits lined with plaster to make them waterproof. Th houses were approximately round in plan and up to meters in diameter, with floors sunk well below groun level and walls lined with stone. No traces of th superstructures survive but they could have been made c branches covered with skins or perhaps thatched wit reeds from the nearby lake. No domesticated plants c animals have been identified here or indeed at any othe Natufian site, nor is there positive evidence even for th collection of wild cereals, despite the presence of num erous grinding stones and sickles. It is generally believed however, that wild emmer and barley are likely to hav formed part of the Natufian diet. Three grains of emme of the apparently domesticated form *Triticum dicoccum* ar reported from an earlier, Late Palaeolithic (Kebaran

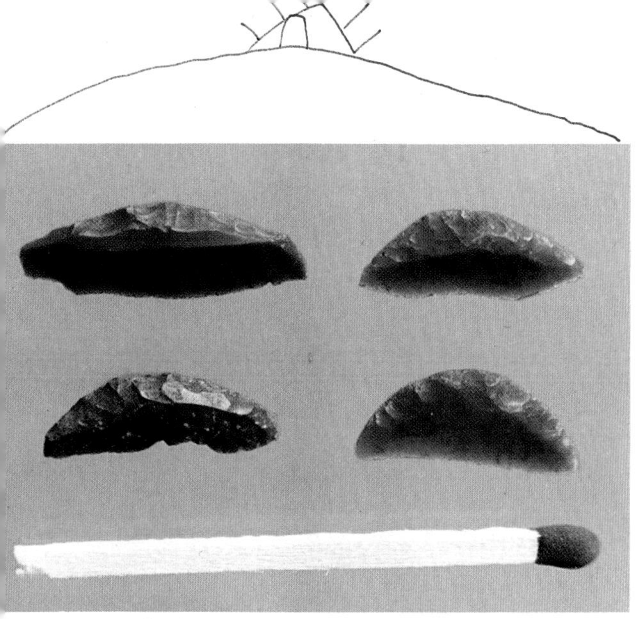

ıbove: Natufian microlithic stone implements from Mount Carmel, alestine, c. 9000 BC.

)pposite: a Natufian carved bone reaping knife from Kebara cave, 1ount Carmel, Palestine, c. 9000 BC, length 32 centimeters ₹ockefeller Museum, Jerusalem).

ontext at Wadi Fellah on Mount Carmel, but this is a uzzling find and only one or two grains were found in ıter levels on the same site. At Ain Mallaha gazelle onstituted 45 per cent of the animal bones, while deer, vild cattle and pigs were also hunted. The discovery of sh hooks and gorges suggests that fish were caught in the ıke, but as at other Natufian sites the main source of rotein was undoubtedly animal, and predominantly azelle. Even the cave sites on Mount Carmel, near to the 1ores of the Mediterranean, do not show evidence for the xtensive exploitation of aquatic resources that is often scribed to these Mesolithic peoples.

3urial customs. One of the most interesting features of he Natufian culture is the evidence found in graves of the eriod for personal ornament, religious ritual and almost ertainly for status distinctions. Normally few if any fferings accompanied the dead, but at El-Wad cave on Aount Carmel four communal, possibly family, graves vere discovered in each of which one of the skeletons – nd only one – was elaborately adorned with a headdress nd other ornaments of *dentalium* shells and bone beads.)nly one other skeleton in a total of 34 burials was dressed 1 this manner. Where the sex of the skeletons could be letermined it proved to be male, and it seems more than ıkely that these were heads of families if not of larger kin ;roups. At Ain Mallaha, too, one among a number of ndividual and collective burials can be singled out as elonging to a person of superior standing. The grave, vhich was bordered by a low wall and covered by three ırge stones, was sunk into the fill of one of the circular pit ıouses. The house itself had been an unusual structure, for he face and the top of its stone revetment were carefully inished with red-painted plaster. In the grave were two skeletons, an adult male propped up on stones with his face towards the snowy peaks of Mount Hermon, and a second person, possibly female, wearing a headdress of *dentalium* shells. Earlier burials had been pushed aside to accommodate the new and more distinguished occupants, although the separated skulls had been rearranged, a hint of later funerary ritual at Jericho and other sites.

Jericho provides further evidence from this period. Here the earliest deposit, from which a radiocarbon determination of c. 9000 BC has been obtained, revealed a unique structure which has been interpreted as some sort of sanctuary. This consisted simply of a rectangular platform of natural clay, overlying the base rock and revetted by walls of undressed stone, but which was kept scrupulously clean. Set in one wall were two carefully bored stones that clearly served no structural purpose but may have been sockets for ritual objects, perhaps some form of totem pole. Jericho is situated some 300 meters below sea level, not far north of the Dead Sea, and undoubtedly owes its existence in an otherwise arid landscape to the nearby spring of ʻAin es-Sultan. The excavator has reasonably suggested that some cult associated with this life-giving spring may have been responsible for the earliest occupation of the site. Remains attributed to this Mesolithic phase have been found only in one small area, but elsewhere extensive traces of the apparently succeeding "proto-Neolithic" phase have come to light. No structures were revealed, only surfaces delimited by slight humps, but these were almost certainly the bases of portable or semipermanent huts or shelters. Jericho seems not to have been permanently occupied at this time but was evidently the object of seasonal visits by a hunter-gatherer population over a long period of time, for their debris formed a mound some 4 meters high without the ruins of any permanent structures to accelerate its growth.

Village settlements. It is perhaps necessary to emphasize to the modern reader that life in a village was not necessarily more profitable than life as a wandering hunter and food-collector, and it was often more arduous. Moreover, although we have no evidence on this point, the intensified problems of sanitation and water-pollution in a settled community would probably have increased the incidence and encouraged the spread of disease. The discovery of the site of Ain Mallaha tells us that some people were now living in villages but in no way implies a general rush to conform to this new way of life. Nomadic hunting and, later, herding societies were to remain an important feature of the Near Eastern scene even in historical times, and it is likely that in this early period a large proportion of the population remained essentially mobile. We cannot explain why some groups settled down. What is clear, however, is that from this time onwards increasing numbers of village settlements are to be found in the archaeological record, and that important

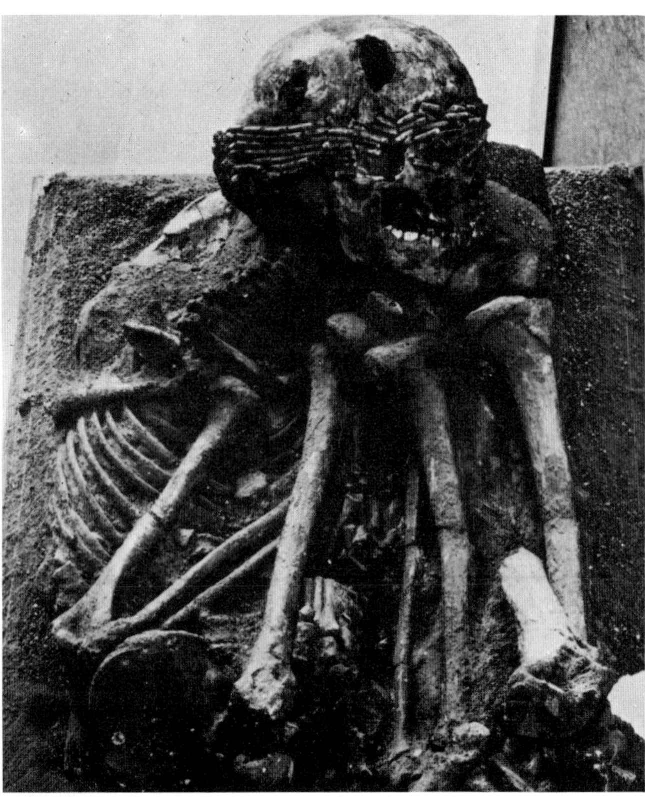

A Natufian male skeleton from the Wadi al-Mughara cave, Mount Carmel. The skull is encircled with a band made up of seven rows of *dentalium* shells (Rockefeller Museum, Jerusalem).

economic changes were soon to take place. The existence of villages that were occupied during most or all of the year implies that their inhabitants were being fed from a very much smaller territory than they would have exploited as seasonal migrants, and therefore that their methods of procuring food had to be radically altered. Indeed succeeding developments at Jericho, to which we shall return shortly, indicate nothing less than a revolution in the local economy.

Settlements that can be dated as early as the ninth millennium have so far been excavated in only two areas outside Palestine. In north Syria two sites, Mureybet and Abu Hureyra, both investigated as part of an archaeological rescue project and both now flooded after the construction of the Tabqa Dam on the Euphrates, produced in their earliest levels materials that can be compared very generally with those of Natufian Palestine. Whether they are truly Natufian is not yet certain, but the assemblages are characterized by Natufian-like geometric microliths and circular structures. Mureybet, first excavated by M. van Loon and subsequently by J. Cauvin, is of particular interest as the first early village site from which extensive information about plant foods was recovered. The published palaeobotanical data come from a late phase of the settlement, roughly 8000–7500 BC, but provide the earliest unequivocal evidence for the collecting, or possibly even the cultivation, of wild cereals. Indeed wil einkorn seems to have constituted a substantial part of th diet of the inhabitants, and wild barley, lentils, vetch an pistachio were also eaten. No domesticated plants c animals occur at any period on the site.

The earliest settlement, in which material resemblin the Natufian was found, is estimated to have been abou one hectare in extent and has yielded a single radiocarbo determination of c. 8640 BC. The inhabitants were un doubtedly hunters who also exploited the resources of th nearby river. Wild fauna include ass (*Equus asinus pale tinae*), cattle and gazelle, and large numbers of bird and fis bones and mollusc shells were recovered. There are als examples of the "fire-pits" which occur in considerab numbers in later levels and are often interpreted a parching pits, suggesting at least the possibility that wil grain was already being collected for food or indeed eve cultivated in this Mesolithic phase, a possibility heightene by the discovery in Mesolithic levels at nearby Ab Hureyra of wild einkorn together with isolated grains c barley, rye, lentil and bitter vetch. These sites lie toda outside the environmental zone in which wild einkor grows, and it seems clear that either the climate at th time was marginally cooler and/or wetter, or these 9th millennium inhabitants of the upper Euphrates valle were among the first deliberately to cultivate cereal crop At Mureybet an interesting discovery on virgin soil was plaster face about 10 cm thick and standing up to 50 cr high, smoothed internally but showing on the outside th impressions of decayed timbers 7–10 cm thick which ha actually formed the structure of a circular house. It important to remember how often such flimsy remains c buildings above ground may have completely dis appeared. In the same level were also found fragments c an ox-skull and two equine scapulae which had bee deliberately buried in a clay bench, perhaps with som ritual purpose, for the practice calls to mind similar bu very much later deposits in the "shrines" at Çatal Hüyü in Anatolia.

Evidence for the beginnings of settlement in the Zagro is less substantial, but several sites indicate lengthy an repeated occupation by groups who were essentiall hunters. Most of these are open-air campsites like Karin Shahir and Zawi Chemi Shanidar, but there was also som seasonal occupation of caves as in Natufian Palestine. Tw radiocarbon determinations of c. 8900 BC for Zawi Chem and c. 8650 BC for the same assemblage in the nearb Shanidar cave show that they were contemporary wit the Natufian settlements. With the single exception c M'lefaat, a mound which lies east of Mosul where th highland zone borders on the north Mesopotamian plain and is only 300 meters above sea level, the early sites so fa identified in this eastern province are in upland valleys a an elevation of 700–800 meters. Here pollen cores sugges that wild cereals may not have been as plentiful as they ar believed to have been in Palestine at this time. None theless, large numbers of querns, grinding stones, mortars and storage pits are characteristic of these sites, and sickle blades occur, although in smaller numbers than in Palestine. Baskets which could have been used for collecting plant food have been tentatively identified in Shanidar cave. One of the most distinctive and economically significant features of this period both in the Levant and in the Zagros is the development of an industry in ground stone. Not only were functional tools prepared by this method, but ornamental objects in polished stone are now found in increasing numbers. Stone celts, often with a ground cutting edge, appear in the Zagros, suggesting that wood was coming into commoner use, perhaps because it was more readily available. As in Palestine, however, the vast majority of tools were still made by chipping flint and chert, but although microliths are found on the eastern sites, the number of geometric shapes is relatively small.

Several features distinguish the two areas. Evidence for house structures in the Zagros is minimal, consisting only of a few enigmatic pits or ovals of stones at Zawi Chemi and M'lefaat, and as yet no settlement has been discovered with the aura of permanence of Ain Mallaha. Perhaps more significant, however, is the proof of wider external contacts on the Zagros sites, especially the discovery of Anatolian obsidian which is already present in small quantity in the Late Upper Palaeolithic, but entirely absent from Natufian Palestine. Also striking is the relatively early evidence in the Zagros for the herding of both sheep and goats. At Zawi Chemi sheep are thought to have been "domesticated" – at least in a limited sense – some 11,000 years ago, because the sheep bones on the site show an unusually high proportion of immature animals. We have already noted that similar data have been interpreted to indicate some human control over gazelle herds in Palestine at an even earlier date, but sheep and goats ultimately proved to be the more useful animals. Genetic changes that were encouraged by husbandry and selective killing – if not yet deliberate breeding – led to increased milk production and, in the case of sheep, the development of woolly fleece in place of the hair that is characteristic of the wild species. Wild sheep seem not to have been native to Palestine, and goat bones do not appear there in any significant quantity until the seventh millennium BC when there is some evidence that they were domesticated.

The situation on the eastern side of the Zagros is more difficult to assess, largely because of uncertainty in dating. At the mound of Ganj Dareh near Kermanshah the lowest level (E) has produced one radiocarbon determination of c. 8450 BC and, more recently, a number of others that all fall within the seventh millennium. But the immediately succeeding levels appear to be dated in the late eighth millennium and the archaeological evidence suggests a gap in occupation between levels E and D, so it is at least possible that level E should be attributed to the ninth millennium. In this level there were a number of "fire-pits" identical with those at Mureybet, but no architectural remains were found, nor any grinding stones or other implements normally associated with the collection or preparation of cereals and other plant foods. Another site near Kermanshah, Tepe Asiab, is thought to belong typologically to this early group but radiocarbon determinations based on bone samples, which are less reliable than charcoal, place it marginally later, in the late eighth millennium BC. It is at Tepe Asiab that evidence indicating the domestication of goats is said to have been found.

We have seen that the earliest village settlements yet known have been found largely in Palestine and the upper Euphrates valley in Syria, while only a few perhaps semipermanent encampments have been identified in the Zagros. But we cannot even guess how far this pattern of distribution represents the true state of cultural development at the time. The Levant has been far more extensively explored by archaeologists than most other areas of the Near East, and even there many of the discoveries are relatively recent. The existence of sites such as Mureybet and Abu Hureyra was not even suspected ten years ago. No comparable sites are known in the corresponding section of the Tigris valley in northern Iraq, but this may be because no one expected to find them on the very limited surveys that have been carried out, and it is in any case difficult in undulating country to identify mounds of this period when there are no potsherds to call attention to them. It is patently improbable that a site like M'lefaat had no neighbors, but they will not be found until the area can be intensively explored. In many parts of the Near East recent research has been unfortunately limited by political problems, and in dealing with the earliest settlements we can be certain only that our existing knowledge is the tip of an iceberg and that there will be many startling discoveries in the years to come.

Developments in the eighth millennium. One discovery that astounded the archaeological world was made by Kathleen Kenyon during her reexcavation of the site of Jericho in the 1950s, in levels following and apparently developing from the "proto-Neolithic" sequence of seasonal occupation. These levels represent the earlier of two phases which the excavator designated Pre-Pottery Neolithic A and B, now generally abbreviated to PPN-A and PPN-B. Radiocarbon determinations from the site are not internally consistent, but suggest that PPN-A began some time around, or even before, 8000 BC. Archaeologically this phase is characterized by the introduction of unbaked mud-brick as a building material, an efficient and economical innovation that heralded a revolution in structural techniques at the time and has not yet been superseded in many rural areas of the Near East. The PPN-A houses were circular in plan, with an entrance porch, and were constructed of handmade bricks of a distinctive "hog-back" shape. At Jericho they were found over an area of some 3–4 hectares (10 acres), representing a

Above: entrance to the internal staircase of the Jericho tower.
Right: Jericho PPN-A: a view of the superimposed walls that encircled the town and, in the foreground, the rock-cut ditch.

considerable expansion of the settlement which was then followed by an astonishing architectural feat, the construction of a massive stone wall which apparently enclosed the whole site. Built without the aid of metal tools, the eighth-millennium defenses of Jericho would have been impressive at any period. The wall itself, originally free-standing, was rebuilt four times as the accumulation of occupation debris raised the level of the settlement within. Around it on the outside ran a rock-cut ditch 8 meters wide and more than 2 meters deep and at one point, where it still stands to a height of almost 6 meters, it was backed by a massive circular tower. The tower, which was also solidly built of stone, is preserved to a height of 9 meters, with a diameter of about 9 meters at the top. The summit was reached by an internal stair of 28 steps, each a single block of stone more than a meter wide, that was approached from the settlement inside the wall. Against the north side of the tower was built a series of well-plastered curvilinear enclosures, with what appeared to be a drainage channel leading away from one group, while a similar enclosure on the south side is said to have been used for the storage of grain.

The existence of these monumental fortifications poses a number of questions to which we do not yet know the answers, but there can be no doubt that the construction of public works on such a scale required not only a substantial

The massive stone-built circular tower built against the interior of the town wall at Jericho, Pre-Pottery Neolithic A phase (eighth millennium BC). The tower is preserved to a height of 9 meters.

labor force but an organizing authority and a surplus of wealth from which the workmen could be supported. Against whom the walls were built remains a mystery. It should be clear from the previous section that no other known sites of this or earlier date even remotely approach the level of achievement that these discoveries imply, but Jericho cannot be viewed in isolation. The only reasonable interpretation must assume a general level of social, economic and even political development in the Levant at this time for which we have at present no other evidence. Of course human behavior is only "reasonable" in the context of a society's own standards which may be quite different from ours, but even a comprehensible – though illogical – motive such as conspicuous display requires the presence of other groups worthy of being impressed.

The sources of Jericho's apparent prosperity are equally mysterious. Very little of the early levels has been excavated, but it is possible that the final publication of the results will provide further clues. We are uncertain, for example, whether the inhabitants engaged in agriculture, although it is clear that the settlement could not have been supported by the natural resources immediately available in the area. Gazelle remained the main source of protein, but for the first time some goat bones are found, though they show no evidence of domestication. Morphologically wild pig and cattle also occur, together with an unusual number of fox bones, as in the "proto-Neolithic" levels. The larger animals would presumably have been hunted in the Judaean hills that overlook the site, and gazelle herds might have been kept by transhumant herdsmen. Palaeobotanical material from the PPN-A levels consists of "only six barley grains, two grains of emmer, forty-six fig pips and three broken pieces of legume," hardly convincing evidence for the intensive agriculture that would have been necessary if it provided the basic subsistence for a community estimated at 2,000–3,000 people. Moreover, Jericho lies in a very arid zone where rain-fed agriculture would have been impossible, whatever climatic fluctuations there may have been. It has been suggested that simple irrigation, drawing water from the spring onto nearby fields, might have been employed even at this very early date, but the area of land that could have been irrigated below the spring is far too small to have supplied the inhabitants of PPN-A Jericho with their basic food requirements. Another suggestion, that the "tanks" adjoining the north side of the tower might have served to provide a greater head of water for more extensive irrigation, seems unlikely in view of their rather flimsy construction and mud-plaster lining. On the other hand, one would not expect to find wild wheat or even barley growing in the environment of Jericho, and the only samples identified are of the domesticated varieties *Hordeum distichum* and *Triticum dicoccum* – possibly the earliest known evidence for domesticated cereals, although we cannot be sure of this until the exact provenance of the finds is published in the final report. If they were local produce, then they must have been grown by irrigation, and this would certainly be the first instance of a technique on which the economy of important areas of the Near East was later to depend.

But agriculture is not the only possible basis for the economy of Jericho at this time, and some of the large bins next to the tower and the town wall may have been used for the storage of imported grain. Moreover, other certain imports can be identified among the finds in the PPN-A town, even in the relatively small area that has been excavated. These include obsidian that is thought to have originated near Kayseri (the Çiftlik source), some 500 miles to the north, nephrite and other greenstones that probably also came from Anatolia, turquoise from Sinai and cowries from the Red Sea. Jericho is an oasis site, strategically situated in relation to trade routes between the Red Sea and Anatolia, and not far from Dead Sea sources of such useful commodities as salt and bitumen. The most satisfactory explanation for its early prosperity and apparently unique development, even perhaps for its need for security, almost certainly lies in trading activities in which the community played a vital and possibly an entrepreneurial role.

Mureybet. The only other excavated site to provide important evidence of eighth-millennium occupation is

Mureybet. We have already mentioned the earliest "Mesolithic" levels, while the second and third phases of settlement are at least partly contemporary with the earlier levels at PPN-A Jericho. Like Jericho, Mureybet appears to be an unusually large site for this period, perhaps some three hectares in area. The Phase-II houses continue the round plan of the earlier Mesolithic occupation but in Phase III, attributed approximately to the first half of the eighth millennium, substantial multiroomed rectangular houses make their first appearance side by side with the round buildings. One of the latter was decorated with geometric designs painted on its walls, the earliest mural ornament so far discovered. Mureybet has yielded no direct evidence for cultivation or animal husbandry, but extensive palaeobotanical data from Phase III indicate heavy reliance on a cereal diet, especially einkorn, which, as we have seen, indirect evidence suggests may already have been under deliberate cultivation in the upper Euphrates valley at this time.

Perhaps the most unexpected find at Mureybet, made during the latest season of excavation, consisted of five lightly fired clay vessels. Four of these come from House 47, ascribed to the beginning of Phase III, which also produced a radiocarbon sample of c. 8000 BC, and the fifth piece comes from a neighboring structure. This crude pottery is 500 or perhaps even 1,000 years earlier than any other examples yet identified in the Near East. Surprisingly, no other ceramic vessels have yet been found in later levels on the site. Clay is both a readily available and a remarkably versatile material, and it is difficult to understand why the discovery that a variety of portable containers could be manufactured from it was not immediately and more widely adopted. One obviously relevant consideration is that until closed kilns were invented and higher firing temperatures could be attained, clay vessels would have remained soft and porous. They were less useful and – if they were used – their remains might have disintegrated or been overlooked by archaeologists. Containers of stone and wood, reed or wicker baskets may well have been more satisfactory, especially for the needs of people who moved frequently from place to place. But even in later periods when the potter's craft was more fully developed we find on some sites an apparent preference for other materials. For instance at Çatal Hüyük, described in the next chapter, the preponderance of wood over pottery vessels must surely reflect a local taste or tradition.

Before leaving the Levant we should mention one other site where eighth-millennium material has been found. This is Wadi Fellah, now known as Nahal Oren, where we have already mentioned the apparent – and anomalous – occurrence of the domesticated form of emmer in a late Upper Palaeolithic level. Here in the Natufian period there was what is described as a "stone-walled campsite," and a settlement of terraced oval houses, varying from 2 to 5 meters in diameter, is attributed to a slightly later phase. Despite the apparently permanent houses this cannot have been a settled agricultural community because only 7 percent of the surrounding countryside is arable land, the terrain is unsuited to the cultivation of cereals and there is a general lack of other local resources. The high percentage of gazelle bones among the faunal remains reproduces the pattern of earlier periods and suggests that the inhabitants of this settlement, like their predecessors, may have been herding gazelle. Wadi Fellah is worthy of mention because it points the contrast between different social groups and economies in the Near East as early as the eighth millennium BC. On the one hand we have the apparently urban community of Jericho and on the other the smaller settled or migratory groups whose traces can be found in the villages of the period. These different communities, and many others of whom we have no knowledge, must have been involved in economic and social relationships that we shall never be able to reconstruct from archaeological evidence.

Early farming villages. By 7000 BC there is increasing and for the first time unequivocal evidence from many parts of the Near East for the deliberate planting of wheat, barley and certain leguminous crops. Signs of the morphological changes that characterize the domestic species are now found among palaeobotanical specimens at a number of sites. At the same time there is evidence for domesticated dogs, sheep and goats, and possibly even cattle, and a growing number of apparently permanent villages appear in the archaeological record. It has been suggested that cultivation began when man found that the supply of his favorite wild plants was insufficient in their

natural habitat, and so attempted to grow them where they had not grown before. If this very neat theory is correct, we should find the early evidence for domesticated forms in areas marginal to their natural distribution. The discovery of domesticated varieties of wheat and barley at Jericho might support the theory, but the minute quantity of grain found is hardly sufficient evidence and elsewhere there is virtually none. Indeed our present information is so limited, and possibly even misleading, that no sweeping generalizations can possibly be justified. We have already mentioned two important sources of uncertainty. We cannot assume that the structure or the behavior of modern wild populations, plant or animal, necessarily parallel those of their ancestral forms. Nor have we any idea of the length of time that would have elapsed between, for example, the first deliberate planting of wild grain and the evolution of an essentially domesticated form. The reader should also remember that our knowledge of the sites themselves is woefully inadequate. The results of recent surveys suggest that many more remain to be discovered, and of the known sites very few have been touched by excavators. Moreover on those that have been "excavated" often only a minute part of the total area – on prehistoric sites commonly less than 1 percent – has actually been explored. In these circumstances it is more than likely that some centers of early agriculture remain entirely undetected. The most we can say at present is that some, at least, of the first farming villages do lie well within the existing natural habitats of their principal crops.

Opposite: Arab woman at Nimrud in northern Iraq pounding grain into coarse flour with a large stone pestle and mortar.

Below: a human skull with features molded in plaster and cowrie shells inset for eyes, from Jericho, PPN-B phase (seventh millennium BC).

One of the earliest of these is Çayönü Tepesi in southeastern Turkey, an area well within the primary habitats of wild barley and wild einkorn, at least in the eighth millennium, and almost certainly of wild emmer (*Triticum dicoccoides*) which was once thought to have been native only to Palestine and southern Syria. At Çayönü both emmer and einkorn were cultivated from the earliest phase of settlement, dated by radiocarbon to the latter part of the eighth millennium and possibly as early as 7500 BC. Barley is virtually absent from the very large number of seed specimens, suggesting that it was deliberately excluded from the diet even though it must have been locally available. Leguminous seeds, peas, lentils and vetches seem to have been consumed in considerable quantities. Pistachios and almonds were a valuable source of vegetable fat, and specimens of linseed, almost certainly the wild *Linum bienne*, were also found. This wide variety of plant foods is characteristic of the diet of early farmers. A number of animals were hunted, in particular those that were later to prove useful domesticates. Domesticated dogs were present from the beginning of the settlement – so far their earliest appearance in a Near Eastern village, although the jaw of a domestic dog has now been identified in a Late Palaeolithic context at Palegawra – and evidence for domesticated sheep and probably goats has been found in later levels at Çayönü. Only preliminary reports are available but these suggest that there was a shift from dependence on large game animals to the herding, predominantly, of sheep.

Two other features of the site are of considerable

interest. Unusually sophisticated building techniques were observed in a variety of eighth-millennium structures of which only the stone foundations are preserved. The earliest well-documented type is the so-called grill plan, in which narrow foundation walls were probably spanned by a floor of clay-covered saplings, reeds or even stones, leaving ventilation spaces below. These structures are interpreted as house foundations, but such buildings could very well have served as granaries, ingeniously insulated against damp. Remains of a second house type consist of cell-like foundations, on several of which an apparently accidental fire has preserved portions of mud-brick superstructures. Yet another "large-room" plan occurs, and in one instance the broad central chamber was floored with a high polished terrazzo-like pavement of patterned salmon-pink and white stone chips, the earliest known example of such a decorative paving technique. From Çayönü also comes by far the earliest evidence for the use of native copper, perhaps not surprising since the site is less than 13 miles from the Ergani copper mines, in later antiquity one of the most heavily exploited of Near Eastern copper sources. Throughout the settlement are found examples of simple tools and ornaments made by cold hammering of the native metal, considerable quantities of which could probably have been picked up on the surface near the site of the later mines. It is a reflection of the idiosyncratic progress of technology that the people of Çayönü appear to have made no use of clay vessels.

Ganj Dareh. Further evidence for technical facility in building by the late eighth millennium comes from the Iranian site of Ganj Dareh. We have already noted the absence of architectural features from its earliest level, E, but in level D a number of very small rectilinear structures, abutting one against another without connecting doorways, have been found. These were built of long handmade mud-bricks with a rounded upper surface. It has been suggested that the buildings were of two stories, with the lower cubicles supporting an upper living floor. Like Mureybet, Ganj Dareh provides evidence for lightly fired pottery already in the eighth millennium, and a more extensive use of clay can be seen in the figurines, both human and animal, which are abundant from level D onwards. Such objects are sporadically found on earlier sites, but at Ganj Dareh and later Zagros settlements they appear in unprecedented quantities. Without texts to help us we cannot be sure what their purpose was, and the contexts in which they are found are rarely meaningful. A "religious" function or significance is often attributed to such figures, but in some parts of Asia today comparable clay objects, even when they clearly depict religious subjects, are no more than children's toys.

At Ganj Dareh careful search has so far failed to yield any quantity of informative palaeobotanical specimens, though many blades with "sickle sheen," rubbing stones, pestles and mortars, items commonly associated with a plant diet, are found as early as level D. We have already noted that such equipment was completely absent from the earlier level E. As at Çayönü, goat, sheep, cattle, deer and pig bones occur, apparently belonging to morphologically wild forms, although the finding of caprid hoof prints on a number of mud-bricks almost certainly indicates the presence of husbanded herds, presumably of the more common goat. An unusual discovery, reminiscent of both Mureybet and later Çatal Hüyük, was a cubicle with a small niche built against one wall. Two skulls of wild sheep had been attached one above the other to the plastered interior of the niche. Certainly the later evidence

Left: a hand-made mud-brick from Jericho, PPN-B phase, with finger marks for keying the mortar.

Below: another human skull from PPN-B Jericho seen coming to light.

from Çatal Hüyük suggests that the deposition of animal skulls in this apparently formal manner, so widespread in time and space, may have had a religious or magical significance, but we must emphasize that there is no reason to postulate any direct tradition linking these diverse examples. Ganj Dareh's lack of contact with Anatolia – it lay well to the east of the main route along the western flank of the Zagros – is indeed illustrated by the complete absence of obsidian on the site.

Jericho. At Jericho the Pre-Pottery Neolithic A settlement came to an abrupt end, for reasons that are not clear, some time around 7000 BC and was followed by an abandonment of the mound, marked by a period of erosion. The succeeding Pre-Pottery Neolithic B population are thought to have been newcomers, unrelated to the previous inhabitants. The new phase is marked by rectilinear houses of several rooms grouped around courtyards, and built of flattened, cigar-shaped mudbricks unlike the "hog-back" form employed in the PPN-A levels, but comparable with those at Ganj Dareh and later Choga Mami. The Jericho bricks were marked with deep finger impressions on one side to aid in keying the mud mortar. Floors were surfaced with burnished gypsum plaster and often painted red or sometimes pink, cream or white. Several buildings are interpreted as shrines, the simplest consisting of a room with a niche in which a stone pillar was set.

More evidence has been recovered of the economy than in the preceding phase. It would appear that the PPN-B inhabitants were at least partly dependent on agriculture, although, as we have seen, it would not have been possible without lift irrigation to feed the entire settlement, which had grown still larger at this time. Of particular interest is the presence of einkorn, which is henceforward found regularly and abundantly. The primary habitat of this cereal is thought to have lain well to the north of Palestine, and its appearance at Jericho has been considered by some to indicate a northern origin for the PPN-B peoples, but the absence of einkorn from the eight cereal grains found in the PPN-A levels is hardly evidence that it was unknown in the earlier phase. Gazelle, cattle, pig, goat and various small mammals were still being hunted, while one or two twisted horn cores of goat, a feature probably present as a rare mutant in wild populations but apparently encouraged by selective breeding in domestic herds, suggest that goats may now have been herded. A similar process of selection is thought to have put the curl into the tail of a particular breed of prehistoric dog. Despite these hints of domestication, however, it was not until the much later "Pottery Neolithic" phase at Jericho that goats and the less common sheep replaced gazelle as the primary meat source.

Undoubtedly the most fascinating discovery in PPN-B Jericho is a group of ten human skulls on which the facial features had been delicately and sensitively modeled in clay and the eyes inset with shells, in one case with cowries. It is thought that these skulls must have played a role in some form of ancestor cult, and we may recall that the separation of the skull from the body and its ritual rearrangement are attested in Palestinian burials as early as the Natufian, while evidence for a "skull cult" was also found in the PPN-A phase at Jericho. But the remarkable modeled skulls are known only from PPN-B levels, not only at Jericho but also slightly later at Beisamun near Ain Mallaha and at Ramad, at the foot of Mount Hermon south of Damascus, where an example is dated by radiocarbon to c. 6200 BC.

Beidha. The presence of 26 successive occupation floors suggests a fairly lengthy occupation of PPN-B Jericho, and radiocarbon determinations span a period from the late eighth millennium to c. 6600 BC. Comparable dates come from the site of Beidha, which has been extensively excavated by Diana Kirkbride. This small village – its surviving area is less than half a hectare – is situated more than 100 miles south of Jericho, in a wide valley in the hills above Petra. An earlier Natufian occupation is overlaid by 2–3 meters of wind-borne sand, above which lies the PPN-B settlement. Beidha provides our most extensive knowledge of this phase, with considerable evidence for craft specialization, trade and some form of communal religious activity. The economy was based on hunting and collecting, the cultivation of emmer and barley, and almost certainly the herding of goats. The emmer is said to represent a series of types morphologically intermediate between the wild and domesticated forms while the barley, the more important crop, is still entirely wild. The country around the site is now generally too arid for cereal agriculture, but it was probably never more than marginally suited for farming.

The architectural remains are of especial interest, both for their rare state of preservation and for the light they throw on the development of building techniques within a single village. In the earliest levels were found floors with a large number of post-holes but no walls, clearly the remnants of temporary shelters. The first houses of more permanent aspect came in level VI. These consisted of circular rooms, partly sunk into the ground and walled with dry stone built around an inner framework of timber. The rooms were arranged in separate clusters like cells in a honeycomb and each cluster had its own encircling wall. One such honeycomb building contained nine chambers, both living and work rooms, with small store-rooms tucked into the thickness of the walls between them. One work room (XLIX on the plan) contained mainly bone tools with the raw materials for making them and a number of lumps of various coloring substances. In another (XVIII) were found polishers and grinders, abrasives, and traces of an oval wooden box that had contained 114 flint arrowheads and points in mint condition ready for their final retouching.

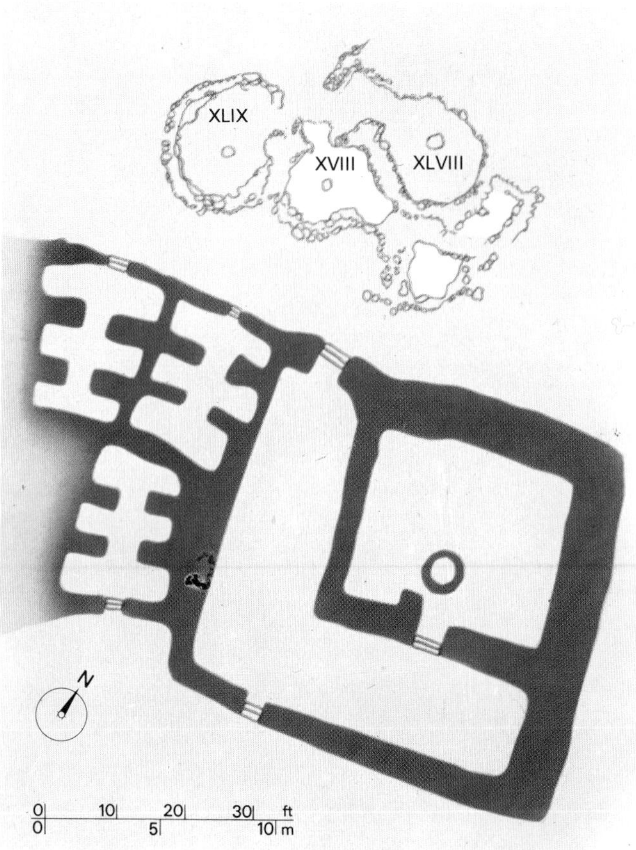

Plan of a level VI (*above*) and a level II (*below*) house at Beidha, Pre-Pottery Neolithic B (seventh millennium BC).

During the following two levels, V and IV, we see the development of free-standing houses, often single-roomed, still curvilinear but in some cases almost rectangular in plan. As confidence in their masonry grew, less reliance was placed on the internal wooden frame that had supported the roof in the earlier houses. Then in levels III and II we find large rectangular units to which were attached groups of very regular, rectangular "corridor buildings." These developed plans appear very unlike the earlier house forms but a closer examination shows that in function they differ very little, since both types comprise a living unit and a workshop area. A fascinating variety of industrial activity can be reconstructed from the debris in these later buildings, and we cannot do better than quote the excavator's description.

"The workshop of a specialist in bone tools and beads contained an untidy clutter of the raw material, animal long bones and ribs, lying in depth in the corridor and in his workroom. The tables on which he worked were flat sandstone slabs lying on the floor, together with his tools and with beads of stone, bone and shell in every stage of the making. Some stone beads were found with the grinding process unfinished, others with the perforation just begun. By the table lay a slender long bone, the shaft divided by incised grooves into nineteen fairly equal sections; nearby were separated slices or rings, rough and unworked, as well as the finished products, smooth and polished. The bone tools also provided a fine view of the worker's art: beautifully polished spatulae, slender points and long (?) weaving implements of aurochs' ribs. One worker in horn left his workroom with a magnificent pair of horns lying on the table; nearby was another pair in readiness for use. In a corner lay a neat pile of ground stone tools. This man kept his basement tidy in marked contrast to most of the others. In one cubicle of the butcher's shop was a great heap of animal bones, some jointed, and horned heads, while the room opposite was piled with heavy implements, choppers, grinders and pounders. Other workshops showed a more general activity; one contained a mixture of horn and bone working, with ground stone tools in quantity and beads as well. Querns were abundant everywhere and when worn out were frequently used as building material."

We shall never know what caused the sudden abandonment of this beehive of activity, but seldom do we get such a vivid glimpse of everyday human life so long ago.

The superficially striking architectural change from the early to the later levels at Beidha has been thought to indicate a change of culture, with newcomers arriving in level III. Indeed it has been suggested on the basis of modern ethnographic parallels that basic differences in social structure can be inferred from the two house types, the early curvilinear plan, which as we have seen is prevalent in the first known settlements throughout the Near East, and the later rectilinear layout. We have already pointed out that in their essential functions the two types at Beidha are indistinguishable. Moreover an analysis of the chipped stone industry, at this period the most significant criterion of a change in population, suggests strongly that no such change took place. This aspect of the Beidha sequence shows how cautious we must be in using cultural change as an explanation even for apparently abrupt developments in style or technology, and cross-cultural analogies to support inferences about ancient society. There are, for example, instances of the replacement of round by rectangular houses in West Africa because the newly imported and prestigious European furniture would not fit conveniently against a curved wall. At Beidha too there is a simpler explanation of the change. From the earliest level onwards we can observe increasing permanence of occupation coupled with increasing confidence in building techniques that seem to have been recently developed. The first structures were simple timber-framed huts, which were later sunk into the ground and revetted with stone, although the roof was still supported on wooden posts. When free-standing stone masonry replaced timber as the load-bearing element in the structure a new method of roofing was developed, and the simplest form of roof is carried on parallel rafters resting on a rectangular wall plan.

These advances in building technique would hardly

have been made at the small site of Beidha itself and were probably copied from more important settlements of which, at present, we have no evidence outside Jericho. But the extraordinary industrial character of Beidha strongly suggests that it was essentially a manufacturing, and possibly a commercial, center serving wider markets than its own immediate and arid countryside would provide. In addition to the game that yielded bones and hides, its local resources included rich supplies of haematite and malachite, and limestone and flint were readily available. Moreover Beidha lay on the same trade route from the Red Sea and the Hejaz to the Jordan valley and the Mediterranean coast that was later controlled by Petra, and was certainly importing Red Sea cowries and mother-of-pearl, though northern imports such as obsidian are rare.

Settlement related to the PPN-B levels at Jericho and Beidha has been found at a number of sites, notably in levels 6–3 at Munhata, south of the Sea of Galilee, at Beisamun near Ain Mallaha and even as far north as Ramad near Damascus, though at Ramad some of the material is more characteristic of coastal sites in northern Syria. Abu Hureyra on the Euphrates, which we have already mentioned as a Mesolithic settlement, appears to have been an unusually large village at this time, perhaps as much as 11 hectares in area. Here as at Beidha there is considerable evidence for craft specialization and trade, and at both Abu Hureyra and Ramad domesticated forms of barley have been found, accompanied at Ramad by the first known specimens of *Triticum compactum* or club wheat, a hexaploid form, and domesticated linseed, and at Abu Hureyra wild vines which must have grown in the valley bottom. The end of this pre-pottery ("aceramic") phase is something of a mystery. Although occupation continued at more northerly sites such as Ramad and Ras Shamra on the Syrian coast, nowhere in Palestine has any continuity yet been established between settlements of this time and those of a very much later Neolithic phase when pottery was in use. Even such established and prosperous sites as Jericho and Beidha were abandoned, and there follows a long interval for which we have at present no archaeological evidence. Some scholars have suggested that the whole of Palestine was deserted, but it seems more likely that the population, always more inclined to herding than to cultivation, reverted for some reason to a nomadic way of life whose traces are almost impossible for archaeologists to detect. The abandonment of the sites seems to have coincided with a dry phase in the climate that offers a possible explanation, if not for the disappearance of the population, at least for their reversion to nomadic herding, for their agricultural techniques were not sufficiently developed to cope with worsening climatic conditions. Indeed it is significant that when settlements reappear in the fifth millennium, their distribution is associated with soils especially suited to agriculture, a pattern quite distinct from that of the earlier cultures.

The site of Jarmo during excavation showing *tauf* walls on stone foundations and one of the grill-plan buildings.

Jarmo. Although Jericho may yet prove to be the earliest known agricultural community, the first extensive evidence for agriculture comes not from Palestine but from the northern and eastern parts of our region. In Anatolia and the Zagros, and in southwestern Iran (Khuzistan) where we now find settlements for the first time, the situation is significantly different. As at late eighth-millennium Çayönü, the majority of seventh-millennium settlements that have been investigated yield, from their earliest levels, unequivocal evidence for the domestication of both plants and animals, although hunting and food gathering continued to provide an important source of food

Jarmo, in Iraqi Kurdistan, is undoubtedly the best known of these early farming sites and was the first to be discovered. Originally covering an area of some two hectares, Jarmo has seven meters of archaeological deposits, in the upper third of which pottery is found for the first time in any quantity. The economy was based on settled agriculture, hunting and gathering. Land snails (*Helix salomonica*) were eaten in vast numbers, and were evidently a very popular taste at other Zagros sites. Barley, einkorn, emmer and several large-seeded annual legumes were cultivated and goats were herded. In the upper levels we have the first certain evidence for domesticated pig, which is of particular interest because pigs, like dogs but unlike the grass-eating ruminants, eat the same range of foods as man and are not adapted to nomadic herding. Domesticated animals provide a form of food bank for their owners, but human populations derive more energy from eating the primary foods themselves than from feeding pigs for their meat. Only when food is plentiful can domestic animals of this type be tolerated.

A grill-plan building on the site of Çayönü with part of a plastered floor surviving in the foreground.

The cereals found at Jarmo and Çayönü are of especial interest, not only as the evidence by which we identify two of the earliest known farming communities, but for the way in which they illustrate one of the fundamental problems we have mentioned – the difficulty of reconstructing the ancient distributions of wild resources and in particular of cereals. It is generally assumed that emmer must first have been domesticated in Palestine, more precisely in the upper Jordan valley, and einkorn in southeastern Anatolia because that is where the wild forms are found today. But when we look at the evidence in detail it does not support these apparently obvious assumptions. No morphologically wild emmer has yet been discovered on any Palestinian site, and indeed it has been found only at Çayönü and Jarmo. Furthermore, wild einkorn has been found at both these sites and in Khuzistan, but it is the small single-seeded variety (*Triticum boeoticum*, subspecies *aegilopoides*), a race that is today characteristic of the cooler Balkans and western Anatolia, not the larger two-seeded *Triticum boeoticum*, subspecies *thaoudar*, that now grows in the warmer, dry-summer areas of southern Anatolia, Mesopotamia and Iran. Yet it is the larger variety that is found in antiquity at Mureybet, in Palestine, and as the predominant crop on sixth-millennium sites in western Anatolia. There would appear to be, on present evidence, a complete reversal of the ancient and modern distributions.

It is estimated that the total population of Jarmo was approximately 150 persons. Rectangular houses, each consisting of several rooms and a courtyard, were built of *tauf* or packed mud. The clay walls were often founded on stone, and clay floors were laid over beds of reeds. Grill-plan foundations similar to those at Çayönü were found, as were bins for storage and domed clay ovens, perhaps for parching grain. One of the most characteristic features of Jarmo, indeed of the "Zagros assemblage" that this site exemplifies, is the quantity and variety of clay figurines, both human and animal. Tools made of chipped stone occur in enormous quantities, as at all sites before the use of metal, and a high percentage of obsidian to flint reflects the site's relative proximity to obsidian sources in eastern Anatolia. There is a great expansion in the ground stone industry, and a variety of very attractive stone bowls were made. The pottery is mostly plain, though often burnished.

The occupation of Jarmo certainly falls largely in the seventh millennium but more precise dates are difficult even to estimate. Many of the available radiocarbon determinations were run when the technique was in its infancy; indeed they are among the first from the Near East. Recent refinements in method have tended to produce earlier determinations on such samples, but those from Jarmo remain a very inconsistent group. Braidwood suggests a date of c. 6750 BC for the earliest occupation, while comparisons with Tepe Guran on the eastern side of the Zagros, where similar archaeological materials including the distinctive painted pottery have been found, confirm that the ceramic levels at Jarmo should be placed somewhere between 6300 and 5900 BC. Pottery provides the archaeologist with a very useful criterion for relative dating between sites, particularly within fairly homogeneous groups and in the prehistoric periods when it was often elaborately decorated. This is because pots are easily broken but their sherds are virtually indestructible, and styles of decoration had a relatively short life. Indeed as evidence for chronological and cultural relationships pottery is quite different from, for instance, chipped stone. Chipped stone tools were made by the same techniques and in almost identical forms not only for long periods but over very large areas. They consequently provide valuable evidence for widespread cultural connections, but are much less useful than pottery as precise chronological markers.

At Tepe Guran the earliest levels (c. 6500 BC) seem to represent an encampment of transhumant or seminomadic herdsmen who kept goats and also hunted gazelle and, in season, waterfowl. There is no evidence for cultivation or for summer occupation of the site at this time. The herdsmen lived in wooden huts with matting floors, but in

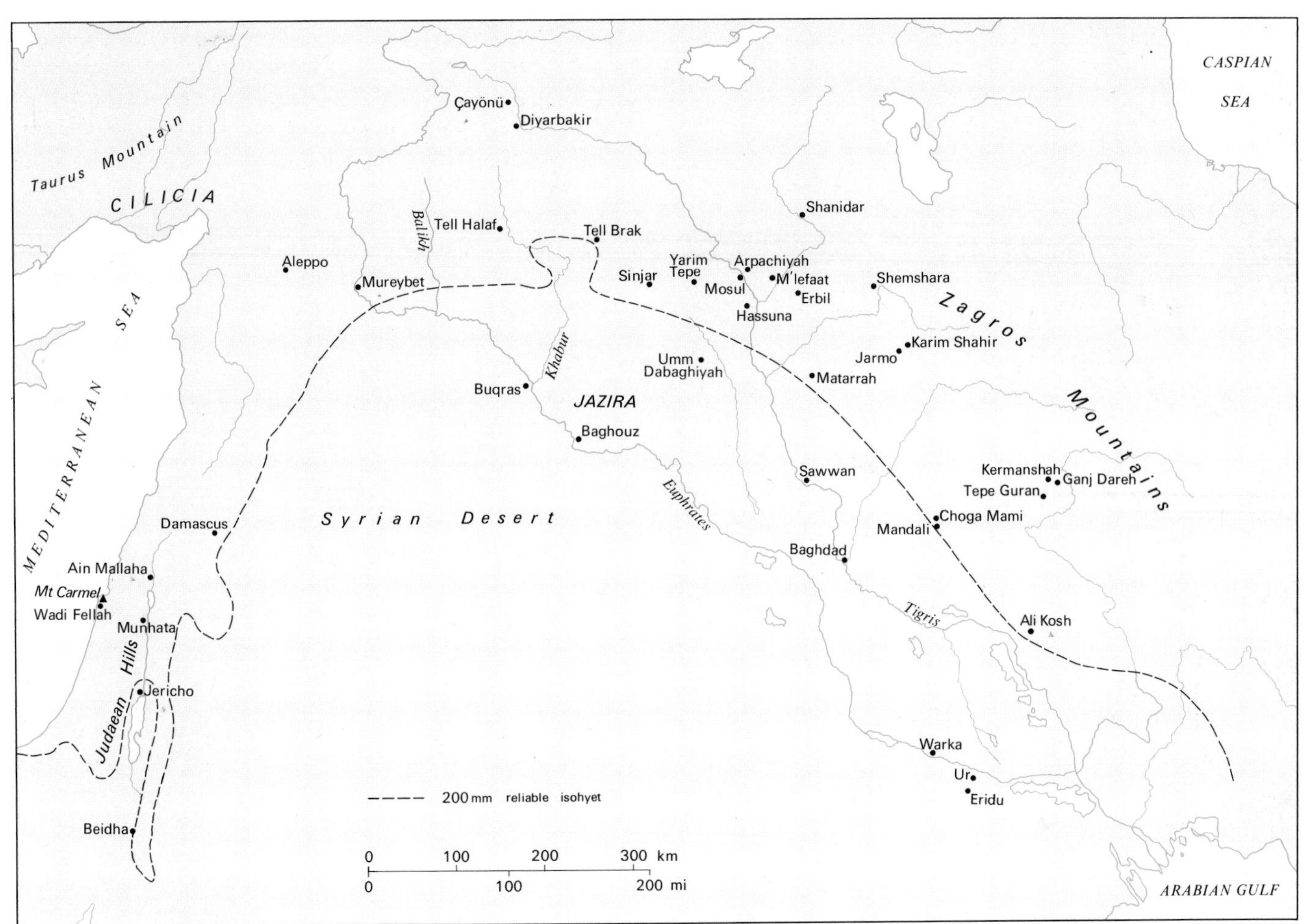

Mesopotamian sites down to 5000 BC.

later levels there are remains of mud-walled houses with terrazzo paving like that at Çayönü, a change that undoubtedly reflects the establishment of a more permanent farming village. Barley was now cultivated, and the inhabitants were using pottery like that found at Jarmo. At the same time, at the mound of Ali Kosh in Khuzistan, we find the first evidence outside Palestine and northern Syria for a farming community in a lowland area, for Çayönü, Jarmo and Tepe Guran are all highland sites. Ali Kosh probably also lay outside the primary habitat of emmer, which constitutes the major food crop from the earliest period of the settlement. Wild two-row hulled barley (*Hordeum spontaneum*) was also present, presumably cultivated. A few grains of "naked" – and therefore domesticated – barley and of wild and domesticated einkorn, of the small single-grained race, were recovered in the earliest (Bus Mordeh) phase.

The Bus Mordeh people herded goats and smaller numbers of sheep, and supplemented their diet by hunting, fishing and collecting wild food. No acceptable radiocarbon determinations exist for this stage of occupation, but the succeeding Ali Kosh phase appears to be dated some time between 6500 and 6000 BC. How closely these determinations can be related to those in the Zagros, Anatolia and Palestine must remain uncertain at present. Although there is growing confidence in the reliability of radiocarbon techniques, it must be admitted that in later periods when close cultural parallels can be found between sites in Khuzistan, such as Tepe Sabz, and in Mesopotamia, there is roughly a 500-year discrepancy between radiocarbon determinations for almost identical materials in the two areas, with Khuzistan yielding the earlier dates. Both the Bus Mordeh and the Ali Kosh phases were aceramic, but this need not indicate an especially early date. Indeed, the general level of development suggests that the first settlement at the site of Ali Kosh should be placed somewhere in the early seventh millennium, roughly contemporary with early Jarmo and early PPN-B Palestine.

In the second (Ali Kosh) phase there is increasing evidence for the cultivation of emmer and barley. By this time the village is thought to have been about one hectare in area and to have had a population of about 100 people. External contacts seem to have increased, for obsidian was brought from Anatolia and seashells possibly from the Arabian Gulf, while a single bead of hammered copper probably came from some Iranian source. Pottery first appears in the next (Muhammad Jaffar) phase, perhaps 6000 to 5500 BC, together with several types of artifact that

The mound of Aşıklı Hüyük close to the Çiftlik obsidian deposits in western Anatolia.

are very like later sixth-millennium materials in Mesopotamia, particularly at the site of Tell es-Sawwan. The decorated pottery from Ali Kosh seems to have been an entirely local product, unrelated either to the "tadpole" wares of the Zagros or to contemporary painted pottery in northern Mesopotamia.

Western Anatolia. One further area must be briefly discussed to complete our survey of seventh-millennium settlement. This is the western plateau of Anatolia, a vast area bordered on the north by the mountains along the Black Sea and on the south by the Taurus range, through which several routes lead to northern Syria and the river valleys of Mesopotamia. The plateau itself consists of a number of separate basins divided by higher land. The average rainfall nowhere drops below 200 millimeters per annum and is generally above 300 millimeters, so it is not surprising to find early farming villages in the fertile and well-watered basins, although they at present appear to be confined to the south of the area. The earliest of them seem to be contemporary with the PPN-B phase in Palestine, Ali Kosh and Zagros sites such as Jarmo and Tepe Guran.

As yet very little earlier evidence for occupation has been found, with the exception of some material from caves along the Mediterranean coast, particularly in the neighborhood of Antalya. What is particularly surprising is the apparent absence of earlier occupation in the very extensive and fertile Konya plain, when we remember that obsidian from sources at its northeastern end was found at Jericho and elsewhere as early as the ninth millennium. Who were the purveyors of this obsidian remains a mystery. We do know, however, that these Anatolian basins had been occupied by very extensive lakes that appear to have diminished in size towards the end of the Pleistocene, and it has been suggested that the rich alluvial land around two of the earliest agricultural sites, Çatal Hüyük East and aceramic Hacılar, was exposed only in the eighth millennium.

The earliest of the western Anatolian sites from which we have archaeological information is Aşıklı Hüyük, 16 miles east of Aksaray and just over 30 miles from the Çiftlik obsidian deposits. The mound has not been excavated, but it has been eroded on one side by a river and much valuable material, including radiocarbon samples, was extracted from the exposed section. The radiocarbon determinations place the site early in the seventh millennium, slightly later than the beginning of Çayönü and approximately contemporary with Beidha and PPN-B Jericho, but we do not know what point in the sequence of occupation they represent. No pottery was found, nor is there evidence for agriculture, but in the absence of excavation such negative information may be misleading. Very large numbers of obsidian tools were recovered, and mud-brick and red lime-plaster floors like those on PPN-B sites in the Levant could be identified in the section.

The earliest farming settlement so far known in this area is represented by an early mound found below the later ceramic Neolithic settlement at Hacılar near modern Burdur. Only a very small part of the earlier aceramic settlement was explored in a brief sounding at the end of the final season of excavations. Samples of domesticated two-row hulled barley, emmer, lentils and wild einkorn were found in the fifth of seven occupation levels which yielded a radiocarbon determination of c. 6750 BC. The only domesticated animal identified is the dog, but bones of sheep, goat, cattle, fallow deer and hare were also recovered. The cattle were small in size, a possible indicator of domestication, but the number of bones found is too small to justify any certain conclusion. The earliest undisputed evidence for domesticated cattle in our region also comes from Anatolia (Çatal Hüyük), but towards the end of the seventh millennium, approximately contemporary with similar evidence from Argissa Maghula in Greece. Like Aşıklı this early settlement at Hacılar appears to have had no pottery; mud-brick was in use and burnished red lime-plaster floors were found. Another feature at Hacılar reminds us of PPN-B Palestine, for human skulls with no associated burials seem to have been deliberately installed at the edge of hearths or in courtyards.

Other sites such as Suberde in the mountains near Lake Suğla, apparently a "hunting settlement," and Can Hasan III near Karaman are attributed to a later phase of the seventh millennium. The evidence from Can Hasan is very limited and in the absence of radiocarbon samples cannot be dated with precision. The site, apparently without pottery, would appear to be an agricultural settlement like aceramic Hacılar, but the presence of the hybrid hexaploid bread and club wheats may suggest a rather later date. Cattle were the most important source of meat, but it has not yet been established whether any of the animals exploited were domesticated. It is clear, however, that the western Asiatic farming economy based on sheep, goats, cattle, wheat (including hexaploid bread wheat) and barley had reached both Crete and Greece (Knossos and Franchthi cave) by the end of the seventh millennium, and this undoubtedly suggests a far more extensive development of farming communities in western Anatolia than the very few known sites have so far revealed.

Çatal Hüyük

VISUAL STORY

The site of Çatal Hüyük was discovered by James Mellaart in 1958 and excavations were carried out under his direction in 1961–63, with a fourth season in 1965. The results of this work have caused archaeologists completely to revise their views of Neolithic development in western Asia. Not only is Çatal Hüyük the largest Neolithic site yet discovered, but the remarkable state of preservation of the material found and the unparalleled artistic achievements of its inhabitants remain for the moment a unique tribute to the skills and ingenuity of man long before the invention of writing and other supposed attributes of civilization. Like eighth-millennium BC Jericho, Çatal Hüyük in the late seventh and early sixth Millennia stands out as an apparently isolated phenomenon. But this is far more likely to reflect the limited state of our archaeological knowledge than the true state of human development at the time. Certainly there is much yet to be learned of the early prehistory of western Asia.

Among the objects found were a great variety of figurines. Illustrated *below* is one of the most extraordinary examples in baked clay, an enthroned female, possibly meant to represent a goddess, giving birth. Two cat-like animals, probably leopards, support her on either side. Discovered in a grain bin in the latest "shrine" (level II, c. 5500 BC).

Left: a view from the north of the site of Çatal Hüyük, which lies in the Konya Plain some 25 miles southeast of Konya, at an altitude of c. 3,000 feet. The site consists of two mounds, the earlier eastern one covering an area of about 32 acres. It rises 17·5 meters above the plain; 15 meters of these deposits are Neolithic. Only $\frac{1}{30}$ of the site has been investigated, and it is thought that several meters of deposit lie below level XII, the earliest so far explored. Çatal Hüyük was a settlement of farmers and cattle-breeders whose inhabitants must have included a number of skilled craftsmen. The variety of objects found on the site and the raw materials employed suggest that trade was an important element in the economy. Among the imported raw materials was obsidian, extensively used for the manufacture of chipped stone tools and luxury goods such as mirrors. One of the sources of this volcanic stone was Acığol, 100 miles to the northeast (*opposite below*). *Below* is a view of the excavations showing several houses and, in the center, one of the level VI structures which because of their unusual painted or plaster decoration have been interpreted as shrines.

Çatal Hüyük revealed a unique series of buildings which because of their unusual ornament have been interpreted as sanctuaries or shrines. In plan and fittings these buildings are identical with the ordinary houses, among which they are found. Nor are there altars or any of the other appurtenances usually associated with Near Eastern shrines. It is their decoration alone that distinguishes them, but this is such as to leave little doubt as to their special nature. Three different methods of ornament were employed, painting, reliefs modeled in plaster, and cut-out figures, that is figures, usually animals, actually cut out of the wall plaster. No two shrines are alike and the variations are extensive. In level VI only there occur groups or rows of bulls' horn cores set in benches (*opposite above*). In this photograph traces can be seen of the heavy burning that was responsible for the remarkable state of preservation of many of the shrines and their contents.

Below right: a pair of leopards with heads in high relief, which decorate the wall of a level VII shrine. These had been frequently repainted with different geometric patterns. Seven successive layers of paint separated by thin white plaster were recorded. This view shows the topmost painted layer. Below the right-hand leopard are traces of wall painting depicting ibexes and what are interpreted as animal tracks.

Above right can be seen two plastered bulls' heads, set in a niche on the west wall of a level VII shrine, the plaster incorporating the actual horn cores of wild bulls (*Bos primigenius*).

Opposite below is a reconstruction of the north and east walls of the so-called Second Vulture Shrine, level VII. The vultures have human legs and are

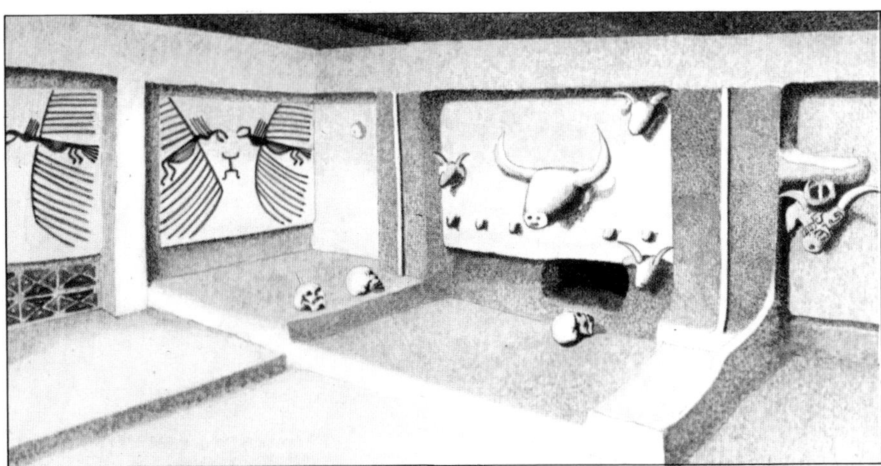

interpreted as "priests" in disguise; a headless corpse lies between them. In other shrines are scenes of more bird-like vultures picking at corpses, possibly reflecting the practice of exposing dead bodies for the purpose of excarnation. The presence of human skulls in this shrine is unusual and may again reflect the funerary aspects of the vulture scene. On the east wall are an enormous bull's head with 3 rams' heads and a row of human breasts below. To the right is a large ornamented ram's head supporting a model of a horn and breast from which protrudes the lower jaw of an enormous wild boar.

Opposite: a white clay figurine, partly blackened by fire.

Left: the function of the wall paintings at Çatal remains obscure. Although a large number were found, it is clear that they remained visible only for brief periods, the painted walls being replastered with plain white layers. Thus some buildings bore painted decoration for only one or two years within a life span of perhaps as much as a century. This "hunting" scene (reconstructed *center left*) decorates the north wall of a level V shrine. A great bull, some 2 meters in length, dominates the scene, with a frieze of wild asses and a dog below. On the other walls were other animals, in one instance followed by a long procession of "dancers." The men are dressed in skins with one or more tails. They carry bows and arrows, clubs and axes, but do not appear to use them. The general impression is one of levity. The men caper about and even "tease" the animals. Thus the paintings appear to portray ritual festivities rather than hunting.

Below: this scene, reconstructed from the north and east walls of a level VII shrine, is unique and would appear to depict the buildings of a town, perhaps Çatal Hüyük itself, with its closely packed terraces of houses. In the background is an erupting volcano, perhaps Hasan Dağ, a now extinct volcano that lies at the eastern end of the Konya Plain, clearly visible from the site.

Left: a unique schist plaque from a shrine in level VI, showing four figures in bold relief. On the left two figures embrace; on the right a mother holds a child whose head is unfortunately lost. It is possible that the two scenes relate a succession of events, the union of the couple on the left and the desired result on the right. (Ht. 12 cm.)

Below: baked clay "stamps" are a prominent feature at Çatal Hüyük. They occur from level VI to level II. They have a flat lower surface and bear incised patterns, among which spirals and meanders are common. Most are oval, round or roughly rectangular; this example (c. 5 cm across) is flower-shaped, a pattern common on the textile or kilim paintings. These "stamps" were probably used for applying patterns to plain cloth.

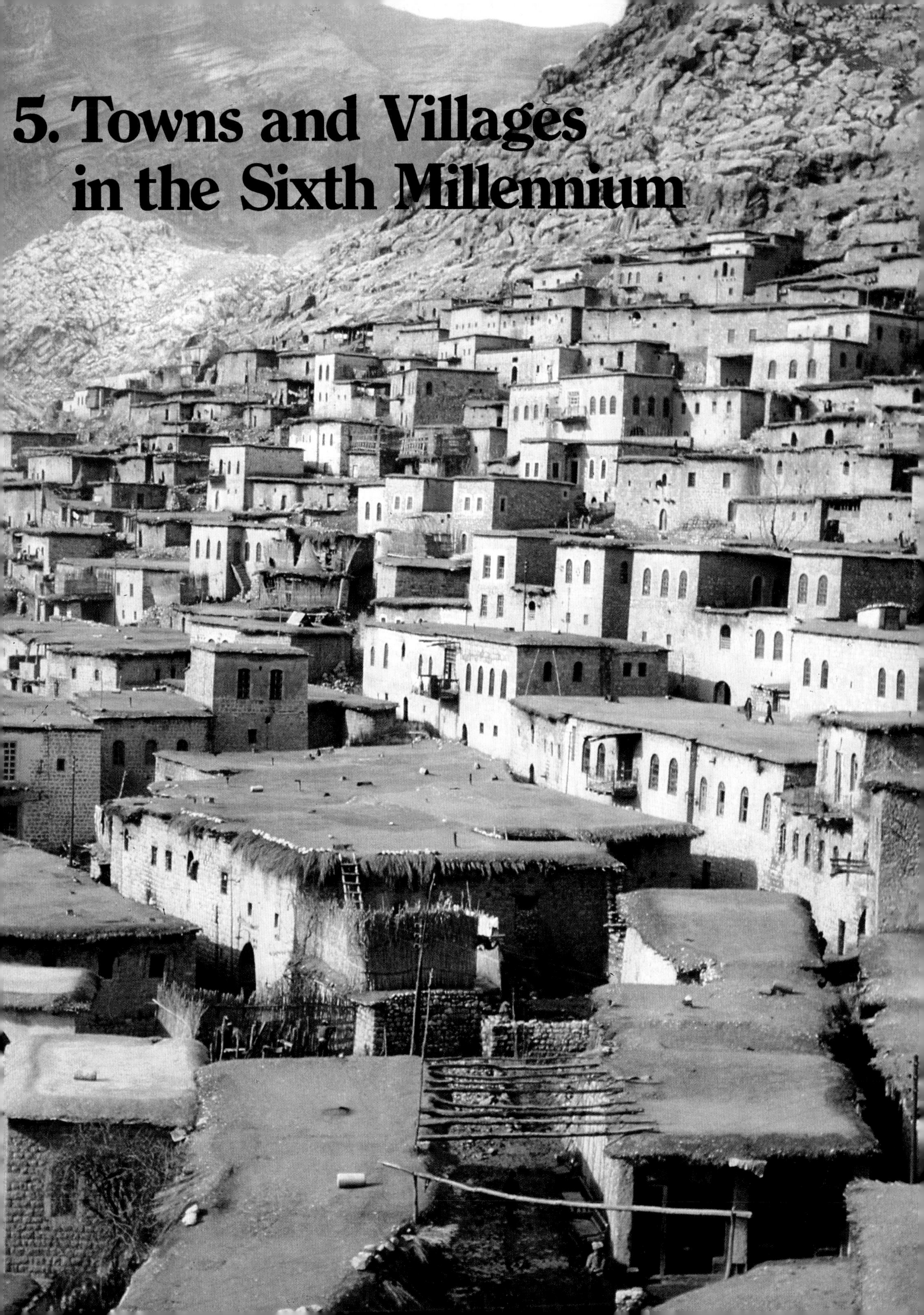

5. Towns and Villages in the Sixth Millennium

In the last chapter we have outlined the often diverse and controversial evidence for the development, in several areas of the Near East, of what can certainly be described as farming villages. By 6000 BC, on a conservative interpretation of the radiocarbon evidence, settled agricultural communities are found from the Mediterranean to the eastern Zagros. Two areas provide exceptions to this, Palestine, where we have already referred to the apparent hiatus in settlement following the PPN-B phase, and southern Iraq, where for climatic reasons cereal cultivation was impossible before the introduction of relatively sophisticated irrigation techniques. Indeed, in Palestine the evidence for cultivation is minimal before the fifth millennium, and it is clear that hunting and herding were of far greater importance throughout the period with which we are concerned. Elsewhere, however, not only was the herding of sheep, goats, pigs and cattle now widely practiced, but crops such as wheat, barley, lentils and certain legumes were extensively grown. With the exception of Jericho, the known settlements are all modest in size and equipment. But at some time in the seventh millennium a village grew up on the Konya Plain in Anatolia that was to eclipse all others known up to that time, and indeed for two millennia thereafter.

Çatal Hüyük. This was the site of Çatal Hüyük, situated along a small river 30 miles southeast of Konya, which by the middle of the sixth millennium had grown to over 12 hectares (32 acres) in area, three times the size of PPN-A Jericho. Not only is Çatal Hüyük the largest known "Neolithic" site in the whole of western Asia, but it has yielded by far the most convincing evidence for the evolution of a highly complex society. Discovered in 1958 by James Mellaart, the site consists of two mounds. The earlier eastern one rises to a height of 17·5 meters, of which 15 meters represent entirely Neolithic deposits. Four seasons of excavation from 1960 onwards have revealed 14 building levels, but only one-thirtieth of the total area of the mound has been investigated and several meters of deposit lie below level XII, the earliest so far explored. A small sounding has penetrated a further four meters below present plain level without reaching virgin soil.

Radiocarbon determinations from levels VIII to II span the first half of the sixth millennium. The site is thus contemporary with the latest PPN-B materials in Palestine and, as we shall see, with the earliest phase of village occupation yet discovered on the Mesopotamian plain. It has been suggested that the economy of the site was based on irrigation agriculture, but the evidence for this consists of the presence of certain crops with high water requirements such as hexaploid wheat and naked six-row barley, that were to become important irrigation crops but are also known from contemporary sites where rain-fed agriculture was practiced (e.g. Ramad near Damascus in Syria where a hexaploid wheat and linseed, another crop usually associated with irrigation agriculture, were grown).

Previous page: the modern town of Aqra in Iraqi Kurdistan. The use of flat roofs for access and for living space recalls their similar function in ancient settlements such as Çatal Hüyük.

Evidence for cattle-breeding is found in the earliest levels at Çatal, the first unquestionably domesticated cattle in western Asia, although, in view of their presence in Crete before 6000 BC, earlier evidence is almost certain to be found in western Anatolia from which the Cretan cattle presumably came. The importance of cattle in the Çatal economy is clear not only from the extremely high proportion of cattle bones – over 90 per cent – but also from the widespread occurrence of bulls' horns, either real or modeled in clay, in numerous "shrines" found from level X onwards. Large numbers of morphologically wild sheep bones were also recovered from the site, but the presence of woolen cloth in level VI suggests that sheep too must have been domesticated, although this is not apparent from the bones. Studies of the human skeletal material show that the population was already a mixed one, as might indeed be expected in view of the evidence for contact between this area and Palestine as early as the ninth millennium. Even the farming economy at Çatal is thought to have been imported in the sense that the cereals grown by its inhabitants were apparently not indigenous.

The houses at Çatal were constructed of timber and mud-brick. Their most unusual feature was a highly standardized plan, each occupying some 25 square meters of floor space and consisting of a living room and a smaller storeroom. Access was from the flat roof and impressions of wooden ladders were found, always on the south wall of the house. The houses were built directly up against one another with very few intervening courtyards, and these usually represented the sites of ruined houses of previous levels that had not yet been rebuilt. There were no streets or even lanes, and all communication was at rooftop level. The large number of broken bones among the human skeletal material may well reflect this difficulty of access. The furniture was "built-in." Common to all houses were a bench, and a series of platforms which may have been used for sleeping, sitting and working, and under which the dead were buried. At the kitchen end were the ladder, a hearth, a flat-domed oven and a fuel cupboard. Otherwise identical buildings were identified as "shrines" only by their extraordinary ornament and by the "high-status" burials associated with them.

Bodies were exposed after death and, after the flesh had been stripped from the bones – presumably by the vultures illustrated on the wall paintings – were wrapped in cloth and buried under the sleeping platforms. A number were covered with red ocher, some even with blue azurite of green malachite. One red ocher burial in level VII had large sliced cowries set into the eye sockets in the manner of PPN-B skulls at Jericho and Ramad. Most were buried without grave goods but some personal ornaments were found. One young woman buried in a level VI shrine wore a string skirt, the ends of which were encased in small copper tubes to weight it down. Another piece of cloth found in a grave had been mended, and the sewn edge was still clearly visible. Burials in the shrines were accompanied by precious objects such as stone vessels, ceremonial daggers, cosmetic sets, obsidian mirrors, polished mace-heads, metal beads and quivers; offerings of food also occur but never figurines or pottery. Wooden boxes and other containers were also found. Wood is rarely preserved in the Near East outside the unusually dry conditions of Egyptian tombs, and the unexpected discovery of wooden vessels at Çatal serves to emphasize that, on the vast majority of sites, archaeologically recoverable material probably represents only a small proportion even of the utilitarian equipment of such Neolithic peoples.

The archaeological evidence from Çatal is fascinating in a number of respects. We have already commented on the unusual size of the site. A conservative estimate suggests perhaps 1,000 houses with a population of 5,000–6,000 at the height of the settlement's prosperity. The extraordinary standardization, indeed deliberate planning, seen in the architecture and furnishing of the houses, is also striking and suggests a high level of cohesion and cooperation within the community if not an organizing authority. Unique too – for this period – is the extensive evidence for organized ritual activity, accompanied by the elaborate plaster ornament in the "shrines," a word that we put in quotation marks only because it is not clear that they were exclusively devoted to religious activities.

Specialization of labor is already evident at earlier seventh-millennium sites such as Beidha and Abu Hureyra, but the craftsmanship of Çatal attains an unusually high level, illustrated particularly among the luxury grave goods. Among the specialized crafts the chipped stone

Above: Ceremonial dagger of flint from a male burial in a level VI shrine at Çatal Hüyük. The serpent handle is carved of bone.

Below: reconstruction of houses in level VI at Çatal Hüyük and diagrammatic reconstruction of a typical main room showing the characteristic furnishings.

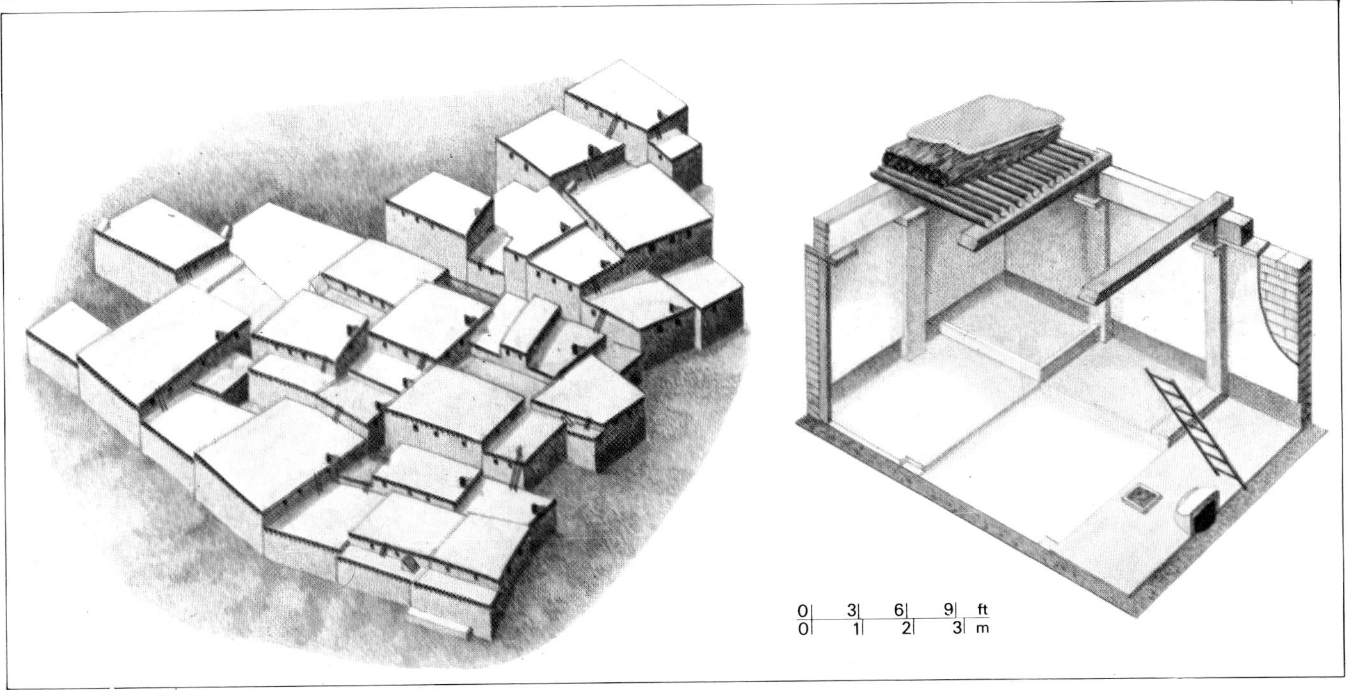

industry is by far the most elegant in western Asia, as may be seen from a number of prestige or ceremonial weapons, while in polished stone the craftsmen achieved such technically difficult products as ground obsidian mirrors. Another highly developed craft was evidently the production of excellent textiles of different weaves in wool or linen. Moreover, the presence among the wall paintings of geometric patterns very reminiscent of those employed today on the thin woven rugs of Anatolia (*kilims*) seems persuasive evidence for the manufacture, as early as the sixth millennium BC, of these very attractive objects which are now used as wall, bench or floor coverings.

Metal was known at Çatal, as were the techniques of smelting both lead and copper. Lead pendants occur as early as level IX, while copper slag in level VI-A shows that by the middle of the sixth millennium – a minimal estimate based on uncalibrated radiocarbon dates – copper was being extracted by this process. Comparable and approximately contemporary evidence comes also from Yarim Tepe in northern Iraq, discussed below. Undecorated pottery is found in small quantity from the earliest levels, but it becomes common only from level V onwards, while decoration is virtually unknown even in later levels. It is clear that at Çatal the production of pottery was never a craft of more than utilitarian interest. The earliest ware found in the excavations so far is cream colored, but this is replaced about level VII by dark burnished ware that is characteristic of Neolithic sites in Cilicia and northern Syria.

There can be no doubt that specialized and even luxury craftsmanship in certain materials was an important feature of the Çatal economy. The fact that many of the essential raw materials had to be brought from elsewhere points to a commercial connection from which much of the wealth of this town – village is surely no longer a suitable term – must have been derived. Indeed the unusual size of Çatal itself strongly suggests that it exercised some form of political control over its surrounding territory.

The site appears to have been occupied from some time in the late seventh until the latter part of the sixth millennium when, for reasons unknown to us, it was totally abandoned. Somewhat later a new site across the river, now the western mound, was occupied, but little of this settlement has been investigated. The "later Neolithic" in Anatolia is best illustrated at the site of Hacılar near Burdur, where we have already noted the presence of an early, apparently aceramic, occupation. Of 13 ceramic levels at Hacılar, level VI, which was burned some time after 5400 BC, would appear to be approximately contemporary with the abandonment of Çatal. By contrast with the latter site, the potters of Hacılar were highly skilled, and from the earliest level decorated vessels of excellent quality were manufactured. The houses are also unlike those of Çatal, having ordinary doorways and no sleeping platforms or internal decoration, nor even the red plaster floors of the earlier aceramic levels. The later settlements at Hacılar are walled (level II) and megaron-like houses appear. It is suggested that newcomers arrived in level I (probably some time after 5000 BC). These were builders of two-storied houses of which the basement rooms alone survive, entered from above in the old Çatal style. Perhaps the best-known artifacts from this occupation are the seated "Toby jugs" now to be seen in many western museums, although unfortunately not all of these are genuine. They remind us very strongly of the earlier Samarran "face-pots" from Mesopotamia.

Painted pottery anthropomorphic jar from Hacılar, level I, c. 5000 BC.

We have already remarked that on the Konya Plain the early settlement at Çatal was succeeded by that on the western mound. Can Hasan near Karaman was also occupied at this later period, and in general it would seem that the pattern of settlement is now one of small sites; no settlement approaching the urban proportions of the eastern mound of Çatal emerges again until the third millennium. The reasons for this remain obscure, and indeed it is very difficult to explain why advanced though apparently isolated developments such as early Jericho or Çatal came to nothing in terms of further social and economic development. It has been suggested that the extraordinary growth and eclipse of Çatal were the result of efficient exploitation that had reached an optimum, perhaps even a maximum, within the resources of the Konya Plain. But this is not an answer to the real question of why new techniques of exploitation, indeed new methods of acquiring both food and raw materials, were not developed. Early farming villages in Sumer were situated in an area far less economically viable than Anatolia, yet it was in this very arid zone, virtually devoid of natural resources, that urban civilization was first to develop. From this point onwards we turn our attention to

Mesopotamia. Despite the many and sometimes startling developments we have traced in earlier periods and other areas, from the sixth millennium onwards Mesopotamia was to be the center of social, technological and political progress that led to the world's first truly urban society.

Sixth-millennium settlement in Mesopotamia. Very early evidence for settlement in the Mesopotamian plains is extremely sparse. Indeed, with the exception of the site of M'lefaat, there is little to suggest occupation even of the northern rain-fed zone before about 6000 BC, although this is not to say that it was not inhabited. It is virtually certain that groups of hunters and collectors had roamed throughout this area for thousands of years, although the traces of their passage are exceedingly difficult for archaeologists to detect. Moreover, much of the area remains almost totally unexplored. Recent work on the plain west of Mosul and to the south of Jebel Sinjar has yielded entirely new information and there can be no doubt that comparable efforts elsewhere would add equally to our knowledge of prehistory. No sites like Mureybet and Abu Hureyra have yet been found, but the existence of such sites in Syria was unsuspected until the last decade, and in recent years geographically comparable areas of Iraq have been largely inaccessible to archaeologists. New discoveries are certain to alter radically the picture we sketch here, and indeed the first part of that sketch derives entirely from investigations of the past five years.

The excavation of Hassuna, to which we have referred in Chapter 3, was the first to provide detailed knowledge of what was then believed to be the earliest phase of farming settlement in the northern plain, and still affords our only sequence for this phase, which has come to be known by the name of the site. At Hassuna six levels of occupation represented the life of a small (perhaps one hectare) but flourishing village that resembled in many ways the little farming settlements that dot the plain today, nearly 8,000 years later. Houses, built of packed mud or *tauf*, consisted of a number of rooms opening on to a courtyard in which were ovens, grain bins and so on. A variety of very distinctive types of pottery, decorated with

Top: mud-brick houses with pitched roofs in a modern village in northern Iraq.

Above: the "campsite" level at Hassuna (Ia) with the remains of burials and large storage jars.

Below: Hassuna level V: suggested reconstruction of a house and sketch plan of the level as found.

painted or incised patterns or a combination of the two, were found from the last phase of level I (Ic) onwards. In level Ib, and in small quantity through levels II and III, there occurred an apparently earlier "Archaic Painted Ware" on which either the body of the pot or the painted decoration, or both, were burnished. This ware is thus readily distinguished from the "Standard Painted Ware" on which both paint and surface are always matt, though many design elements are common to both. In the earliest excavated level, Ia, there was no trace of buildings, but there were three superimposed ground surfaces over a total depth of about a meter with occupation debris on them, referred to by the excavators as "campsites." The pottery from the three encampments consisted almost exclusively of large coarse storage vessels of a dark-cored ware tempered with straw. Many of these have a very distinctive shape, with a carination low on the body profile and a shallow ogival curve below, and this type has come to be associated specifically with the earliest phase of settlement at Hassuna. Lugs and other applied ornament are not uncommon.

Our knowledge of this "archaic" phase, which was here revealed only in a very small area, has been much expanded by the recent excavations at Yarim Tepe, some 50 miles west of Mosul at the foot of the Sinjar hills, and at Umm Dabaghiyah, a small site (0·85 hectares) southwest of Mosul on the border of the steppe and at the very limit of possible rain-fed agriculture. At Umm Dabaghiyah four meters of archaeological deposits have revealed material which is clearly related to that of Hassuna and seems to represent an early phase of the "archaic" assemblage. This interpretation has been confirmed at another small site, Tell es-Sotto near Yarim Tepe, where material like that from Umm Dabaghiyah has been found in a context where both its chronological position and cultural affiliation are clear.

Four seasons of excavation at Umm Dabaghiyah have revealed a number of unusual features. One is the presence of extensive buildings consisting of very regular rows of small cell-like rooms, undoubtedly planned and constructed for a special purpose and difficult to interpret other than as communal storehouses. Certainly the rooms contained no traces of domestic occupation, nor indeed did they have any obvious means of access. Two such storage units adjoined a large central courtyard, and their extraordinary character is emphasized by comparison with the ordinary houses that were also found. Their rooms too were small, but had low interconnecting doorways through which the inhabitants must have had to crawl or wriggle. Of special interest among their internal fittings are the hooded chimney-breasts and plastered cupboards. In two houses hand and toe holds for climbing to the roof are visible in the wall above the cupboards, but external doorways are known, of which one led to a narrow lane.

Some of the painted pottery is identical with examples from the "archaic" phase at Hassuna, but at Umm Dabaghiyah a much greater quantity of material and thus a much wider range of motifs are known. On the coarse wares a variety of appliqué ornament occurs, including animal and human figures. Similar but less elaborate examples are known from several sites including Hassuna (level Ia), Tell es-Sotto, Yarim Tepe (in an "archaic" Hassuna context) and the earliest levels at Telul eth-Thalathat near Tell Afar. Among the chipped stone objects were a few arrowheads of Syrian type and some tools that are more in the Zagros tradition, but it is clear that the local flint industry does not derive directly from either area. A number of attractive stone bowls were found – again a feature of Zagros sites – but the Umm Dabaghiyah vessels are much more reminiscent of Samarran polished stone work as exemplified at the slightly later site of Tell es-Sawwan.

The economy of Umm Dabaghiyah appears to have been at least partly agricultural. Traces of emmer, einkorn and barley, and single examples of pea, lentil and bread

Reconstruction of three houses in levels III–IV at Umm Dabaghiyah showing chimneys and foot holes leading to the roof.

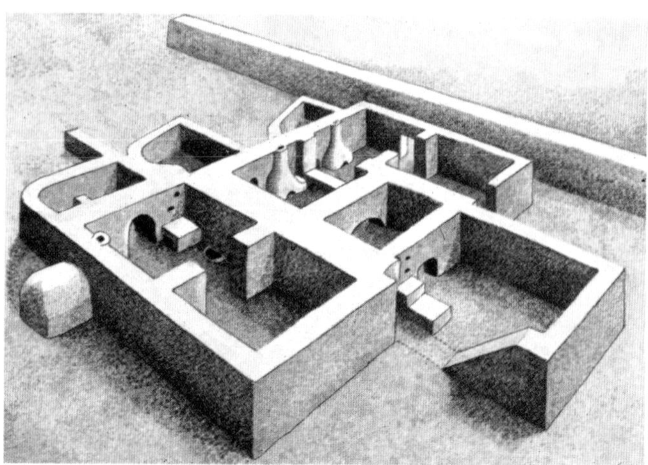

One of two communal storehouses enclosing three sides of a central courtyard in level III at Umm Dabaghiyah.

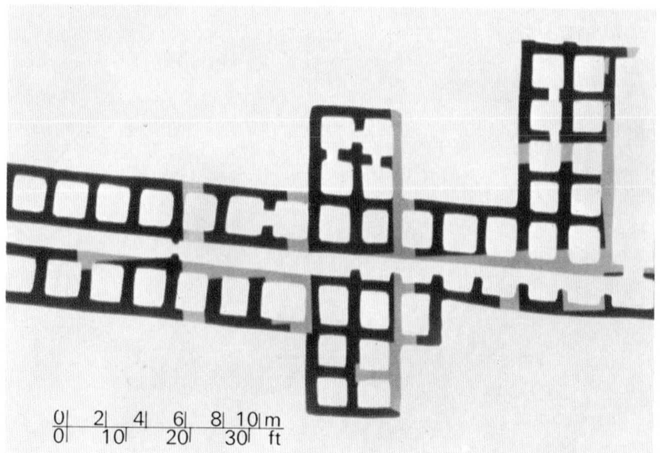

wheat together with indeterminate "groats" were identified among the palaeobotanical specimens. Animal bones include the full range of domesticated species, cattle, pig, sheep, goat and dog, but by far the largest number of bones are those of onager and gazelle (84% of the total). Wall paintings found in the final season appear to represent the hunting of onager and emphasize the importance of this animal in the local economy. Indeed the excavator, Miss Diana Kirkbride, interprets the site as a trading outpost exporting onager skins and perhaps other animal products to some major and, regrettably, unidentified center. This theory provides a possible explanation for the communal storehouses as repositories for such potential exports.

Certainly Umm Dabaghiyah lies in an area that is today agriculturally unprofitable and, judging by the distribution of sites, was at the southern limit of settlement even in the sixth millennium. Nevertheless, the presence in this area of some 40 prehistoric mounds, most of which have yielded Hassuna material, strongly suggests that at this particular time rainfall must have been, if not greater, at least more reliable than at the present day. We know not only from historical sources but also from patterns of settlement that there have been minor climatic fluctuations throughout the Holocene. We know too that their effect is greatest in climatically marginal zones. Irrigation agriculture is not possible here, but climatological evidence is too imprecise to allow us to eliminate beyond question the possibility of effective rain-fed farming at least for a brief period in the sixth millennium. But hunting has always been of major importance in the steppe and clearly was to the inhabitants of Umm Dabaghiyah. Buqras, an approximately contemporary site on the middle Euphrates in Syria, is another example of a hunting settlement, in this case well beyond the possible boundary of rain-fed agriculture.

Yarim Tepe. No radiocarbon determinations are yet available for Umm Dabaghiyah, but we may reasonably assume on the evidence of the Soviet excavations at Yarim Tepe and Tell es-Sotto that the occupation of the site – almost certainly quite brief – should be dated around or not long after 6000 BC. Identical materials occur in the lowest level at Sotto, where they are followed by two later phases of "archaic Hassuna" and one attributed to "late Hassuna." Thirteen levels, all of the Hassuna period, have been excavated at the larger mound of Yarim Tepe I nearby, and it is clear that Yarim Tepe will provide a new chapter in the prehistory of Mesopotamia and a new basis for future work.

Among the most interesting revelations so far from Yarim Tepe I are the evidence for metallurgy, including the smelting of both copper and lead, and a hitherto unsuspected level of industrial specialization, illustrated by the discovery of a large number of two-stage, domed pottery kilns – the earliest so far known – situated in clearly demarcated manufacturing areas. Storehouses identical with those at Umm Dabaghiyah are found, clearly demonstrating that whatever economic purpose they served, these distinctive buildings were widely used in the Hassuna period. The excavators' very careful analysis of house plans in individual levels has shown that each reconstruction of a part – not necessarily or even probably the whole – of the settlement began with the building of relatively small houses for single families, separated by open spaces that provided adequate room for circulation. The original houses were then gradually extended, perhaps to accommodate married children and their families, until much of the open space was built up and access through the streets and lanes was blocked. After perhaps two generations, which is in any case a long life for a *tauf* house, circulation became virtually impossible within that part of the settlement and it had to be laid out afresh, producing what archaeologists call a new "building level." We know nothing of landownership, but the idea of property seems to be reflected in the first appearance of genuine stamp seals, presumably used, as they were later, for the identification of portable objects to which a clay sealing could be attached.

It is not surprising to find a full and almost certainly transhumant agricultural economy representing a fairly

Clay figurines from level 7 at Yarim Tepe I. The elongated headdress is reminiscent of earlier Zagros types but the "flounced" skirt is peculiar to Yarim Tepe.

advanced stage of both agriculture and animal husbandry. Of the hexaploid wheats spelt is unusual for it apparently does not occur elsewhere in the Near East, although there is in general some disagreement about the identification of the subspecies of *Triticum aestivum*. No radiocarbon determinations are yet available from the early levels at Yarim Tepe or Sotto, but the middle levels at Yarim Tepe I have produced figures in the latter part of the sixth millennium.

The excavations at Yarim Tepe have greatly expanded our knowledge of the Hassuna phase, and clearly indicate levels of social and technological development not apparent at the type site. It should be recognized, however, that we are unlikely ever to know the full extent of cultural development at this time. The nature of settlement in the northern plain is such that the more important prehistoric centers inevitably lie buried and inaccessible under enormous mounds like Nineveh and Erbil, where even if their presence was detected – as in the deep sounding at Nineveh – one could never afford to explore their nature. If Miss Kirkbride is correct in interpreting Umm Dabaghiyah as a "trading outpost," the missing emporium on which it depended almost certainly lies buried under one such vast and complex tell. The "campsite" levels at Hassuna also suggest at least the possibility that in the sixth millennium there may already have been nomadic herdsmen or hunters contemporary and probably in some sort of economic relationship with the settled villagers, a pattern well established by the time of the earliest written records some 3,000 years later.

It is of course possible that at Hassuna the small area excavated simply lay in an area which had not been built over, like the open courtyards for which there is evidence at Umm Dabaghiyah and Yarim Tepe, but two facts suggest that the "campsites" may genuinely represent a seminomadic population. One is the existence of apparently sterile deposits between the three "campsite" levels, indicating genuine breaks in occupation, and the other is the association of digging tools commonly described as "hoes" exclusively with level Ia. These implements were clearly not agricultural, for they do not occur at any of the other farming sites of this period. Whatever function they served was relevant only to the economy of the first, probably semipermanent, inhabitants of Hassuna. Unfortunately we do not yet know what this economy was, largely because techniques for the recovery of seed and plant remains had not been evolved at the time when the site was dug.

Hassuna farming villages have a wide distribution coinciding with the lower elevations of the plain and steppe on either side of the upper Tigris valley, roughly between 150 and 350 meters above sea level, and within the present limits of rain-fed agriculture. Up to now we have no evidence for the existence of Hassuna settlements in the mountainous homeland of the Zagros assemblage which is known from sites such as Jarmo and Tepe Guran

Above: clay figurine from the Late Zagros site of Tepe Sarab, Iran, early sixth millennium. Height 6·4 centimeters. The elongated stalk-like head is particularly characteristic of figurines from this site.

Opposite: excavations at the sixth-millennium site of Tepe Sarab near Kermanshah in Iran, a Late Zagros type settlement contemporary with villages of the Hassuna phase on the northern plain of Mesopotamia.

and is indeed partially contemporary with the Hassuna phase. This contemporaneity is especially clear at sites like Guran and Tepe Sarab near Kermanshah, where radiocarbon determinations of the first half of the sixth millennium have been obtained. It is therefore virtually impossible to accept the common view that farming communities in the plains were first established by people descending from the hills. The rolling plains of Assyria are a rich winter grazing ground, more than likely to have been inhabited by hunters, collectors and perhaps even herdsmen long before we find actual traces of settlement. The industries in chipped stone and pottery and the techniques of building associated with the Hassuna settlements differ strikingly from those characteristic of the Zagros group of sites and indeed sites in neighboring areas of Anatolia and Syria. It seems clear that the cultural assemblages in each of these areas represent discrete local developments, independent from though undoubtedly in contact with one another.

The Samarran phase. Following the Hassuna phase but at least partly contemporary with it, permanent settlements are found for the first time throughout the country.

The earliest of these new developments has come to be called Samarran after the Islamic city beneath which in 1911 Herzfeld first found the attractive and very elaborately painted pottery that defines this stage of Mesopotamian prehistory. Similar pottery was found at Nineveh, and at Hassuna in levels III–VIII, where it was thought to represent an extraneous element. For a long time "Samarran" defined nothing more than this elaborate ceramic style which came to be considered an "imported" or "luxury" ware, and later simply "one aspect of the later phase of the Hassunan assemblage." Recent excavations at Tell es-Sawwan and Choga Mami, however, have confirmed what was suspected earlier from the evidence at Baghouz on the Euphrates, that Samarra must be considered a separate assemblage and that the people it represents flourished some time in the sixth millennium north of Baghdad along the fringes of the alluvium. Although this "Samarran assemblage" has now become a reality, we still lack coherent knowledge of its development. Further excavation at Sawwan and Choga Mami will certainly fill this gap.

Excavated Samarran sites include Matarrah, south of Kirkuk, which was interpreted originally as an impoverished southern variant of the Hassuna complex, and Shemshara in the Rania plain east of Erbil, where the material was also originally described as Hassuna. Both can now confidently be attributed to the Samarran phase. Ceramic types include painted, incised and painted-and-incised varieties in many ways comparable with the standard Hassuna wares, but the excavations at Sawwan and Choga Mami have provided a clear basis for distinguishing the two. At Sawwan Hassuna sherds are rare and at Choga Mami virtually non-existent.

At Sawwan five building levels have been excavated. Level I, the earliest, yielded very little pottery, and that entirely coarse or plain undecorated vessels. It is possible that this reflects the function of the buildings so far exposed in this level, in which it is said that no household debris was found and beneath which were discovered the graves discussed below. Stratified pottery from level II continues predominantly coarse or plain, but in the 1972 season of excavations a quantity of painted ware was recovered from this level which was undoubtedly related to later Samarran types. Levels III–V are characterized by standard Samarran pottery, while some later Halaf pottery was found unstratified in the latest level. At Choga Mami the earliest level so far exposed has yielded standard Samarran materials, but here a sequence of Samarran levels is succeeded by a phase with atypical traits which find their closest parallels in the earliest al-'Ubaid levels in southern Mesopotamia, to be discussed in the next chapter. This phase at Choga Mami has been termed "Transitional," but it is impossible yet to establish whether the transition is genuinely developmental or whether it merely reflects the geographical position of the site, midway between the apparent areas of distribution of the northern and southern prehistoric cultures. Samarran terracotta figurines from Choga Mami provide another important link with the south.

Perhaps the most important single discovery from these new excavations pertains to the Samarran economy. By contrast with sites of the Hassuna phase, Samarran sites are found well to the south of the zone where rain-fed agriculture is now possible. Some, like Baghouz on the

Euphrates, Samarra and nearby Sawwan on the Tigris, lie far beyond any conceivable boundary of dry farming. Others, such as Matarrah and Choga Mami near Mandali, are closer to the present 200-millimeter isohyet, but in the vicinity of Mandali irrigation is necessary at least at the present day. Palaeobotanical evidence from both Sawwan and Choga Mami suggests that it was practiced in both areas in the sixth millennium, and in the Mandali area the distribution of Samarran sites follows an artificial alignment along low contours parallel with the nearby hills and at right angles to the natural flow of water into the plain. Indeed we know that by the fifth millennium there was a canal along this line, and the excavations at Choga Mami revealed the cross-section of what was evidently an earlier version of this canal, together with a number of small channels skirting the settlement which probably also served for irrigation. All were certainly of Samarran date.

Dr Hans Helbaek has suggested that agriculture at Sawwan was probably conducted on the basis of seasonal flooding, but the floods come as the crops are ripening in the spring and not at the time of planting. Linseed was cultivated, a crop which probably could not have been grown in such a climate without artificial watering, but "the poor size of the cereal grains makes it improbable that regular canalization was instituted at the time" (Helbaek). At Sawwan irrigation would have been feasible *only* on the river flood plain below the site which lies on a high bluff, now immediately overlooking the river, and crops on this land would have needed extensive protection against the spring floods. At Choga Mami, on the other hand, the physical configuration was ideal for an early canal system since the site lies in a triangle between two rivers that flow out of the hills, the Gangir providing a head of water and the Ab-i-Naft a natural drainage outlet at a lower level. It is, in fact, the lower Tigris–Euphrates basin in miniature, with the problems of drainage and stagnation at least partly eliminated by the more rapid drop in land levels that results from its position on an alluvial fan on the outer slope of the foothills.

At both Sawwan and Choga Mami emmer, bread wheat, naked six-row barley and hulled two-row barley have been identified, together with considerable quantities of linseed. At Choga Mami lentil was one of the most important crops and a large-seeded pea was grown, while pistachio was collected, probably from the nearby hills. It is clear that the Samarran villagers exploited a well-developed range of cereal types as well as other high-protein foods. They were, as far as we know, among the first deliberately to employ the techniques of irrigation without which their climatically marginal area could not have been effectively settled, and which were fundamental to widespread cultivation on the rich but very arid soils of the southern alluvium. There is some indication that these techniques were transmitted from the Mandali region, directly or by intermediate contacts, to Khuzistan in southwestern Iran, where the botanical evidence at Chagha Sefid suggests the introduction of irrigation at a slightly later date, established by the occurrence of typical Choga Mami "Transitional" sherds; but we have for the present no comparable evidence for the diffusion of irrigation techniques within Mesopotamia.

The faunal evidence from Choga Mami, like its botanical counterpart, suggests fully developed domestication. At Sawwan fish and fresh-water mussels from the river were eaten, and at both sites onager, gazelle, aurochs and probably fallow deer were hunted. It is particularly striking that by 6000 BC domesticated cattle are associated with all lowland sites, both in Anatolia and Mesopotamia, while there is no comparable evidence from contemporary highland sites. By the fifth millennium the percentages of cattle bones on alluvial sites would appear to be very high indeed, and one cannot but speculate whether some form of primitive plow was already in use, with oxen to pull it. Certainly plowed fields are more suited to simple, uncontrolled irrigation than those prepared for planting solely with hoes or digging sticks. Indeed, even under rain-fed farming conditions, more efficient methods of digging and tillage would have been a prerequisite for the expansion of settlement that is apparent during the Hassuna phase. The earliest actual evidence for plows comes late in the fourth millennium, and by this time at least two types, including a seeder-plow, were in use.

Both Sawwan and Choga Mami are large villages compared with those known from earlier periods (Samarran Choga Mami extends over an area of some 4 to 5 hectares). At Sawwan a ditch and a wall, constructed in level III, surround the site except on the west where it falls away steeply to the river, while at Choga Mami a tower guarded the only excavated entrance to the village at least as early as the end of the Samarran period. Entry to both settlements was gained by dog-leg approaches, later a well-known defensive device. At both sites sun-dried mud-bricks were employed, for the first time in Mesopotamia and in contrast with the exclusive use of *tauf* at more northern villages like Matarrah, Hassuna and Yarim Tepe.

Above: alabaster female figurine from a level I grave at the Samarran site of Tell es-Sawwan (Iraq Museum).

Opposite: mold-made mud-bricks drying in the sun in Turkey.

Below: alabaster vessels from level I graves at Tell es-Sawwan, mid-sixth millennium BC (Iraq Museum).

At Choga Mami the bricks were long and cigar-shaped, and were laid in alternate courses along and across the axis of the wall. Many of the houses at Sawwan and Choga Mami are very regular in plan, T-shaped at the former and rectangular at the latter site. The rooms remain surprisingly small, rarely more than two meters in length, but this is a feature common to other prehistoric sites, as we have already noted at Umm Dabaghiyah. The employment of external buttressing at the corners of buildings and opposite internal wall junctions marks the beginning of a widespread Mesopotamian building technique that was at first functional and later became a conventional feature of religious architecture. At Choga Mami and apparently also at Sawwan the houses were built on top of, or in some cases within, the walls of their predecessors in earlier levels. A possible motive for this strict adherence to earlier boundaries may lie in the existence of continuing property rights. Moreover, at Choga Mami we think we have detected more massive buttressed walls which did not form part of any particular structure, although smaller buildings were often backed against them. These look like the boundary walls of larger units, perhaps extended households.

As at Yarim Tepe stamp seals suggest the recognition of private ownership, and a more conscious professionalism among Samarran craftsmen is indicated by the widespread use of potters' marks. Moreover, there is no doubt that we are now concerned with a community where surplus wealth was available for non-productive purposes, although we cannot analyze the social situations or motives implicit in such expenditure. This is especially clear at the unique site of Tell es-Sawwan. Here, beneath but clearly associated with several unusually large buildings attributed to the earliest level, were found a large number of graves, many the burials of small infants. These contained an extraordinary collection, now to be counted in hundreds, of ground stone objects, in particular alabaster female statuettes and a variety of elegantly shaped alabaster bowls. In their prehistoric context it is virtually impossible to assess the religious significance – if any – of the buildings, the graves or even the objects within them. Obviously this is no ordinary cemetery and we may well speculate that Sawwan, like Çatal Hüyük, was a settlement with some special significance. However that may be, the evidence both for specialized craftsmanship in luxury materials and for surplus wealth is incontrovertible.

An unusual feature of the Samarran sites is the extraordinary variety of human terracotta figurines, which are markedly dissimilar from one site to another. Those recently found at Yarim Tepe, in levels which have yielded Samarran pottery, include ladies with "flounced" skirts and an unusual "stalk-headed" type. These differ not only from the more naturalistic and 'Ubaid-like examples from Choga Mami but from the several varieties found at Sawwan. Certain traits are shared, for instance the use of "coffee-bean" eyes, elongated headdresses and the appliqué necklaces of the Sawwan and Choga Mami examples, but the differences from site to site remain striking. Evidence for the use of metal is less than at Yarim Tepe, but a few hammered copper objects have been found at Sawwan.

Samarran sites occur in some numbers in a band across Mesopotamia north of Baghdad and south of the rain-fed lands occupied by the Hassuna peoples, although limited within this band to locations where a perennial water supply was available – none are known, for instance, in the steppe between the Euphrates and Tigris valleys. Some occur in the hills to the northeast, and to the north and northwest Samarran materials are found as an intrusive element on Hassuna sites in the Mosul area and on the plain southwards from Jebel Sinjar to the neighborhood of Umm Dabaghiyah, where considerable quantities of the pottery have been identified on surface surveys. In spite of the close proximity of Samarran sites to the Iranian frontier, as for instance near Mandali, no ceramic material of this type has yet been reported from adjacent areas of Iran, although in Khuzistan, as we have noted, pottery resembling the Choga Mami "Transitional" has been found. In this context one should observe that both Mandali and Deh Luran in Khuzistan lie on the route of the much later Achaemenid Royal Road, which clearly served in this sector as an "obsidian trail" at least as early as the seventh millennium BC.

We have remarked above that we know very little about the early development of Samarra. We cannot identify any archaeological assemblage ancestral to that of level I at Sawwan, but it seems certain that this represents an early stage in the material culture of the people who later produced the Samarran style of painted pottery. Undoubtedly some relationship exists between the ceramic traditions of Hassuna and Samarra, and many similar traits are found at settlements of both types; but Samarra does not derive from Hassuna, for the two groups are at least partially and probably wholly contemporary. It is conceivable that population pressures in the Assyrian plain, where there is extensive evidence for settlement in the Hassuna phase, may have provoked movement to the climatically more marginal areas to the south, but we cannot say how much earlier such a movement may have taken place. Although in the Samarran areas widespread agricultural settlement would have been inconceivable without some recourse to irrigation, even if rainfall was marginally more reliable, catch-crop cultivation, hunting and fishing could have supported earlier less settled populations.

The Halaf culture. One further cultural assemblage is widely represented in northern Mesopotamia during the latter part of the sixth and well into the fifth millennium. It takes its name from the site of Tell Halaf near Ras al 'Ain on the Syrian-Turkish border, where the very beautiful and distinctive painted pottery that characterizes this phase was first found. The same ware was later identified in the deep sounding at Nineveh, following upon Hassuna in the latest stage of what was then designated "Ninevite II," and – as we have recounted in Chapter 3 – the next year, 1932–33, saw the excavation by M. E. L. Mallowan of the small site of Arpachiyah just outside the walls of Nineveh, where quantities of Halaf sherds had been found on the surface. This was the first deliberate excavation in the Near East of a small prehistoric mound in order to elucidate the way of life of its inhabitants, and it is a great pity that circumstances beyond the excavator's control limited his operations to one season.

Nevertheless the results were spectacular, and still remain our only substantial published evidence for the character of a Halaf settlement. We must consequently remember that Arpachiyah is not necessarily typical of the villages, still less of the towns of the period, and Mallowan himself thought that it might have been a specialized settlement whose principal function was the production of pottery for some larger center such as nearby Nineveh. Certainly many of its inhabitants were highly skilled artisans. A potter's workshop in the latest Halaf level, TT 6, contained some of the finest prehistoric pottery ever found, including polychrome vessels painted with elaborate designs in black, red and white. A large lump of red ocher was discovered, together with flat palettes for mixing the paint and bone implements for trimming and burnishing the clay.

One of the most interesting features of Arpachiyah is the architectural evidence. In the earlier levels, TT 7–10, was a series of circular structures with *tauf* walls which

Opposite above: clay figurine from Tell es-Sawwan, level II. Height 11·5 centimeters (Iraq Museum).

Opposite below: reconstructions of Halaf round structures or "tholoi" at Arpachiyah, levels TT 7–8, c. 5000 BC.

Below: Halaf bowl from Arpachiyah, level TT 7 (British Museum).

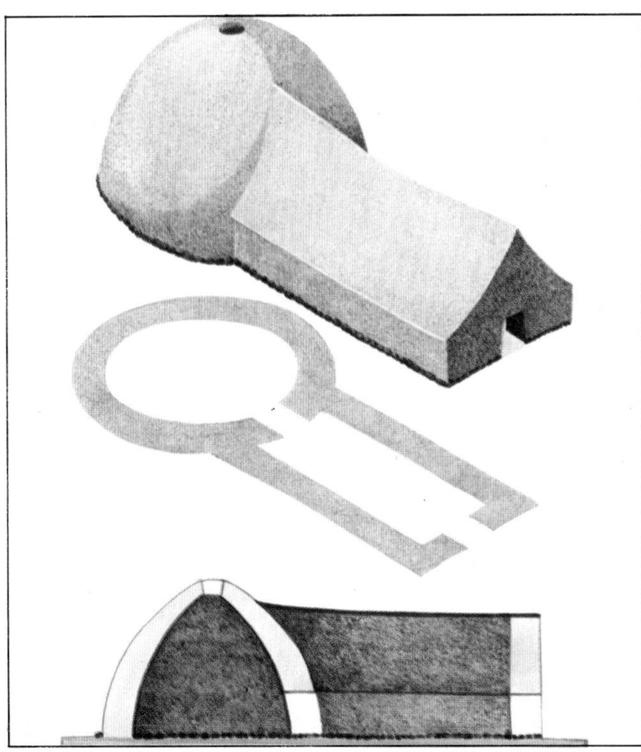

seem originally to have been domed like the modern beehive houses of north Syria. The earliest of these were some 4 meters in diameter, and they became progressively larger and more elaborate, until the most imposing example in level 7 consisted of a round chamber almost 10 meters across, approached by way of a rectangular anteroom 19 meters long. These buildings are commonly though misleadingly referred to as "tholoi" because of their resemblance to Mycenaean tholos tombs, but the use of the name does not of course imply even a remote connection between northern Mesopotamia around 5000 BC and second-millennium Greece. Indeed, as we have seen, round houses are found in some of the earliest settlements in the Levant from the Natufian period onwards and represent, with rectangular houses, one of the two simple forms of permanent structure that might have evolved from different traditions of construction in the temporary dwellings of a mobile population.

But although rectangular buildings do occur, the tholoi are a conspicuous characteristic of the Halaf sites so far excavated, in marked contrast with Hassuna and later 'Ubaid villages in the area which contain occasional round structures but show a marked preference for multi-roomed rectangular houses. The purpose of the tholoi has been the subject of considerable discussion. At Arpachiyah the stone foundations of seven of the ten discovered had been left undisturbed by later builders, and one contained a large number of figurines interpreted as "mother-goddesses." For these reasons it has been suggested that they had some religious function, but even if the large Arpachiyah tholoi were designed for some formal purpose, there seems no doubt that the smaller examples found elsewhere were essentially utilitarian buildings.

A sequence of Halaf occupation was found at Hassuna overlying the original settlement but was not published in detail because it was said to reproduce the evidence from Arpachiyah, and it was not until 1969 that the Soviet expedition to Yarim Tepe began the excavation of another significant Halaf site, the mound known as Yarim Tepe II some 200 meters distant from the Hassuna village of Yarim Tepe I. The work is continuing and our information comes only from preliminary summaries and, like much else in this book, from personal communication with the excavators. This site will undoubtedly supplement and extend the picture derived from Arpachiyah, and its great depth of stratified occupation, amounting to at least 8 meters, may well provide a longer sequence. The latest Halaf pottery appears to be later than anything found at Arpachiyah, and more comparable with late Halaf types known from north Syrian sites such as Tell Brak, but so far the Soviet excavations have not reached levels corresponding with the earliest known occupation of Arpachiyah. But, apart from the possibly specialized nature of Arpachiyah as a satellite village of Nineveh, there are significant differences between the two sites.

At Yarim Tepe II a long series of circular structures was found, and the material in them was much more clearly domestic than in the Arpachiyah tholoi. The most popular type was a simple, single-roomed building, although houses with rectangular annexes are known. Wholly rectangular buildings have been found, but these are thought to have had some special – that is non-residential – character. Among the most interesting discoveries are those relating to funerary practices. A Halaf cemetery, dug into the abandoned Hassuna village, revealed the earliest known examples of "shaft graves" in which a small lateral compartment opened off the bottom of a vertical shaft. Two instances of cremation were also found within the settlement itself. In the first case, the cremation of a 12- or 13-year-old child was carried out in a specially constructed oven. At the time of the cremation, six clay and three stone vessels were intentionally broken into pieces and thrown into the oven together with a clay spindle-whorl, a stone seal, two cowrie shells and about a hundred beads of gypsum, clay, rock crystal and obsidian. After the performance of this ritual the burned remains of the bones were collected and placed in a large painted vessel under a tholos floor. The remains of the second cremation were also found in a painted pottery vessel, and a thick ashy layer remained to show where the cremation hearth was situated. Here were found an intricately formed alabaster bowl, a large alabaster cup and three clay vessels, one painted, all of which had been deliberately broken at the time of the cremation and thrown into the hearth.

Other evidence for ritual observances among the Halaf people is rare, but it is interesting to notice that for them – as for the inhabitants of Çatal Hüyük – the ox seems to have had some special significance. The ox-head pattern known as the "bukranium" is, in more or less stylized form, an extremely common motif on their pottery, and at Tell Aswad in the Balikh valley of northern Syria an ox skull with spreading horns was found installed in an

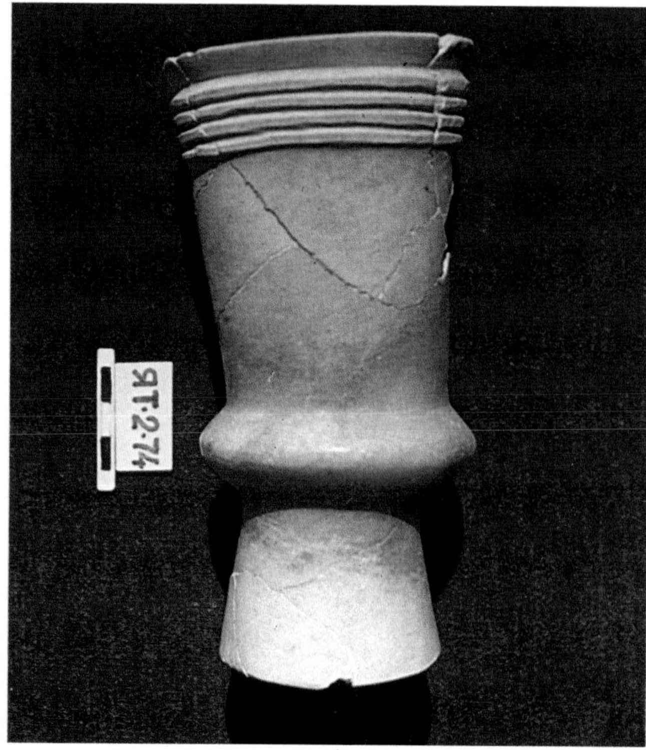

Above: painted baked clay Halaf figurine from Chagar Bazar. *Below:* an alabaster vessel ritually broken in association with a Halaf cremation burial in level 7, Yarim Tepe II.

Stone amulets of the Halaf period from Arpachiyah.

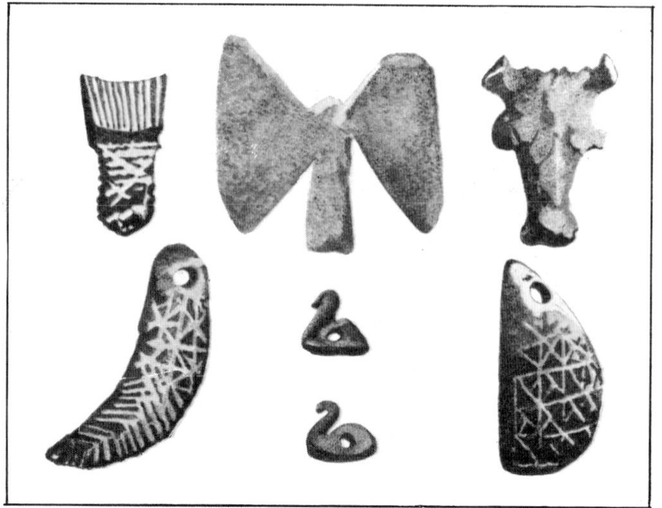

nternal doorway of a small building that the excavator ook to be a shrine.

Unfortunately our knowledge of the Halaf economy is also very incomplete. The sites lie within the boundary of the rainfall zone and were presumably dependent on rain-fed farming. We may assume that not only cattle but most of the already full range of domesticated animals and cereals were exploited, but we do not know in what proportions, or whether the pattern varied from one locality to another within the very large area over which Halaf pottery is found. The very wide distribution of Halaf pottery is one of the most puzzling aspects of what is still a problematic "culture." As far as we know from incomplete surface surveys the greatest concentration of sites occurs in the north Mesopotamian plain, including the Hassuna homeland but extending well beyond it. To the west it is common in the upper Khabur basin, to the east it is found on highland sites such as Banahilk and Bagum, and to the north it occurs in eastern Anatolia particularly in the neighborhood of obsidian sources (Tilki Tepe near Lake Van), and north of Diyarbakr near the Ergani Maden copper mines (Gerikihaciyan). A northern connection is especially emphasized on sites in the Sinjar area – the only ones in northern Iraq that have been extensively surveyed – by the quantities of obsidian associated with them. Later Halaf materials occur as far west as the Mediterranean and the Cilician plain, while to the east of Mount Ararat and south of the Caucasus some Halaf pottery has been found in association with round buildings (Kültepe and Tegut in the Araxes valley).

Every occurrence of pottery, even of unmistakably Halaf style, does not necessarily imply that the site on which it is found was occupied by people belonging to one large, ethnically and culturally homogeneous group. Trade and imitation are always possible explanations. Yet where neutron activation analysis of sherds has been carried out, mainly on material from sites in northern Mesopotamia but including the most southerly known occurrence of Halaf pottery at Choga Mami, it is clear that despite the striking superficial differences between the lustrous burnished Halaf wares and the matt pottery of Hassuna and Samarra, when they occur together at the same site they are locally made and of the same clay. At Choga Mami in particular, all varieties of matt-surfaced Samarran painted, incised and plain wares and much of the fine polychrome Halaf material employ identical clay sources. In Mesopotamia at least, there was obviously no break in the exploitation of known raw materials for this highly professional craft, yet – and this is the intriguing problem – new techniques of manufacture and decoration were suddenly introduced. It is also clear from the contrast in domestic architecture that new people had arrived on the scene, and that the Halaf culture is not a direct descendant of Hassuna or any other of its known predecessors in the north Mesopotamian plain. Moreover we have noticed that on many sites such as Yarim Tepe the Halaf people chose to found a new village rather than to reoccupy an existing one, and this again suggests that they were newcomers. But present archaeological evidence from neighboring areas gives us no hint of their origin.

A cruciform complex in level 7 of the Halaf mound Yarim Tepe II, consisting of a circular mud-brick structure with rectangular buildings abutting onto it on four sides.

VISUAL STORY

The Uruk Achievement

The Uruk period in Mesopotamia saw the growth of the first literate urban society. By the late fourth millennium BC there were in Sumer a number of cities, each with its central temple or temple complex, each with a high degree of craft specialization and an economic authority centered in the temple organization. We know most about this period from the site of Warka, the Sumerian city of Uruk, though it is clear that Kish, in the northern part of southern Mesopotamia later known as Akkad, was of equal if not greater political importance at this time. By the third millennium Nippur was undoubtedly the most important religious center, but we know little of its earlier development.

The site of Warka is pictured below. The Erech of Genesis, it lies some 150 miles southeast of Baghdad and 12 miles from the Euphrates, of which a branch skirted the ancient city. Pottery found there includes, as at Eridu, some of the earliest known in Sumer. It has been suggested that Uruk grew out of two settlements, Kullaba and Eanna, the former centered around an important sanctuary dating back to the late 'Ubaid period. Eanna appears to have developed in a different fashion, and by *c.* 3500 BC was endowed with a unique complex of vast ceremonial buildings elaborately decorated with pilasters and cone mosaic.
By the end of the fourth millennium BC the two sites had coalesced to form one unit, surrounded from the beginning of the third millennium by a city wall almost 6 miles long, enclosing an area of some 3·5 square miles.

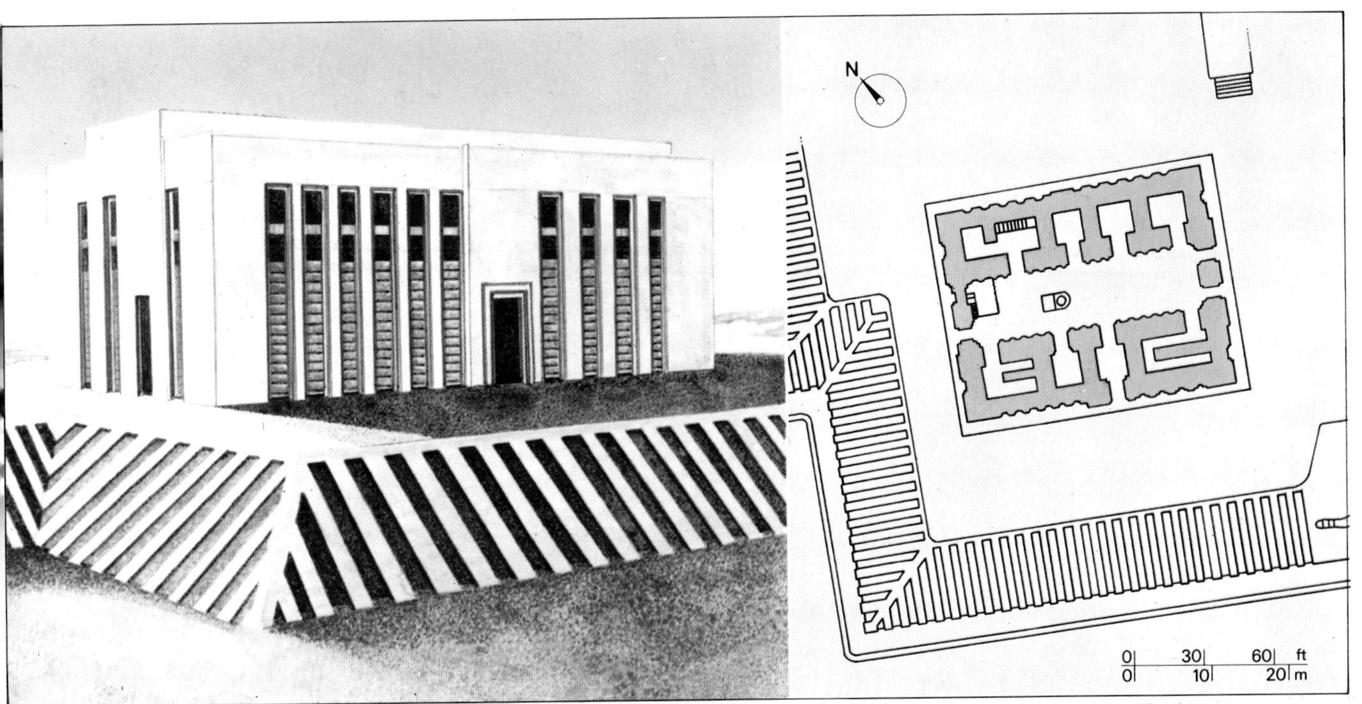

Top: reconstruction and plan of the "White Temple" at Warka, late fourth millennium BC, the best example of the Sumerian "high temple," built on a high terrace which enclosed the remains of earlier religious structures on the same site, a ritual method of construction dating back to the 'Ubaid period both here and at Eridu. The plan is "tripartite," a form of religious building also dating from the 'Ubaid period. Temple furnishings include a stepped altar at one end and a central table for burned offerings. Staircases on the south side gave access to the roof, where Sumerian ritual prescribed the saying of certain prayers. The White Temple and its predecessors are situated in the Kullaba area of Warka, where a later shrine was dedicated to the god Anu. The terrace, at this time some 40 feet high, is sometimes referred to as the "Anu Ziggurrat," though there is no evidence for its dedication to Anu at this period nor is it a true staged tower.

Above: stone bowl with horned woolly sheep in high relief, a type common in the Late Uruk period.

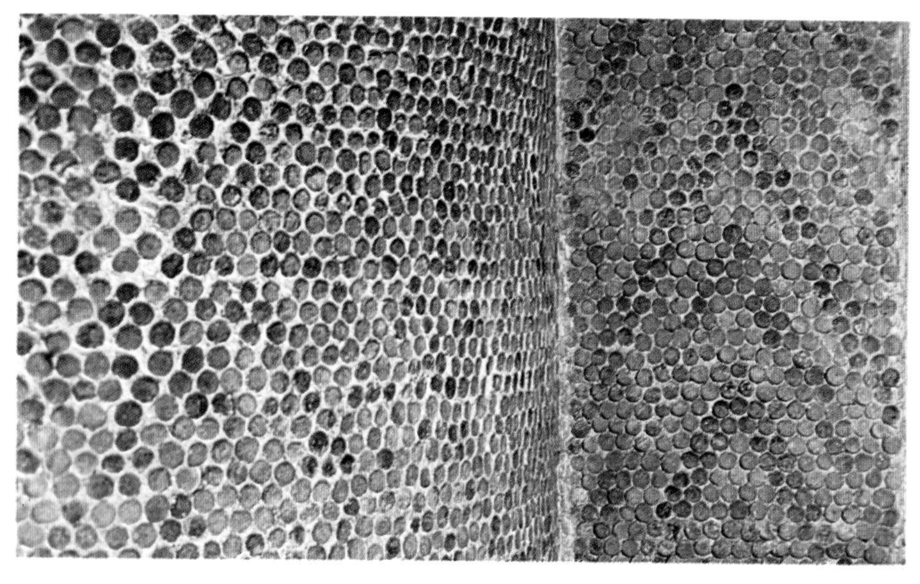

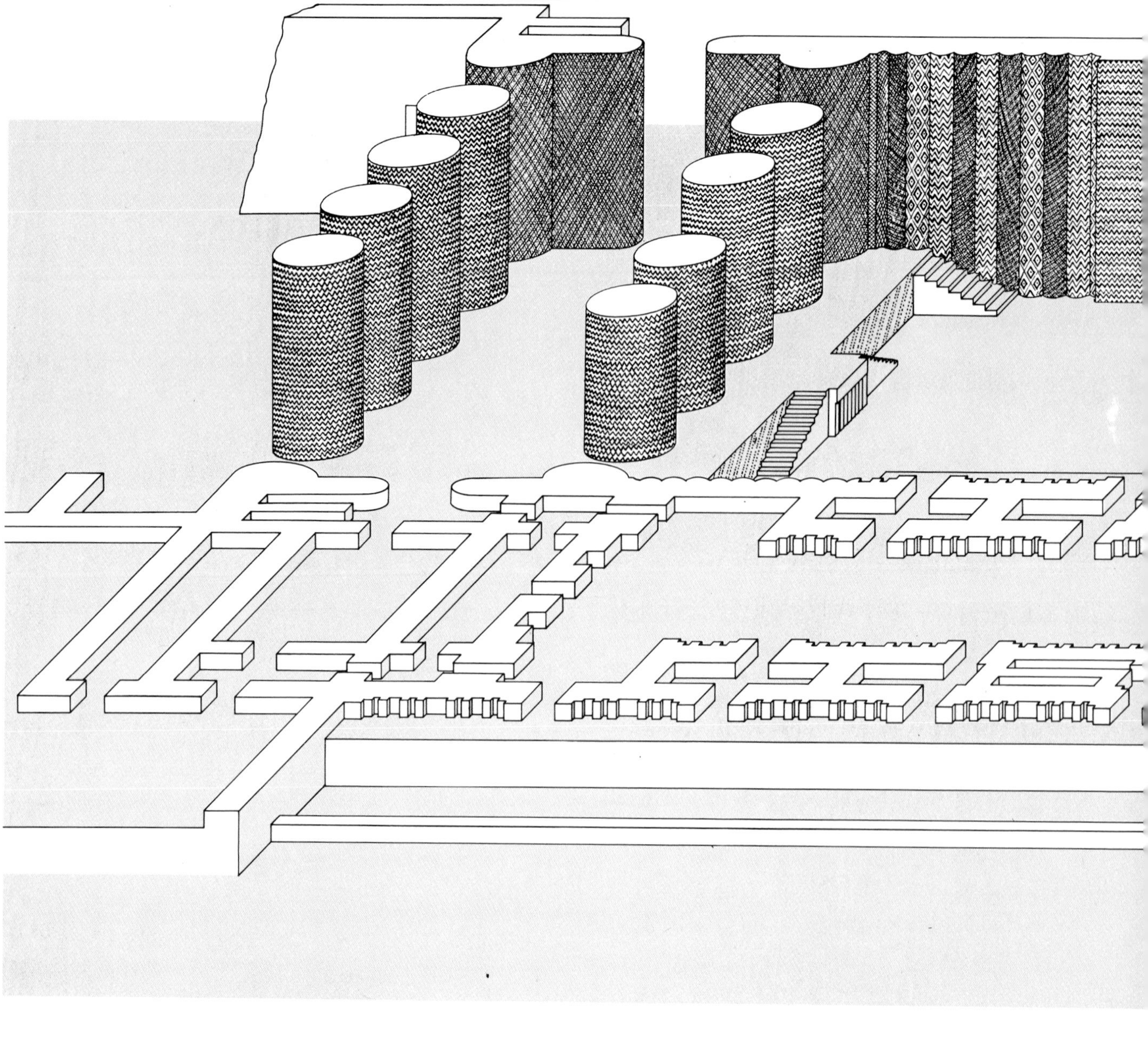

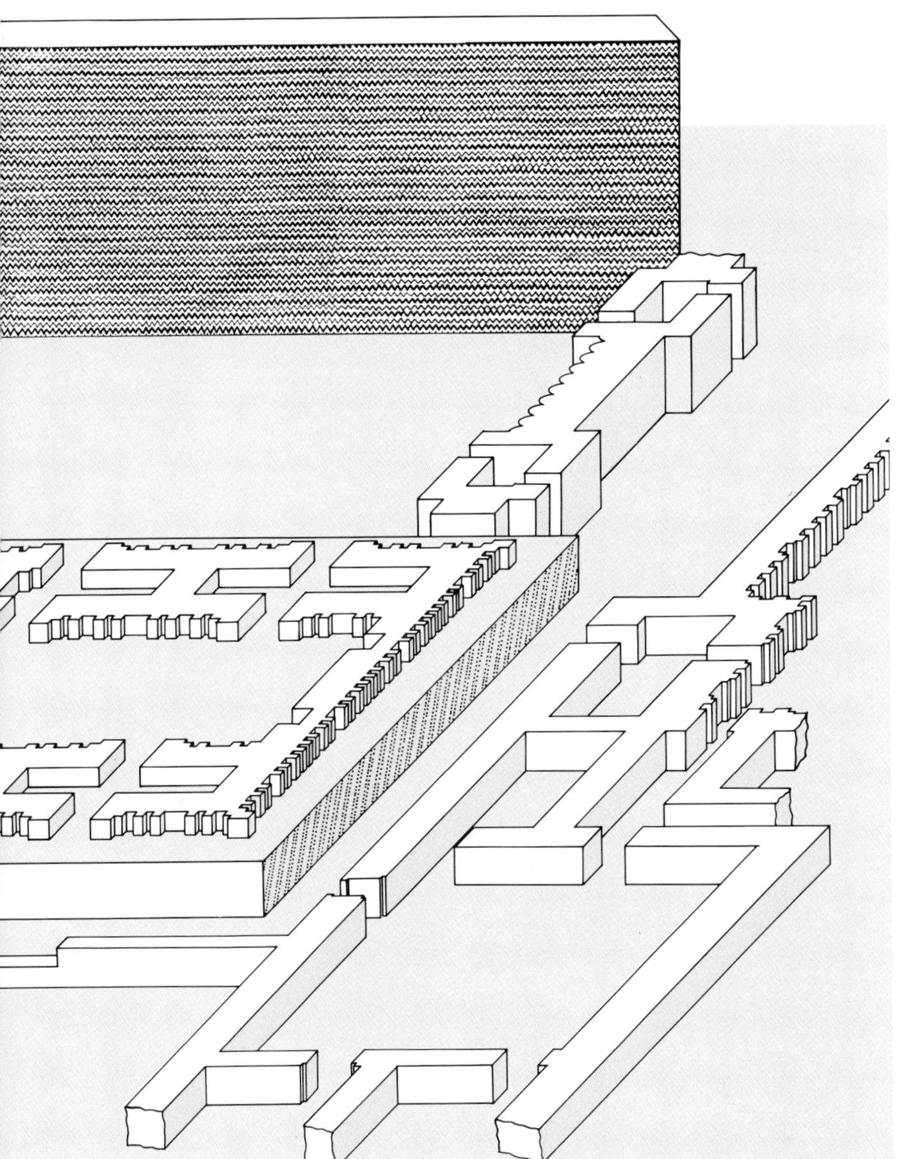

Left: by the Late Uruk period a high degree of artistry and skill was displayed in the cutting of stone, particularly in the miniature representation of animals. This amulet-like stone seal from Tell al-Rimah (ht. c. 2 cm) is characteristic of a type commonly found in Jamdat Nasr levels. The flat underside of the seal is engraved with two highly abstract cat-like figures.

Below left: reconstruction of the columned hall and northeastern side of the famous cone mosaic court at Warka (Uruk IV b); in the foreground, a reconstructed plan of the contemporary temple situated on a terrace bordering the southwestern side of the court. These impressive and highly ornate buildings are but part of a vast ceremonial complex built at Warka in the latter part of the fourth millennium. The court is entirely decorated with cone mosaic, of which an example is illustrated (*opposite above*). The colonnade is some 30 meters wide and the columns themselves over 2 meters in diameter. They once supported the roof of a hall and represent the earliest known instance of the use of columns in a monumental building. The mosaic pattern consists of clay cones with the heads colored black, white and red, set into the mud-brick walls. Hundreds of thousands of such cones were used in the adornment of a single building. The cone mosaic court and associated buildings were completely leveled and replaced, like the other buildings of Eanna. with no concern for the preservation of their remains. In level III, representing the so-called Jamdat Nasr phase at the very end of the Uruk period, the whole precinct was apparently leveled once again and equipped with a series of buildings of quite different character, including, for the first time in Eanna, a high terrace of the type found earlier in Kullaba.

Opposite: one of the most striking pieces of Late Uruk art, a white marble mask, almost life-size (ht. 20 cm), found in the Eanna precinct at Warka, in a pit of the Uruk III (Jamdat Nasr) period. It is uncertain whether this finely modeled female head, which had been carelessly thrown into the pit, belonged to a statue or to a relief composed of several parts. The back is flat, with four holes drilled in it to fasten it to some background. Eyes, eyebrows and perhaps also the hair parting would have been inlaid with some colored material, while the hair may have been covered with gold or some other precious metal. Indeed the finished piece would have appeared to us overornate compared with the sensitively modeled head we now see. Two holes above and below each ear could have served for attachment or perhaps for the insertion of earrings such as are found on the strikingly similar prehistoric clay head from Choga Mami illustrated elsewhere. The scalloped hair style too resembles that of the Choga Mami head which can be dated over 2,000 years earlier.

Right: alabaster vase from Warka, found as part of a treasure hoard in a late Jamdat Nasr context, but probably to be dated slightly earlier (overall ht. 1·05 m). Perhaps the most interesting single object found at Warka and the earliest representation in Mesopotamia of what can certainly be interpreted as a religious or cult scene. The produce of the fields and the increase of the herds, both symbolically represented in the lowest register, are presented to the goddess Inanna, who is represented on the vase just to the left of her reed standards, top register left. Two lesser figures are shown standing on the back of a ram, apparently praying or sacrificing, and behind them are displayed some of the temple offerings. On the other side of the vase, a ritually nude priest advances towards the goddess carrying a large bowl of fruit; behind him is a damaged figure wearing a net skirt who is possibly the *En* or head of the temple community. The middle register shows a procession of nude attendants or "priests" carrying offerings of food and wine. The vase was treasured in antiquity as it was at one time repaired with copper rivets.

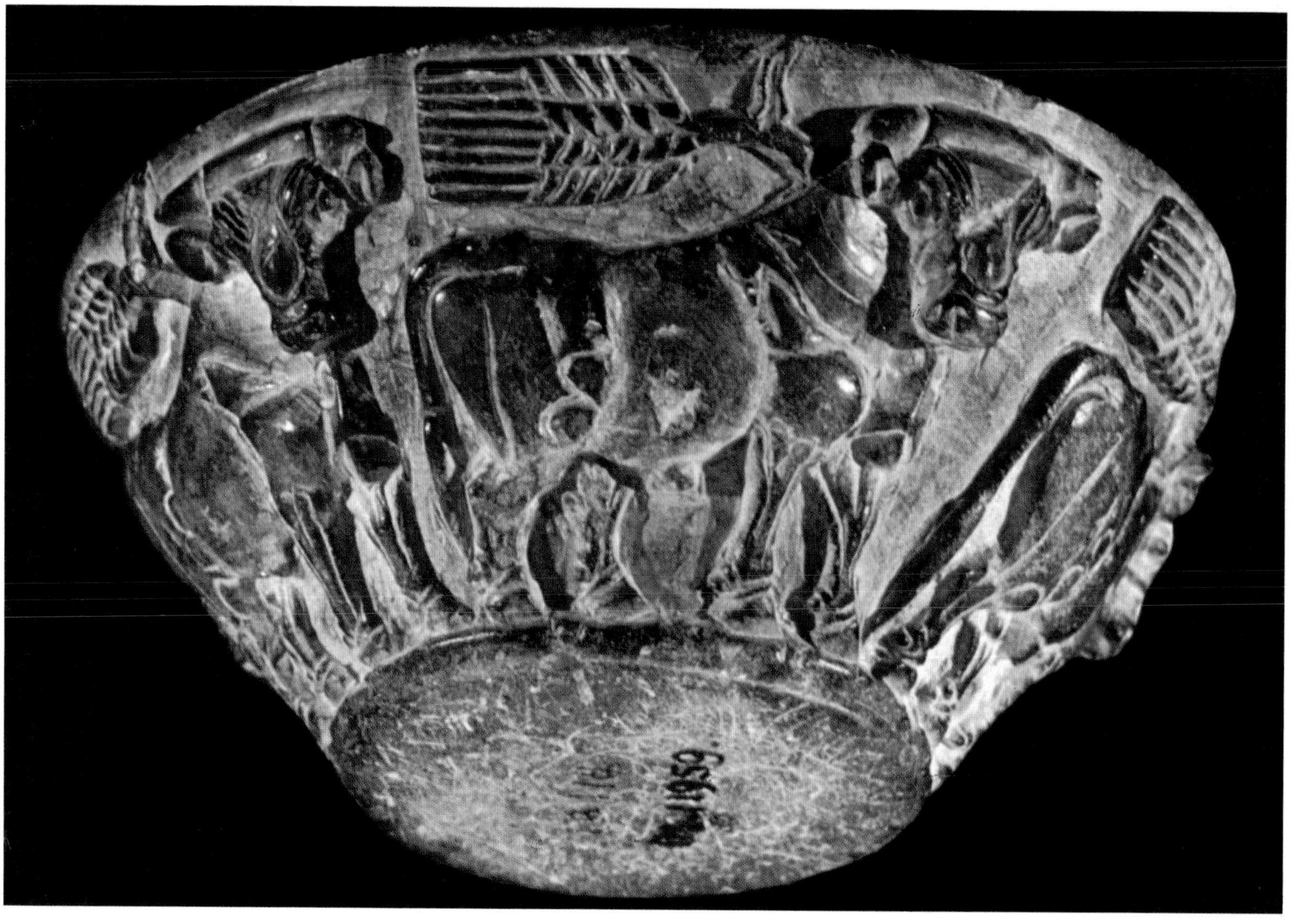

Opposite above: this stone rosette formed part of the facade ornament of the late third-millennium Eye Temple at Tell Brak in northeastern Syria. The petals are of white marble and black shale, the center of pink limestone. Brak lies over 750 miles upstream from Warka, yet the basic features of its temples, including the tripartite plan and the use of cone mosaic as well as these rosettes, closely parallel those of the Late Uruk period in Sumer. The Eye Temple was so named because of the discovery within earlier temple remains incorporated in its platform of many thousands of small "eye-idols" such as the one illustrated *below*. Made of black or white limestone, some examples have more than one pair of eyes, others wear a high headdress. Most are c. 4–6 cm in height. They were probably offerings dedicated to the god worshiped in the temple.

Opposite below: stone bowl of the Late Uruk period, found at Ur, decorated with bulls and ears of corn in high relief.

Right: stone jar with shell mosaic inlay, Jamdat Nasr period, ht. 15 cm, found in the same deposit as the Warka vase. Such jars were often made in several parts; the spout of this one had been lost and has been replaced by another found separately.

Reverse side of a pictographic tablet of the Jamdat Nasr period from the site of Jamdat Nasr, near Kish (c. 3000 BC). It is an administrative tablet, a list of accounts involving animals and various commodities including bread and beer. The circular, crescent- and D-shaped signs represent numbers. The earliest form of writing is a pictographic script in which each sign signified some concrete object or a closely related meaning. At the slightly later time when this tablet was written, grammatical elements were still not normally indicated and there was still no convention as to a correct order of writing. This tablet would have been read in columns from right to left, though later cuneiform was written from left to right.

Late Uruk pottery from the site of Habuba al-Kabira on the Euphrates in northern Syria. This fortified settlement has many characteristics that are distinctly Mesopotamian, including the use of pottery and mud-bricks that are identical with those employed at contemporary Warka. Especially characteristic are the jars with curved spouts and the four-lugged jars with ornament of incised triangles on the shoulders. Habuba al-Kabira is a large site, half a mile in length, which appears to have been an outpost established from the south, perhaps to control the Euphrates trade route.

6. The Growth of Cities in Mesopotamia

Our final chapter spans a period of about 2,000 years from approximately 5000 to 3000 BC which saw the development in southern Mesopotamia – historic Sumer and Akkad – of a civilized society based on an irrigation economy, and the expansion of its influence over neighboring lands. When we remember that this period alone is equal to all the time that has elapsed since the birth of Christ, and reflect on the great vicissitudes that have marked the history of European civilization in that time, this may seem an impossible task. But although there are many gaps in our evidence, the emergence of urban civilization in Mesopotamia from the still rural communities we saw in the last chapter does seem to have been a more coherent process, and certainly we hold the view that it was an essentially self-contained one. There were of course innovations, without which no development could have taken place, but we can trace a basic continuity in many aspects of culture over very long periods. It is thus possible for the first time in this book to treat some features of the emerging society, such as the development of formal architecture or of representational art, in general summaries rather than the piecemeal presentation which the nature of earlier evidence has so far imposed on us.

One of the most serious defects in our information, however, is the lack of any overall chronological framework. Indeed, the number of radiocarbon determinations available in the Near East for these last two millennia of prehistory is very small, and some of them are mutually inconsistent. This is not as surprising as it may seem, for many of the excavations on which we rely came to an end before the technique was introduced, and at others such as Warka work has been concentrated largely on monumental buildings where determinations would be invaluable but which yield no carbon. Indeed within Mesopotamia we have effectively only two figures, one of c. 4900 BC for the end of the Samarran occupation at Choga Mami and the other of c. 4200 BC for a late phase of the 'Ubaid period at Warka. Both of these are determinations from single samples and so not wholly satisfactory though generally consistent with the lowest range of figures for comparable material from Khuzistan and Saudi Arabia. They are plausible in their uncorrected form, but if they are corrected in accordance with the recent proposals for the calibration of carbon "dates," the end of Samarra at Choga Mami, which was closely followed by the appearance of 'Ubaid 2 material representing an early stage in the southern sequence, would be moved back to an absolute date closer to 6000 BC. Since the first date in Mesopotamian history that can be at all reliably calculated from historical evidence is the foundation of the dynasty

Right: the sequence of 'Ubaid temples at Eridu with debris of the third-millennium ziggurrat at the top (5000 BC onwards).

Previous page: lizard-headed clay female figurine from Ur, 'Ubaid 4 (late fifth millennium). The appliqué decoration may represent tattooing (British Museum).

of Agade about 2370 BC, we would then be left with three and a half millennia to be filled by the 'Ubaid, Uruk and Early Dynastic periods. This is at best an unresolved problem and for the present we prefer, as we have done hitherto, to retain uncalibrated "dates" and to recognize that the whole sequence may need substantial revision.

The two cultures with which we are now concerned are those known as 'Ubaid and Uruk, and as a very approximate guide to the reader we suggest that the 'Ubaid phase lasted through the fifth, and the Uruk phase through most of the fourth millennium. We have already said that our story has no definable ending, since writing in its earliest pictographic form as an ingenious device for tallying accounts was of some economic use but little social importance. We therefore treat the "Jamdat Nasr" phase, when writing in this limited sense was already in use, as a late stage of the Uruk culture, although we also regard it as a forerunner of the Early Dynastic period since much of the archaeological material is indistinguishable from that which was in use in Early Dynastic I.

Early settlement in Sumer. It is only at a relatively late stage, around 5000 BC, that we begin to find archaeological evidence for settlement in southern Mesopotamia, but this is not to say that the area was previously uninhabited. Recent discoveries of substantial hunter-gatherer populations in the undoubtedly more arid eastern province of Saudi Arabia leave no doubt about the viability, and indeed the likelihood, of a comparable and contemporary pattern of subsistence in Sumer long before the earliest surviving evidence for occupation. Moreover in Sumer the presence of lagoons and marshes, attested from the earliest excavated levels in the alluvium, provides the further possibility of relatively settled communities, perhaps comparable with those of today's non-agricultural Marsh Arabs. In these marshes fish, wild fowl and wild boar would have been available in abundance, together with the giant reeds from which the modern inhabitants still make their houses and rafts.

A further valuable resource that must have existed at least in parts of the southern alluvium is the date palm. This tree needs liberal quantities of water at its roots but matures its fruit only where there are long, hot and rain-free summers. It is thus perfectly adapted to the lower reaches of the Tigris and Euphrates where natural fresh-water irrigation results from the pressure of tides in the Arabian Gulf. At the present day such natural tidal action extends over 100 miles upstream, affecting 112,000 acres of land through 70 major creeks in the estuary area. The date palm is without doubt one of the most useful plants known to man; the Greek geographer Strabo refers to a Persian poem extolling 360 uses of this impressively versatile tree. Apart from the fruit, the palm sprout is still a popular vegetable, while the sap can be made into a honeylike syrup for sweetening and indeed a potent alcoholic beverage. Date stones provide a high-quality fuel, used in later times for smelting. The palm trunk, though notable for elasticity rather than strength, today provides timber for light building construction, boats, furniture and even small bridges, while the fiber is extracted for rope making. The fronds are widely used to build temporary shelters and the individual leaves for weaving baskets. Most important of all, the fruit provides even today, in areas where it is widely grown, not a mere sweetmeat but a staple food. Harvested in late summer, dates can be dried and stored, affording year-round supplies of carbohydrate and thus eliminating the need for more common staples such as cereals. Dates together with fish, another local product that can also be dried and stored, afford a completely adequate human diet.

Archaeological evidence for such a postulated pattern of occupation, however probable, is unlikely to be easily found. Heavy silting combined with a shifting pattern not only of lagoon and marsh but also of the river courses themselves has made prehistoric investigation in the south extremely difficult. Indeed, with present archaeological techniques there is little likelihood of recovering reliable data even concerning the distribution of early settled villages in the area. The discovery of Ras al 'Amiya, a small prehistoric site near Kish and Babylon, strikingly illustrates this point. Found only by accident in the excavation of a modern irrigation canal, the *top* of the ancient mound lies 1–2 meters below the modern plain, and there remained no surface indication whatsoever of the ancient site. Nonetheless, the fact remains that a hunting and fishing economy would have been viable in the marsh areas of the south long before the development of the simple gravity-flow irrigation techniques needed to support the settled village populations for which we do have evidence sometime before 5000 BC. Moreover, when we remember that one of the principal exports of the Marsh Arab communities at the present day is reed matting, an important element in traditional roof construction, it cannot be maintained that the surplus wealth necessary for the purchase of imported commodities was not available in this area before the introduction of agriculture.

Whatever may have been the early history of occupation in Sumer, it is clear that the techniques of cereal cultivation must have been introduced from elsewhere. This is not to say that the people themselves were immigrants, as is so often supposed. Indeed the very minimal evidence we possess for the earliest cultural assemblage in the area suggests that, like the early farming assemblages we have described in other geographically distinct areas of Mesopotamia, it represents an essentially local development. Known to archaeologists as the 'Ubaid culture, this earliest manifestation of settled farming in the southern alluvium is divided – for the convenience of archaeologists – into four easily recognized chronological phases. The earliest of these, 'Ubaid 1 or Eridu as it is often called, has a very limited geographical distribution, approximately between the sites of Warka and Eridu in the very southernmost part of Sumer.

Eridu. The site of Eridu itself provides our only excavated sequence for the 'Ubaid period as a whole. Here a sounding under a corner of the late third-millennium ziggurrat revealed 19 levels of occupation, of which levels XIX–VI were attributed to the 'Ubaid period, characterized by a very distinctive monochrome painted pottery, often greenish in appearance. The earliest 'Ubaid 1 or Eridu phase, identified in levels XIX–XVI, was once thought to define a distinct archaeological culture, the most recognizable feature of which was its elaborately ornamented, often glossy, monochrome painted pottery. Identical ceramic types have been found at nearby Ur and Tell al 'Ubaid, and at several smaller sites in the vicinity of both Eridu and Warka. Many parallels can be observed with the post-Samarran "Transitional" pottery at Choga Mami, which we described in the last chapter as related both to the earlier Samarran ceramic and to probably contemporary early 'Ubaid types in the south. Some Transitional pottery has been found at two small sites in Sumer, and it occurs in quantity also in Khuzistan. Nevertheless, there is no evidence to suggest that the earliest 'Ubaid pottery derives from it. In fact the Choga Mami data can be interpreted to suggest that 'Ubaid 1 was at least partially contemporary with and perhaps even earlier than the so-called Transitional levels. We have to mention this complex evidence because many attempts have been made to derive the 'Ubaid assemblage from elsewhere on the almost certainly mistaken assumption that the early inhabitants of Sumer must have been immigrants. Undoubtedly many of their ideas were derived from external contacts – even the pigments for painting their pottery must have been imported – but there is on present evidence no reason to suppose that these early farming communities in Sumer represent other than an essentially local development.

In the marshes of southern Iraq: Suq al-Shuyukh.

Perhaps the most interesting feature of the earliest 'Ubaid settlements at Eridu is the presence, for the first time anywhere in Mesopotamia, of buildings that can certainly be identified as non-secular in function. In levels XVII and XVI were found the remains of small square structures, that in XVI being the more complete. Projecting from one wall was a deep recess within which was a small square pedestal, while a second similar pedestal in the center of the building bore traces of burning and was surrounded by ash. Such features are common in all later Mesopotamian temples and it seems clear that at Eridu we can identify an early stage of what was to be a very long religious tradition. The "shrine" in level XVI was built of long prismatic mud-bricks, similar in general proportions to those employed at Choga Mami, while bricks in the succeeding and larger shrine in level XV bore a row of double thumb marks on their upper surface, a feature found also in approximately contemporary Transitional levels at the latter site and which served to improve the bond of the mud mortar.

In level XV a ceramic style was recognized identical with that already known from the small site of Hajji Muhammad near Warka. This continued in quantity through level XII, defining a second 'Ubaid phase, 'Ubaid 2, which is commonly referred to as "Hajji Muhammad" after its original place of discovery. Archaeological material of this phase has a wider *known* distribution than that of 'Ubaid 1, being found further to the north at Nippur and almost certainly as far as the district of Mandali east of Baghdad. From level XII onwards the pottery includes a substantial quantity of rather more simply decorated varieties, many of which have an enormously wide distribution over the whole of Iraq and into adjacent areas of Syria, Iran and Saudi Arabia. In levels XII to VIII,

however, a significant number of Hajji Muhammad types persist, a fact that has led to many identifications of "'Ubaid 2" pottery which are undoubtedly of the later 'Ubaid 3 (Eridu levels XII–VIII) phase. Identical early 'Ubaid 3 ceramic types, including many specimens that would be described stylistically as "Hajji Muhammad," are found as far afield as Choga Mami (in the so-called 'Ubaid well deposit), at Ras al 'Amiya and among the earliest pottery discovered far to the south in the eastern province of Saudi Arabia. Here this undoubtedly Mesopotamian ceramic appears on some 40 sites as an intrusive element among the debris left by the local stone-tool-using hunters and collectors. Soundings have been carried out on three of the four large mound sites in this region by Abdullah Masry, now Director of Antiquities in Saudi Arabia. It is approximately at this same time ('Ubaid 3) that distinctively 'Ubaid pottery types first appear in northern Iraq, on sites such as Tepe Gawra and Qalinj Agha. We shall return to these sites later.

At Eridu levels VII and VI constitute a late phase, 'Ubaid 4, within the development of this cultural assemblage, while a still later stage, apparently not represented at Eridu, is marked by the appearance of plain pottery types more characteristic of the later Uruk assemblage and by the very limited manufacture of painted wares of a singularly uninspired and pedestrian variety. This apparent decline in potting skill coincides with an increasing use of the potter's wheel and seems likely to represent a growing "industrialization," indeed mass production, of pottery rather than any real falling off in technical ability.

'Ubaid economy and society. We have no direct information concerning the early 'Ubaid economy, but there can be little doubt that the inhabitants of the settled villages of this phase cultivated wheat and barley with the aid of simple irrigation techniques. This is not as surprising as it once seemed, since we know that the Samarran farmers of central Mesopotamia had been well practiced in such techniques for some centuries and, by the time of the earliest 'Ubaid 1 villages, were capable of constructing and maintaining true canals four to six meters wide and a number of kilometers in length. Along the major rivers, however, the problems of irrigation are more complex than those encountered on fan deltas such as that around the Mandali oasis, where the Gangir river emerges from the hills. We have already pointed out that, unlike the Nile which floods just before the autumn planting season, the Mesopotamian rivers are low at the time of planting and flood in the spring, thus threatening with inundation the crops which they are with difficulty persuaded to germinate. Crops must be protected against the flood, and a 19th-century practice was to farm one bank of the river only, with protection in the form of high embankments, while encouraging uncontrolled flooding on the other bank. The Tigris and Euphrates carry enormous quantities of silt, of which the heaviest particles are deposited almost immediately as the rivers breach their banks. Thus natural levees develop, while the silting of the river bed itself can lead to the raising of the channel above the level of the plain.

In some ways this makes irrigation easier, but the problems of drawing water from an inevitably low river level within the levees at the crucial planting season, as well as the destructive potential of serious flooding before the harvest, are much increased. Silt clogs the artificial water channels as well as the rivers, making yearly cleaning an essential task that requires not so much an enormous labor force as a level of community cooperation which must certainly have influenced the development of social structure in this area. Perhaps more important, irrigation led to differential land values and thus differential wealth, since land closest to the water source was the most desirable, and tended moreover to tie people to specific plots of land in a way that would have encouraged the growth of concepts of property and inevitably an increase in the size of settlements. Such considerations would have been unimportant in areas of reliable rain-fed farming where most arable land was of equal value, especially in western Asia where land suitable for agriculture did not – as it often did in Europe – require extensive forest clearance. Irrigation also made possible the reliable crop surpluses that must have stimulated the diversification of specialist craftsmen and the growth of a central economic authority for which we have evidence in the succeeding period.

Mesopotamian sites, 5000–3000 BC.

Although we can be certain that the ʻUbaid peoples were irrigation farmers, we lack precise information about what they farmed. Seed impressions from Ur of unspecified, but certainly ʻUbaid, date indicate the cultivation of emmer, barley and linseed, while animal bones attributed to the ʻUbaid 3 phase at Eridu include domesticated cattle and wild onager. Faunal samples from both Eridu and Ras al ʻAmiya show a low proportion of sheep and goat by comparison with cattle, in sharp contrast to the heavy emphasis on the herding of sheep and goats deduced from contemporary evidence in nearby Khuzistan. Our very limited data suggest that cattle breeding was normally of greater economic importance in areas of irrigation farming than in the rain-fed farming zone, although we must not overlook the apparently special significance of cattle to the inhabitants of Çatal Hüyük and the Halaf people of northern Mesopotamia.

We have outlined some of the ways in which the special circumstances attending irrigation agriculture probably affected the society and economy that depended on it. More concrete illustrations of some aspects of social development can be drawn from the exceptionally interesting sequence of buildings at Eridu. They not only provide the earliest certain evidence in Mesopotamia for communal religious activity but, more important, an actual sequence of religious buildings culminating in ʻUbaid 4 with temples almost indistinguishable in concept and design from those of the late Uruk period, many centuries later, at sites such as Warka itself and Tell ʻUqair. Moreover, the discovery of fish offerings in these shrines suggests that they were already associated with the cult of Enki, the Sumerian god of the waters under the earth, who was the supreme deity of Eridu in the historical period. It is conceivable, therefore, that as early as the ʻUbaid period such a temple was the focus of an organizing authority, as in later times.

Certainly there is evidence for increasing settlement size

– the 'Ubaid inhabitants of Tall 'Uqair would appear to have occupied some 11 hectares – which would imply an increasing need for some form of centralized control. But evidence for social stratification, which in archaeological terms can sometimes be deduced from differential grave goods or houses of superior aspect, is almost completely lacking at this time. This contrasts markedly with the Levant, where we have noted such evidence as early as the Natufian period (p. 72). We must emphasize, however, the limited dimensions of our knowledge of this phase in Mesopotamian prehistory. From the south, for example, we have no complete house-plans, while a very small and essentially unpublished sounding at Eridu provides the only typological sequence. Many authors have implied that the earliest 'Ubaid farmers of Sumer lived exclusively in reed huts, but we have as yet no archaeological evidence for such a stage. Indeed mud-brick walling is found in the earliest levels at both Eridu and Ur. Such traces as there are of reed structures are found side by side with the employment of mud-brick, and at Eridu one mud-brick house appears to have had a reed annex. It should also be emphasized that the use of reed structures in no way signifies a "primitive" settlement. Reed huts provide very adequate housing in the climatic conditions of southern Iraq and are still in common use today – even in one instance to house an American archaeological expedition!

A reed boat in the marshes of Khuzistan, Iran.

North Mesopotamia: 'Ubaid expansion. More extensive evidence of domestic architecture is available from 'Ubaid levels at sites in northern Iraq, particularly at Tepe Gawra, situated at the foot of the first line of hills northeast of Mosul, and the only 'Ubaid settlement at which more than limited soundings have been carried out. In turning to this site we move well outside the southern "nuclear" 'Ubaid homeland and into the habitat of the Hassuna and Halaf peoples we have previously discussed. Here in fact is the first convincing evidence in western Asiatic prehistory for a cultural intrusion in the sense that a large part of the material culture of one area is brought into or deliberately adopted by another. 'Ubaid pottery, in many respects indistinguishable from its southern progenitor, together with comparable mud-brick building techniques, is found on hundreds of sites throughout the northern plain, in the Zagros to the northeast and to the west across northern Syria, while we have already noted the recent discoveries which have extended this vast geographical distribution to include eastern Saudi Arabia. The mechanism of this cultural dispersion is far from clearly understood but provides one of the most fascinating puzzles of this period.

At Gawra the earliest level excavated (XX) is clearly of Halaf attribution while the succeeding three levels yielded features among the architectural as well as the ceramic evidence reminiscent of both Halaf and 'Ubaid. A similar pattern can be seen among the smaller objects in clay and stone. These apparently transitional levels are followed by a further four in which Halaf traits disappear and the cultural assemblage in many respects closely resembles that in the south. The evidence is less clear at other less well-documented sites but the pattern that emerges by the latter part of the fifth millennium is undoubtedly one of 'Ubaid "cultural" domination, if not domination in any other form. Indeed available data imply a very rapid expansion of southern influence, coinciding with the period designated archaeologically as 'Ubaid 3. What these data really signify in terms of human activity is much more difficult to understand, although they cannot be attributed to the simple interchange of ideas or material objects between culturally discrete regions for which there is evidence in earlier periods. Nor do these phenomena appear to represent any real replacement of one cultural group (Halaf) by another ('Ubaid). Indeed there is convincing evidence of the contemporaneity of some late Halaf settlements with others where the material assemblage is predominantly 'Ubaid, a situation perhaps already parallel with that found today in the northern plain with its many separate villages inhabited by culturally as well as linguistically discrete groups of Kurds, Turks and Arabs.

Changes in ceramic style can be attributed to "fashion" while technological innovations are often adopted for solely practical reasons; but the apparent religious unity, not only in architectural form but in ritual as well, between north and south at this time requires a more complex explanation. Certainly the latest 'Ubaid temples at Gawra (level XIII), discussed below, parallel those known at Eridu far too closely for the similarity to be dismissed as coincidental. This evidence alone would seem to require some southern "presence" in the north at this time. It is difficult to envisage any form of political domination at such an early stage, especially while we lack evidence for any form of political development within Sumer itself. By far the most plausible explanation for these phenomena is also unacceptable to many archaeologists for essentially the same reason, that is the apparently simple level of society with which we are concerned. Nonetheless, it is difficult to explain the pattern of 'Ubaid expansion clearly visible in the archaeological record of the fifth millennium as other than the earliest attempt by the inhabitants of Sumer to control the trade routes on which depended their acquisition of raw materials such as stone, metal ores and timber, totally lacking in their own environment. Developments in subsequent phases confirm the likelihood, while the widespread occurrence of 'Ubaid pottery on sites in northeastern Syria astride the major route to the copper mines at Ergani Maden near Diyarbakr provides some confirmation, of such an economic motive. Moreover, there can be no doubt that our knowledge of social and economic developments in 'Ubaid Sumer is significantly limited by the extreme paucity of excavated evidence. Renewed archaeological investigation of earlier phases of Mesopotamian prehistory has radically altered our view of developments at this time; that we have much to learn about 'Ubaid Sumer seems even more likely.

Above: Temple VIII at Eridu in southern Iraq, late 'Ubaid 3 (second half of the fifth millennium).

Opposite: tholos in level XVII at Tepe Gawra, transitional Halaf-'Ubaid phase (mid-fifth millennium).

The Uruk period. Whatever were the real reasons for the extension of 'Ubaid influence in the latter part of the fifth millennium, a comparable pattern is to be seen in the succeeding archaeological phase, that known as Uruk, the ancient name of the type site (Biblical Erech, modern Warka) and one of a number of important settlements of the period. We have already emphasized the difficulty of interpreting developments during the 'Ubaid period, owing to the lack of excavated data. However, archaeologists in recent years have shown even less interest in the investigation of Uruk settlements, despite an increasing concern with theoretical aspects of the growth of urban society. Undoubtedly the earliest cities so far known acquired their very distinctive character during this phase of Mesopotamian prehistory. The complex cultural processes that led to the growth of cities in Sumer, however, were deeply rooted in its earliest settlements, those we know as 'Ubaid, and indeed in even earlier social and

economic developments, particularly in Samarran areas of occupation further to the north. It was the Uruk phase, however, spanning much of the 4th millennium, that was to see the culmination of these earlier phenomena in the growth of settlements of both urban proportion and function. Yet of the earlier part of this development we know next to nothing. A number of small soundings at Warka have revealed a sequence of levels in which there would appear to have been a gradual change from painted ceramic types associated with a late phase of 'Ubaid occupation to the mass-produced, often wheel-made, plain wares characteristic of the Uruk period. Some red and gray burnished wares are also found, though such pottery is far more common on Uruk sites in northern Iraq than in the south where the plain types are predominant.

At Warka a series of levels under a later sanctuary known as Eanna, excavated by a German expedition in 1930–31, still provides the basic sequence for the Uruk period, despite the fact that some levels yielded almost no material, that much material from the sounding lacks a reliably stratified context and that the sounding was of very small proportions (the lowest levels penetrated an area of only some seven square meters). More recent soundings appear very generally to confirm the sequence previously established but have added little to our knowledge of the Uruk period. The presence of a monumental building of 'Ubaid date under another sanctuary, that later associated with the god Anu, was however established. Beneath Eanna, the earliest and essentially unstratified levels XVIII–XVI contain a number of characteristic Uruk types mixed together with large numbers of 'Ubaid painted sherds, while levels XIV–IX represent an early and so far ill-defined phase of Uruk. Only from level VIII onwards can the Warka sequence be paralleled elsewhere in the south, in as yet unpublished levels under the Inanna precinct at Nippur, while only from levels V–IV, the latest phase of Uruk development, have we any extensive knowledge of what should be one of the most interesting and significant periods described in this book. The earliest written records known anywhere in the world occur in the latest phase of level IV (IVa), while level III (often referred to as "Jamdat Nasr" after a very distinctive polychrome pottery type first discovered at a site by that name and commonly associated with materials of this phase) marks a transitional stage between Late Uruk and the Early Dynastic period, often indistinguishable from the latter. With the Early Dynastic period we leave the realms of prehistory for a stage associated with the earliest Sumerian dynasties known from the so-called King-List, a partly mythological but also genuinely historical document that chronicles dynastic lists associated with a number of Sumerian cities.

Tepe Gawra. In northern Iraq Uruk materials have been excavated more extensively, for example at Grai Resh near Sinjar, at Qalinj Agha near Erbil, at sites excavated by the Iraq Antiquities Department in the Raniya plain north of

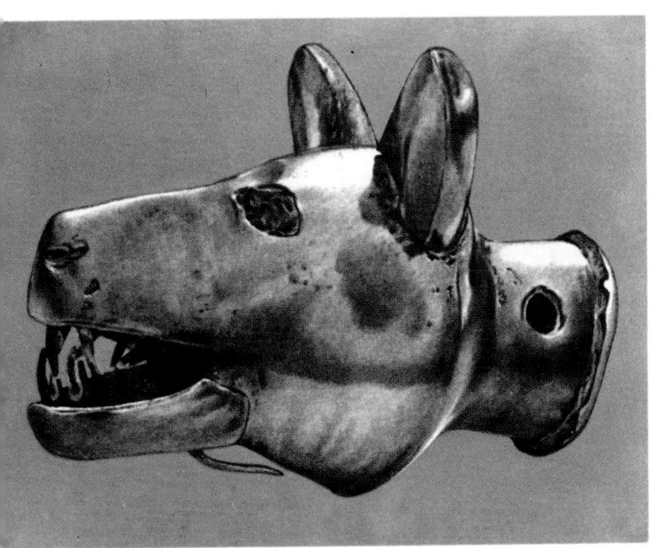

Above: electrum wolf's head from a tomb in level X at Tepe Gawra, fourth millennium, length 3 centimeters.

Opposite: spouted painted jar from Jamdat Nasr, late fourth millennium (Ashmolean Museum, Oxford).

Sulaimaniya and in particular at the site of Tepe Gawra northeast of Mosul. Material from the latter site, however, does not closely parallel the little that is known from the south, nor indeed from Uruk sites further west. At Grai Resh, for example, the pottery is largely identical with that known from southern sites but includes a far greater preponderance of red and gray wares, a feature generally characteristic of early Uruk settlement in the northern plain. At Gawra, on the other hand, the latest 'Ubaid level (XIII) is followed by one in which painted wares continue, though in shapes and patterns very different not only from the preceding 'Ubaid and Halaf styles, but also from contemporary pottery in the south. One very distinctive type, with sprig-like patterns painted in black over a red slip, has a very wide distribution at this time across northern Iraq and Syria. Levels XI–IX form a related group, united both by ceramic and other types of object and by the temple architecture, to which we shall return later.

In level VIII are many features characteristic of so-called Jamdat Nasr levels in the south, while its latest phase (VIII-A) is possibly to be equated with the earliest stage of the Early Dynastic period. Thus Gawra levels XII–VIII correspond roughly in time to the Uruk phase as inadequately defined at Warka, while it is only from Gawra that there is any extensive body of evidence documenting the early phase of Uruk development. The main thrust of Uruk expansion would appear to lie further to the west, however, and although it is clear that material from sites like Grai Resh, Tall Brak in northeastern Syria and Habuba al-Kabira on the Euphrates closely parallel that known in the south, that from Gawra is undoubtedly atypical and cannot necessarily be taken as characteristic of the period as a whole. It is difficult to imagine, however, that such a peripheral site, situated as it is at the foot of the first range of hills northeast of Mosul, should be significantly in advance of its neighbors to the south and west, in what were clearly more major areas of development at other better-documented periods. And it is at Gawra that we find the first convincing evidence for differential wealth and a complexity of society not previously attested in the Mesopotamian archaeological record. This is most striking among the grave goods excavated in a number of mud-brick or stone-built tombs associated with levels X to VIII-B. Three tombs, believed to have originated from stratum X, were especially rich, containing unusually large quantities of gold, electrum, lapis lazuli and ivory. One tomb alone yielded over 200 objects in gold and some 450 lapis beads. Ordinary graves found in these levels were relatively poorly furnished, though the contents of a child's grave in XI-A, perhaps that of a shepherd boy, are of interest in providing an early example of a musical instrument, a playing pipe made of bone.

The contents of the Gawra tombs suggest not only significant social differentiation but also a very considerable increase in trading activities. Indeed at Gawra evidence of a growing demand for luxury goods such as lapis lazuli and gold appears already by the end of the 'Ubaid period, perhaps some confirmation of the economic motivation we have already postulated for the widespread expansion of southern contacts at this time. A further feature of this phase at Gawra is the first convincing evidence for some form of economic activity associated with the temple. This too can be dated to the latest 'Ubaid phase with the discovery in a well associated with the Eastern Temple of the level-XIII "acropolis" of a large number of clay seal impressions, whose function had clearly been to identify some form or forms of portable property brought to or belonging to the temple. The lumps of clay bearing these impressions frequently preserve also the imprint of the cord, reeds or cloth by which they were attached. Although seals are found throughout the excavated levels on the site – and indeed as early as the Hassunan village at Yarim Tepe – at Gawra they first come into extensive use in level XIII, while, in the succeeding two levels over two-thirds of the site's rich deposits of 600 seals and impressions were found, many now bearing elaborate human and animal designs.

Perhaps the clearest hallmark of the Uruk period, and one of the least attractive of ancient objects, is a crudely made flowerpot-shaped bowl known to archaeologists as a "beveled-rim bowl." Found in profusion on sites of this phase, especially in its latest levels, this mass-produced container is of much greater interest than its mundane appearance would suggest, and provides yet another clue to the growing complexity of centralized economic activity. Unlike most pottery of this time, which was produced on a fast wheel, these unattractive but clearly functional objects were mold-made. This fact, together with their widespread distribution, particularly in associ-

General view of the Late 'Ubaid (level XIII) acropolis at Tepe Gawra, with the stone foundations of the level XIV house under the open court (looking north).

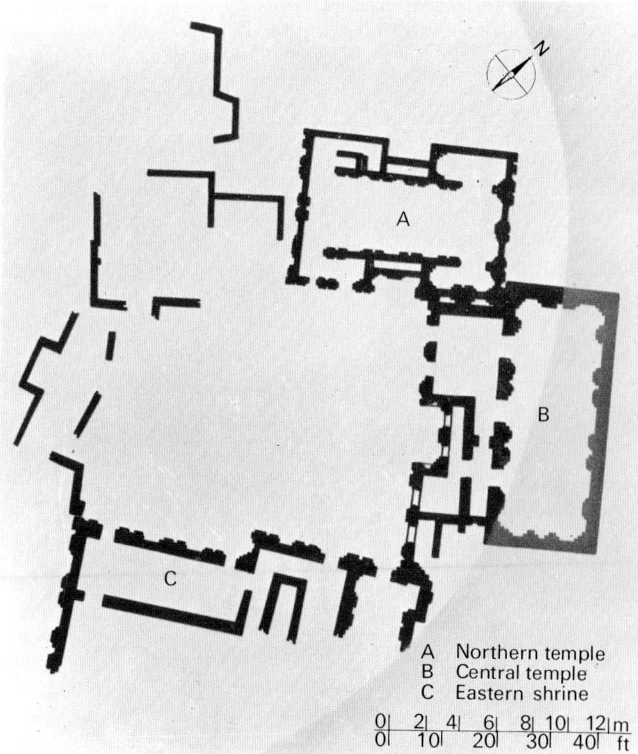

ation with major settlements, strongly suggests that these vessels may have been ration measures used in the "payment" of personnel "employed" by the temple or other large estates. Later texts testify to such a practice and list specific quantities, especially of barley and oil, issued to workers engaged in various manufacturing and agricultural pursuits. As early as Uruk III one text from the Eanna precinct at Warka lists daily rations of bread and beer for some 50 individuals, while other fragments mention barley and fish. It is possible to see in the ubiquitous beveled-rim bowls the earliest widespread standardization of such a practice.

Architecture and art. One of the phenomena that mark the progress of Mesopotamian society towards civilization is the appearance of buildings formally designed for communal functions. We have observed in earlier times the existence of specialized structures such as the wall of Jericho, or more recently the storehouses at Umm Dabaghiyah and Yarim Tepe, but, although these undoubtedly represent the organized efforts of considerable numbers of people, their purpose was practical. In the temples at Eridu, Gawra, Warka, Brak and 'Uqair we have a sequence of "tripartite" buildings which, since they span almost two millennia and a vast geographical area, conform with surprising consistency to a standard pattern of layout and decoration and certainly served a purpose that was largely if not wholly ceremonial.

The creation of, and adherence to, this tradition of religious architecture reminds us strongly of the persistence over a similar period of one of the earliest forms of Christian church, the basilica, and suggests that an important motive behind such conservatism may have been continuity in the general forms of ritual that the buildings were designed to house. This is borne out by the occurrence in many, though not all, instances of certain

The Round House, Tepe Gawra XI-A. This is the earliest house in Mesopotamia that can definitely be identified as having some special function or status; early fourth millennium.

standard features that remained characteristic of Mesopotamian temples throughout the historical period long after the tripartite plan had been abandoned. These include a raised podium at one end of the main chamber faced by an offering table that sometimes shows traces of burning and, on one of the long sides, a stairway leading to the roof. The stairs may have no special significance in the prehistoric period, but in later Babylonian temples they were clearly a formal part of the design, suggesting that some ceremonies were performed on the roof. In the vast tripartite buildings of the Late Uruk period in the Eanna precinct there may even have been two stairways symmetrically disposed on either side of the central chamber, although curiously these structures, which otherwise represent the ultimate and most grandiose development of the tripartite plan, lack the podium and offering table of earlier shrines and

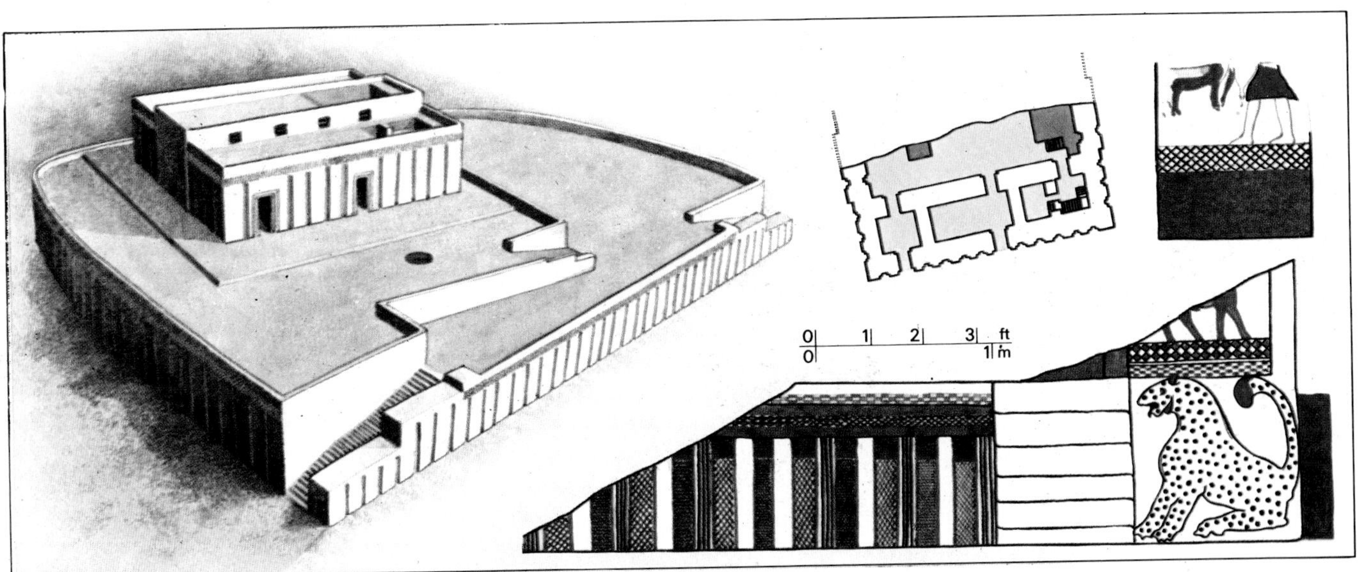

Above: reconstruction of Late Uruk temple at 'Uqair on its high terrace.

Opposite: plan of the temples in level XIII at Tepe Gawra.

obviously served a somewhat different though clearly ceremonial function.

The origins of this distinctive architectural form are still a matter of conjecture. The invention of mud-brick which, by contrast with *tauf*, provided a structural unit of standard size and later of rectangular form, obviously made the construction of precisely rectilinear buildings much easier, and this development is clearly reflected in the very regular house-plans of the Samarran period at Choga Mami and Tell es-Sawwan. Here, too, we see the use of symmetrically disposed external buttresses, undoubtedly in the Samarran period a structural device, but perhaps the forerunners of the elaborate pilasters of the 'Ubaid and Uruk temples which were obviously designed to produce a visual effect that would have been especially dramatic in the harshly contrasting light and shade of Mesopotamia. The increasing complexity of this facade decoration again reflects the introduction of mud-bricks of standard sizes. This point is well demonstrated from the discovery, in the oldest of a group of three temples in the Late 'Ubaid XIII level at Gawra, of terracotta scale models of the bricks employed in the other two shrines and clearly used for preliminary planning of the structural techniques.

Gawra also casts an interesting light on the possible origin of the characteristic plan of these temples, for it is one of the few sites that has produced any considerable number of house-plans of the fifth and fourth millennia; and it is notable that a less formal and undecorated version of the tripartite layout, with a large central chamber flanked by smaller rooms irregularly dispersed on its long sides, was employed in several of the larger buildings as early as the beginning of the 'Ubaid occupation. Two of the earliest examples, in levels XIX and XVIII, are indeed identified as temples by the excavators because of the presence of a low rectangular platform on the axis of the main chamber, but it is clear from their contents that others were purely domestic in character. Since excavation on the mound did not penetrate below a very limited exposure of level XX we do not know whether this house type was current at Gawra before the 'Ubaid period. Level XX produced a single tholos, and another was found in level XVII, showing that these characteristic Halaf buildings not only existed in the pre-'Ubaid phase but continued to be built alongside rectilinear structures; there was clearly no sudden break in architectural tradition.

This is not to say, of course, that the highly conventional tripartite plan of the later temples developed from the house-plan at Gawra or even in its vicinity. It almost certainly did not, for the three temples of level XIII suggest that the formal plan, here adorned both internally and externally with very complex systems of rebated pilasters, had been introduced fully fledged from elsewhere. On the other hand the first formal tripartite building at Eridu, in level XI approximately contemporary with the earliest examples of tripartite structures at Gawra, bears no obvious relationship to its predecessors, and the earliest shrine of which we have any real plan, in level XVI, is of a quite different type. The evidence from levels XV to XII is very fragmentary, and it is possible that tripartite temples in these levels were not found because they lay outside the area of the sounding; but again there is no reason to think that the type was developed in southern Sumer rather than, for instance, in Akkad, and thence exported to the north.

Unfortunately we know nothing of domestic architecture in the south at this time and therefore cannot tell how widespread tripartite houses may have been in the 'Ubaid period. By Late Uruk times they were very widely distributed in the north, and a number of typical examples have been found at Qalinj Agha, Grai Resh and fortified in the large, Late Uruk settlement of Habuba al-Kabira on the Euphrates in northern Syria. Habuba al-Kabira has many characteristics that are distinctly south

Mesopotamian, including even the use of mud-bricks identical with those employed in contemporary Warka, and we suspect it of being a colony established directly from Sumer. If so, it is reasonable to suggest that the house type was also known in southern Mesopotamia by the Late Uruk period and perhaps earlier, but this gives us no clue to its origin and still less to that of the tripartite temple which we regard as its translation into formal architecture. It seems certain, however, that it is a Mesopotamian development. Indeed one of the characteristics of Mesopotamian temples in later times is that they reproduce in many respects the architectural features of secular buildings, for they were regarded in a very real sense as the earthly homes of the gods and consequently designed to accommodate the requirements of divine households – reception, business, storage and the like – just as the houses of ordinary mortals of varying rank and wealth provided for the different functions performed within them.

Although the occurrence of such closely similar temples at Eridu and Tepe Gawra is strong evidence for close contacts, and a basic similarity in ritual observance, between northern and southern Mesopotamia from the fifth millennium onwards, this fell far short of complete standardization. There are obvious changes within the sequence of temples on individual sites, and other features indicate differences in religious tradition. Some of the Gawra temples appear, for instance, to have a special association with groups of graves, a connection not so far observed in Sumer. More striking, however, is the contrast in the treatment of earlier buildings when the occasion for their replacement arose. At Eridu, and apparently in the case of the Eye Temple at Tell Brak, convention clearly demanded that the ruins of one shrine should be preserved beneath the foundations of its successor, a practice that probably explains the appearance of the high terraces on which some of the latest prehistoric temples stood, and which may be the forerunners of the ziggurrats of later times. At Gawra, on the other hand, the earlier temples were razed to make room for their replacements, which did not even occupy the same sites. More surprisingly, the two traditions apparently coexisted within sight of one another in the twin settlements, Kullaba and Eanna, which were united at the end of the prehistoric period to form the city of Uruk. The heart of Kullaba was a tripartite temple – the "White Temple" – which stood in the Late Uruk period on a high terrace that incorporated the remains of earlier shrines going back to 'Ubaid times. In the Eanna precinct, on the other hand, the earliest levels in which we can identify monumental buildings, V and IV, show a complicated sequence of development involving the erection and destruction of vast structures with no concern for the preservation of their remains, a process which has made their excavation the most complex operation in Near Eastern archaeology. In level III, representing the so-called Jamdat Nasr phase at the very end of the Uruk period, the whole precinct was apparently leveled once more and equipped with a series of buildings of quite different character including, for the first time in the history of Eanna, a high terrace presumably with a temple on its summit. By this time the terrace temple in Kullaba had evidently gone out of use and it may be that the ritual it had housed was transferred to Eanna as a part of, or a preliminary to, the fusion of the two religious centers.

There is in prehistoric Mesopotamia no present evidence for monumental buildings that anticipate the largely – though never wholly – administrative functions of the "royal palaces" of historical times. Mesopotamian tradition, which seems to have been founded at least in part on contemporary records although it also incorporated an element of myth, ascribed the beginnings of dynastic kingship to what we now call, for that reason, the Early Dynastic period. It is indeed in the Early Dynastic period, and probably in its latter half, that we find in Sumer the first archaeological evidence for large buildings that reproduce none of the more easily recognizable architec-

Opposite: limestone cylinder seal with copper bull mount, Late Uruk (Jamdat Nasr) phase. Such seals were used for the identification of property (Ashmolean Museum, Oxford).

Above: impression of the same seal, showing cattle in the upper register and sheep below, together with byres built of reed bundles in which young animals alternate with storage jars.

Right: Marsh Arab *mudhīf* or guest house in southern Iraq. It is built of bundles of reeds and is very similar in construction to the byres depicted on the Late Uruk seal (*above*).

tural characteristics of a temple but in their very general layout foreshadow the palaces of later times. This is not to say that no distinction of status appears in houses of the prehistoric period, even in our very incomplete evidence. Obviously there were always rich and poor, and one would expect their relative wealth to be reflected in the size and complexity of their establishments. Our information from southern Mesopotamia is sadly deficient, but from Gawra, early in the Uruk phase, we have the "Round House" of level XI-A which is, in our opinion, a grander version of the traditional tripartite house-plan, surrounded by a massive circular wall that transformed it into a fortified strongpoint. The need for defense is easily explained by Gawra's position on the border between the plains and the hill-country, but it is less obvious why such a fortress should be found only in one level, and to infer from this single example the existence of "rulers" exercising individual authority over their communities is certainly unjustified.

The art of the Late Uruk period does however give us some glimpses of contemporary society, even if only in the rather limited aspect of ceremonial observance. Throughout most of Mesopotamian prehistory its art, as represented by painting on pottery or much more rarely on wall-plaster and by the manufacture of terracotta or stone figurines, was symbolic when it was not purely decorative. Much of the ornament on pottery clearly falls into the latter category, though some of the motifs, for instance the Halaf bukranium, probably had a magical or religious significance. So, clearly, did the representations of onager on the walls of houses at Umm Dabaghiyah, while some if not all of the many figurines may have served a ritual function. In Late Uruk – including Jamdat Nasr – times symbolic motifs were increasingly used both in architectural decoration and in the adornment of temple furnishings. Elaborately pilastered facades were already characteristic of ceremonial edifices. By level IV at Warka engaged columns and free-standing columns had been added to the architects' repertoire – though the latter were never widely adopted – and whole buildings were decorated with stone cone mosaic set in geometric patterns which seem, at least in some instances, to bear a significant relationship to the architectural features. That both columned facades and mosaic decoration had some symbolic meaning is shown by their representation in paint on the front of the podium in the 'Uqair temple, and in stone and precious metals on the Eye Temple podium at Brak. The walls of the latter building were also adorned with stone rosettes exactly like those found at Eanna in level III. The painted decoration at 'Uqair further includes single figures of leopards and bulls, and part of a procession of human figures of which only the feet survive.

The last feature brings us to the major development in Late Uruk art, the representation of scenes involving a number of figures and thereby presenting us with a narrative of a particular, and usually ritual, action. The most numerous examples occur on cylinder seals, now widely adopted in place of the earlier stamp seals and, by virtue of the long rectangular impressions they produced, better suited to a pictorial treatment. Here we see offerings brought to temples, as well as the more mundane activities of life such as plowing, although these too may have been associated with the economic activities of the temple organization. But the outstanding example of this narrative style is undoubtedly the so-called Warka vase, a superb piece of craftsmanship as well as our most detailed representation of a ritual scene. Its bottom registers show symbolically the crops and herds on which the wealth of the city depended, while in the upper registers a procession of naked attendants brings the produce to the temple. At their head in the topmost register is a single figure, unfortunately almost completely destroyed, dressed in a skirt with a long tassel depending from the waist and supported by a servant behind him. He faces a female figure, almost certainly the goddess Inanna, who is backed by the traditional symbols of her cult and a group of objects representing the wealth of her temple. Here the figure in the tasseled skirt is obviously the principal participant in the presentation ceremony, but it is worth noting that although the scene is a ritual one, the activity it portrays is essentially economic, so it would be dangerous to assume that he is a "priest" in our rather narrow sense of that word. We shall return to this point in the next section. A second relief, also from Warka but of much cruder workmanship, is the Lion Hunt Stele. This shows two figures, one above the other, killing lions with a spear and with a bow and arrow respectively, and is of special interest because it is the first representation in Mesopotamian art of a theme – the "hero" defeating a wild beast that embodies the untamed forces of nature – which was much used in later times to illustrate one of the traditional aspects of kingship, and indeed passed into Christian art as "St George and the Dragon." It does not of course justify any assumption that there were "kings" in the late prehistoric period, but it does emphasize the connection between even rudimentary ideas of the function of authority at this time and their formal embodiment in later institutions.

The Lion Hunt Stele from Warka, height 80 centimeters, depicting a figure killing lions, a ritual activity clearly associated in later times with kingship. Late Uruk (Iraq Museum).

City and society. By the latter part of the 4th millennium a number of settlements not only in Sumer but undoubtedly also in northern Iraq and Syria (Tall Brak, Habuba al-Kabira, and very probably sites such as Nineveh for which we have no excavated evidence) can be described as urban in the sense not only of physical size but also of specialized function. Although the focal point of such communities was certainly a temple or temple complex, a pattern whose origins as we have seen are to be identified in 'Ubaid Sumer, it is an oversimplification to explain these societies as "theocratic" or to regard "religion" as a prime cause for the growth of the earliest urban complexes. We must remember that the distinction between "religious," "social" and "economic" activities reflects modern attempts to analyze the structure and behavior of societies, and that such terms would have had no meaning in ancient Mesopotamia. In the historical period authority derived from the gods, and all individuals whom we would classify by their functions as "religious" or "secular" officials acted alike as the servants of their divine overlord. The temple was his earthly residence and accommodated his household, not only his personal attendants who performed what we should term priestly or cult services, but his secretaries ("scribes"), stewards and many servants of lesser status who administered his estates and engaged in commercial or manufacturing activities. In modern terms, then, the Mesopotamian temple functioned largely as an economic organ, a central authority engaged in the collection and distribution of surpluses not only in the form of agricultural produce but also of the products of the specialized crafts and industries it sponsored.

It is impossible to be sure how far such functions were characteristic also of prehistoric temples, but the continuity of cult at Eridu and other sites suggests that a gradual development of the temple as an institution, including its economic activities, is far more likely than a radical change in its character that happened to coincide with the invention of writing, which in itself represents a technical advance in economic administration associated from the beginning with temples. Certainly such a central mechanism for redistribution was vital to the well-being of a society in which foreign trade signified not simply the provision of luxury goods but was an activity essential to its prosperity and technological advance, and there is little doubt that the urgent necessity to look beyond immediate horizons to the outside world was a significant factor in the way in which society developed in Sumer.

The emergence of "priests" or "king-like" figures is well attested, as we have observed, in the representational art of the later Uruk period. But we have no idea to what extent these scenes portray generalized ritual or individuals of real status. At Warka the title *en* appears in the earliest (Uruk IV) texts, and may possibly be portrayed by the dominant though damaged figure on the Warka vase. The *en* was head of the temple community both in its secular and religious aspects, but it is clear that in the period of which we are writing the *en* played not so much a "priestly" role but more that of an "administrator" whose responsibilities were for the economic well-being of the community but whose duties also included related cult ritual. The title often translated "high priest" (*sanga*) appears also at this time, but it is believed that such officials were originally accountants. Neither the title translated "king" (*lugal*) nor the word which later designated a palace (*é-gal*, literally "great household") appears before the Early Dynastic period. It has been suggested that the *lugal* may originally have been selected by an assembly as a temporary war leader, but as the power of the new city-states grew, so too grew the need for a more permanent military establishment. Certainly a number of military terms now appear in the texts while the earliest buildings identified as "palaces" together with the earliest known city walls in Sumer are attributed to Early Dynastic II. We should point out, however, that the excavated evidence is sparse indeed while the presence at Habuba al-Kabira of an elaborately walled southern outpost before the end of the Uruk period makes it less certain that walled settlements were entirely lacking in Sumer at the same time.

Despite these intimations of growing centralized authority there is some reason to believe there may have been a basically "democratic" orientation of society at this time, and even perhaps of the cities themselves. We have evidence for a growing economic complexity, yet that for "ranked" society or differential wealth remains small. Moreover, the word *unken*, denoting an assembly (literally a "circle of the people"), occurs in the earliest texts, while the "Council of Elders" is mentioned as an administrator of estates in Uruk III times. Such local institutions of government are well attested in later texts, but it is difficult to judge their early role or significance in the absence of more informative textual evidence from the periods with which we are concerned.

Also difficult to elucidate are those factors which might be isolated as particularly significant to the development of the first urban civilization. Many authorities have sought for simple single-cause explanations. Among those put forward are a number we have already discussed such as trade, irrigation and religion. Warfare too is cited by some as a major precipitating factor in the growth of complex political systems. Certainly this was an activity indulged in with increasing frequency by Sumerian city-states during the Early Dynastic period, but it is clear that this activity was more a result of than a contributory factor towards urban growth. We should also emphasize that "warfare" is perhaps an exaggerated term to apply to what were often little more than petty squabbles of limited duration, while even in later periods there was rarely a standing army. Perhaps the most popular thesis among present-day anthropologists is a demographic argument in which it is asserted that population growth was the precipitating factor that created the necessity for new techniques of intensified food production which in turn provided the surpluses to support the craft and other specialization that are the generally agreed prerequisites of urban growth. Such a hypothesis is difficult to test in western Asia, however, where no one has yet devised a method by which reliable population figures can be calculated, nor are there any means of distinguishing within the archaeological record between settlement increase that is the genuine result of population growth and that resulting from a change in pattern of subsistence among already existing populations. This presents a serious drawback to any critical consideration of such demographic arguments. Moreover, the changes in society that we have already documented following upon the widespread adoption of irrigation agriculture in Sumer must certainly leave open the possible validity of the old Malthusian view, adapted by Gordon Childe, that new developments in agricultural technology came first, and led to surplus production at a level to support intensive craft specialization and population concentration if not growth. Certainly irrigation agriculture meant that surpluses could for the first time be guaranteed and that mechanisms for their redistribution or other deployment became necessary.

A number of archaeological surveys have been carried out in attempts to trace changing patterns of settlement and to test these various hypotheses. Results so far indicate, perhaps not surprisingly, that no single paradigm

Detail from the large limestone vase from Warka, depicting naked male attendants bearing agricultural offerings to the goddess Inanna. Late Uruk (Iraq Museum).

of urban growth can be applied to Sumer. Indeed different urban forms appear to have evolved for different reasons in different areas, and one can only conclude that a diversity of historical and ecological processes were responsible for the earliest development of city life. Accident of excavation, and the enthusiastic efforts of the German expedition under Professor Lenzen, have meant that we know most about the city of Uruk at this time. Yet Uruk, despite the presence in the Late Uruk period of a vast ceremonial complex in Eanna, was neither a unique religious center nor a city of unusual political importance. If later tradition can be relied upon, these roles were played by Nippur and Kish, where the patterns of urban growth appear to have differed significantly from those observed at Uruk. Unfortunately there are other problems for which the evidence is even less tangible. We can never penetrate the minds of prehistoric populations, and here may lie factors as important as those we can identify archaeologically. Certainly the Sumerians were great "achievers," enthusiastic catalogers of knowledge and, more practically, astute merchants. Whether they constituted the indigenous population of Sumer remains open to question, although the evidence for ritual continuity at Eridu provides a convincing argument for their presence already in the 'Ubaid period. But whoever the original 'Ubaid population were, the external contacts that would have accompanied their far-reaching attempts to acquire raw materials must undoubtedly have been a spur to rapid cultural innovation.

We are unlikely ever to unravel the tangled cultural and linguistic threads that we can identify in Sumer even at the time of the earliest written records. Among the languages represented at this time are of course Sumerian, an agglutinative language related to no other, together with a Semitic language, Akkadian, and possibly – though authorities are not in agreement here – another whose speakers some would credit with the invention of writing despite the fact that the earliest readable texts are in Sumerian. (The language of the Uruk IV tablets is wholly pictographic and thus cannot be identified.) It is indeed likely that a mixed population had long characterized this region and the close proximity of agricultural and grazing land in Sumer has always encouraged contact – and indeed also conflict – between groups pursuing different patterns of subsistence. It would be a mistake, however, to see necessarily in these groups evidence for different ethnic or linguistic populations. Certainly nomadic elements in later periods were largely Semitic, but there is substantial evidence for the presence of Semitic-speaking peoples already in the cities of the Early Dynastic period. It is even more imprudent to speculate about the ethnic composition of prehistoric populations, but certainly there is good reason to associate the Sumerians with southern Sumer, and no longer any convincing argument for deriving them from elsewhere. One might even venture to suggest that the Samarran farmers of central Mesopotamia are unlikely to have been either Sumerian or Semitic speakers, while certainly the peoples of the Hassuna, Halaf and Zagros settlements were essentially different and at least partially contemporary groups whose social development need not in any way have been comparable. It is only with the expansion of the 'Ubaid influence from Sumer that any coherent pattern of development can be identified for the whole of the country, and it is from this point onwards that the rise of urban settlements can be traced.

Perhaps the final comment that should be made in this last chapter is that the Sumerians, whom we believe on the balance of sometimes ambiguous evidence to have been an indigenous element in the prehistoric population of southern Mesopotamia and substantial, though not the only, contributors to the development of its earliest civilization, would not have had the least understanding of the theoretical arguments about urbanization or social organization on which we have attempted to comment. If our readers are equally befogged, they may take comfort from the fact that no ancient Mesopotamian language had words to distinguish between village, town and city, nor indeed does the idea of citizenship in our modern sense exist before the Greeks. Had any Sumerian or Babylonian been asked about the birth of his civilization, he might well have adapted the words of Topsy "It just growed."

Further Reading

Adams, R. McC., *The Evolution of Urban Society* (Chicago, Ill., 1966).

Braidwood, R. J., *Prehistoric Men* (8th ed., Glenview, Ill., 1975).

**Cambridge Ancient History*, vol. 1, parts 1 and 2 (3rd ed., Cambridge, 1970–71).

Clark, J. D., "A Reexamination of the Evidence for Agricultural Origins in the Nile Valley," *Proceedings of the Prehistoric Society*, 37 (1971).

Frankfort, H., etc., *Before Philosophy* (Harmondsworth, 1949).

Jones, T. B., ed., *The Sumerian Problem* (New York, 1969).

Lloyd, Seton, *Foundations in the Dust* (Harmondsworth, 1955).

Mellaart, J., *Çatal Hüyük* (London, 1967).

*—— *The Neolithic of the Near East* (London, 1975).

Mellink, M. J. and **Filip, J.,** eds., *Frühe Stufen der Kunst* (Berlin, 1974).

***Oates, J.,** "The Background and Development of Early Farming Communities in Mesopotamia and the Zagros," *Proceedings of the Prehistoric Society*, 39 (1973).

—— "Mesopotamian Social Organization," in Rowlands, M. J. and Friedman, J., eds., *Evolution of Social Systems,* forthcoming.

***Perrot, J.,** *La Préhistoire palestinienne* (Supplément au Dictionnaire de la Bible, Paris, 1968).

Piggott, S., ed., *The Dawn of Civilization* (London, 1962).

Struever, S., ed., *Prehistoric Agriculture* (New York, 1971).

Ucko, P. J., and **Dimbleby, G. W.,** eds., *The Domestication and Exploitation of Plants and Animals* (London, 1969).

Ucko, P. J., Tringham, R. and **Dimbleby, G. W.,** eds., *Man, Settlement and Urbanism* (London, 1972).

*Works marked with an asterisk have particularly full bibliographies.

Radiocarbon Determinations

Site	*Level*	*Date*	*Lab number*
Zawi Chemi Shanidar (Zagros)		8920 ± 300	W681
Shanidar Cave (Zagros)	B1	8650 ± 300	W667
Jericho (Jordan valley)	Mesolithic	9216 ± 107	P376
		7800 ± 240	F69 (GL69)
		7850 ± 247	F72 (GL72)
	PPN–A VII	7370 ± 150	BM252
	VI	8350 ± 200	BM106
	VI	7440 ± 150	BM251
	late VI	8350 ± 500	BM250
	late VI	8300 ± 200	BM105
	late VI	8230 ± 200	BM110
	post VI	7825 ± 110	P378
	post VI	7705 ± 84	P379
	I	7623 ± 89	P377
	upper	6855 ± 210	F40 (GL40)
	upper	6775 ± 210	F40 (GL40)
	upper	6850 ± 160	F39 (GL39)
	PPN–B early	6708 ± 101	P381
	lower	7075 ± 100	GrN963
	first	6660 ± 75	P380
	middle	7220 ± 200	BM115
	middle	7190 ± 70	GrN942
	middle	7006 ± 103	P382
	middle	6760 ± 150	BM253
	upper	6720 ± 200	GL41 (F41)
	upper	6250 ± 200	GL28
	upper	5850 ± 160	GL38
Mureybet (Syria)	end of phase I (Mesolithic)	8640 ± 140	Lv607
	phase II level I	8142 ± 118	P1216
	level I	8056 ± 96	P1215
	phase II level II	8265 ± 115	P1217
	phase II	8640 ± 170	Lv605
		8510 ± 200	Lv606
		7780 ± 140	Lv604
	phase III level X–XI	8018 ± 115	P1220
	level XVI	7542 ± 122	P1224
	level XVI–XVII	7954 ± 114	P1222
Ganj Dareh (Zagros)	level E	8450 ± 150	GaK807
	level E	6690 ± 90	SI924
	level E	6435 ± 75	SI925
	level E	6675 ± 195	SI923
	level E	6620 ± 210	SI922
	top of level E	6960 ± 170	GaK994
	level D	7018 ± 100	P1484
	level C	7289 ± 196	P1485
	upper	6938 ± 98	P1486
Çayönü (Anatolia – southeastern highlands)		7570 ± 100	GrN4458
		7250 ± 60	GrN4459
		6840 ± 250	M1609
		6620 ± 250	M1610
Aşıklı Hüyük (Anatolia)		7008 ± 130	P1240
		6857 ± 128	P1238
		6843 ± 127	P1241
		6828 ± 128	P1242
		6661 ± 108	P1239
Asiab (Zagros)		7100 ± 300	UCLA1714F
		6950 ± 100	UCLA1714B
		6750 ± 100	UCLA1714C
Jarmo (Zagros)		9250 ± 200	W665
		7090 ± 250	W607
		6880 ± 200	W651
		6000 ± 200	W652
		5800 ± 250	W608
		6575 ± 175	H551/491
		6030 ± 140	UCLA1714E
		5850 ± 120	UCLA1723A
		5320 ± 200	UCLA1723B
(plus a number of 5th-millennium dates that are clearly too late)			
Tepe Guran (Zagros)	c. level U	6460 ± 200	K1006
	level H	5810 ± 150	K879
Sarab (Zagros)	5	6006 ± 98	P466
	"lowest"	c. 5900	UCLA1714A
	4	5655 ± 96	P465
	1	5694 ± 89	P467
Ali Kosh (Khuzistan)	Bus Mordeh phase	7950 ± 200	UCLA750D
		5720 ± 170	I1489
		5430 ± 180	I1496
	Ali Kosh phase	8000 ± 190	I1490
		6900 ± 210	Sh1174
		6460 ± 200	Sh1246
		6475 ± 180	O1816, O1833
		6300 ± 175	O1845
		6150 ± 170	I1491
		5820 ± 330	O1848
		5790 ± 600	SI207
	Muhammad Jaffar phase	6970 ± 100	SI160
		6940 ± 200	SI160(R)
		5870 ± 190	I1494
		5270 ± 160	I1495
Beidha (Transjordan)	PPN–B level VI	6990 ± 160	K1086
	level VI	6765 ± 100	P1378
	level VI	6760 ± 130	K1082
	level VI	6690 ± 50	GrN5063
	level VI	6596 ± 100	P1379
	level V	6690 ± 160	K1083
	level IV	7178 ± 103	P1380
	level IV	6860 ± 50	GrN5136
	level IV	6840 ± 200	BM111
	level IV	6815 ± 102	P1381
	level IV	6780 ± 160	K1084
	level II	6600 ± 160	K1085
	late level II	6942 ± 115	P1382
	upper level II	7080 ± 50	GrN5062
Munhata (Jordan valley)	PPN–B level IVB	7210 ± 500	M1793
	level IVA	5420 ± 400	M1792
Tell Ramad (Syria)	level I	6260 ± 50	GrN4426
	level I	6250 ± 80	GrN4428
	level I	6140 ± 50	GrN4421
	level II	5970 ± 50	GrN4427

Radiocarbon dating is an extremely useful technique, but it is also a very complex one. The reader may be interested in the detailed listing below of radiocarbon determinations that apply to the sites mentioned in the text of this book (between 10,000 and 3000 BC). For the specialist it should be pointed out that all dates are BC, based on 5570±30 half-life. Fuller descriptions of samples can be found by looking up the laboratory numbers given below in the journal *Radiocarbon*. Corrected dates (MASCA), calibrated by dated dendrochronological samples, are not at present available before radiocarbon 4570 BC.

Site	*Level*	*Date*	*Lab number*
	level II	5950±50	GrN4822
Ceramic Neolithic	level III	5930±55 (?reused wood)	GrN4823
Bouqras (Syria)	level I	6190±60	GrN4818
	level I top	6290±100	GrN4852
	level II	6010±55	GrN4819
	level III	5990±60	GrN4820
Çatal Hüyük (Anatolia)	level XII	5807±92	P1374
	level X	6142±98	P782
	level X	6086±104	P1370
	level X	5987±109	P1369
	level X	5965±85	P1372
	level X	5894±102	P1371
	level IX	6240±99	P779
	level VIII	5903±97	P1367
	level VIII	5734±90	P1366
	level VII	5588±89	P778
	level VIB	5986±98	P1364
	level VIB	5962±94	P770
	level VIB	5954±111	P1362
	level VIB	5754±91	P777
	level VIB	5679±90	P797
	level VIB	5574±90	P781
	level VIA	5779±80	P1365
	level VIA	5629±86	P827
	level VIA	5622±91	P772
	level VIA	5555±93	P769
	level VI	5961±103	P1363
	level VI	5711±99	P1375
(a number of these samples come from timbers which are clearly older than the levels in which they were found)			
	level V	5690±91	P776
	level V	5549±93	P1361
	level IV	6087±96	P775
	level III	5581±94	P774
Suberde (Taurus mountains)	level II	5571±77	P796
	level II lower	6326±300	P1387
	level II lower	6299±91	P1391
	level II lower	6226±79	P1388
	level II lower	5634±85	P1389
	level II upper	6045±76	P1386
	level II upper	5957±88	P1385
Hacılar (Anatolia) Late Neolithic	level IX	5393±92	P314A
	level VII	5820±180	BM125
	level VI	5590±80	BM48
	level VI	5399±79	P313A
Chalcolithic	level IIA	5219±131	P326A
	level IA	5037±119	P315
Matarrah (Mesopotamia)	earliest level	5620±250	W623
Telul eth-Thalathat (Mesopotamia)	level XV (early Hassuna)	5570±120	TK24
Tell Halaf (Syria)	early	5620±35	GrN2660
Tell es-Sawwan (Mesopotamia)	level I	5506±73	P855
	level III (?)	5349±150	P856

Site	*Level*	*Date*	*Lab number*	*MASCA corrected date*
	level III	4858±82 (too late)	P857	
Hassuna (Mesopotamia)	level V	5090±200	W660	
Choga Mami (Mesopotamia)	"Transitional" phase	4896±182	BM483	
Arpachiyah (Mesopotamia)	well	6114±78	P585	
	TT 8 (middle Halaf)	5077±83	P584	
Chagar Bazar (Syria)	Halaf c. level 11–12	4715±77	P1487	
Banahilk (Zagros)	middle Halaf	4904±72	P1504	
		4802±85	P1502	
	late Halaf	4359±78	P1501	5060–5090
Gerikihaciyan (highlands, eastern Anatolia)	late Halaf	4515±100	GrN	5245
Tepe Gawra (Mesopotamia)	level XIX	5052±82	P1494	
	level XVIII	4470±61	P1495	5180–5240
	level XVII	4041±72	P1496	4971
	level XII	3837±72	P1497	4761
Saudi Arabia				
Site 18, 'Ain Qannas	level 12	4935±325	GX2824	
	level 11	4705±320	GX2823	5330
	level 9	5110±445	GX2821	
Site 1, Dosariyah	level 7	4950±330	GX2818	
	surface	4185±120	I5786	4910
Site 11, Abu Khanis	level 8	3710±250	GX2820	4410
	level 8	3615±255	GX2819	c. 4340
	surface	3800±65	UGa315	4470
Site 2	surface	4207±238	SI1263	4930
Tell 'Uqair	'Ubaid	4649±107	P1498	4927
Warka	late 'Ubaid	4120±160	H138/123	4770–4870
Tepe Sabz (Khuzistan)	Sabz phase	(7100±160)	UCLA750C	
		4790±190	I1497	
	Khazineh phase	5510±160	I1501	
		5250±1000	SI206	
		4975±200	UCLA750B	
	Mehmeh phase	4520±160	I1493	
		3460±160	I1500	
	Bayat phase	4220±200	SI203	
		4120±100	UCLA750A	
		4110±140	I1502	
		4110±200	SI204	
		4100±140	I1499	
		3910±230	I1503	
		3820±120	SI156	
		3750±250	SI205	
Grai Resh	unstratified Uruk	3219±64	P469	3780
		2989±75	P468	3625
Nippur	Inanna level XVII (Warka VI/V)	2722±74	P530	3350

Acknowledgments

Unless otherwise stated, all the illustrations on a given page are credited to the same source.

Ankara Museum; photo Josephine Powell 47 (bottom)
Ashmolean Museum, Oxford 12, 21 (bottom), 37, 46, 48, 79, 80 (left), 108 (top), 116 (top), 118 (top), 128, 132, 133 (top)
Dick Barnard, London 56 (bottom), 91 (bottom), 97 (bottom), 99 (bottom), 100 (left), 107 (bottom), 108 (bottom left), 111 (top), 131, 133 (bottom)
Bodleian Library, Oxford 25
P. E. Botta and E. Flandin: *Monuments de Nineve´* (1848–50) 31
Professor R. J. Braidwood, Chicago 59, 83, 84, 102, 103
British Museum, London 23, 32 (top), 38 (bottom), 58, 106, 119
British Museum, London; photo Andrew Lawson 45 (top), 47 (top)
Colorific!, London 17 (left)
Elsevier, Amsterdam 120
Roger Gorringe, London 44 (top), 53 (top), 64 (bottom left), 66 (bottom right), 82, 93 (center), 93 (bottom), 100 (right), 130 (top right)
Sonia Halliday Photographs 9, 69, 70, 104
Robert Harding Associates, London 11, 16, 19, 21 (top), 41, 52, 57, 76 (left), 125
Hirmer Verlag, Munich 38 (top), 110 (bottom)
Michael Holford Library, London 92
T. A. Holland 15
Iraq Museum, Baghdad, by courtesy of the Director General of Antiquities 43 (top), 56 (top), 99 (center), 126
Iraq Museum, Baghdad; photo Robert Harding Associates 114
Iraq Museum, Baghdad; photo Picturepoint, Jacket, 39, 136
Iraq Museum, Baghdad; photo Scala 115, 116 (bottom), 117 (right), 134
Israel Department of Antiquities and Museums 74
Jericho Excavation Fund, by courtesy of Dame Kathleen Kenyon, Frontispiece 76 (right), 77, 80 (right)
Andrew Lawson, London 45 (bottom), 72 73, 112 (top), 117 (left)
A. H. Layard: *Nineveh and its Remains* (1849) 32 (bottom), 33
Lovell Johns, Oxford 14, 64 (bottom right), 85, 124
Mansell Collection, London 35
Malcolm McGregor, London 129
James Mellaart, London 22, 60, 87, 88, 89, 90, 91 (top), 93 (top), 94, 97 (top), 98
D. & J. Oates 17 (right), 34 (bottom), 42, 43 (bottom left), 43 (bottom right), 44 (bottom), 62, 63, 64 (top), 64 (center), 65, 66 (top), 66 (bottom left), 67, 68, 78, 95, 99 (top), 101, 105 (bottom), 108 (bottom right), 109, 113 (top), 118 (bottom)
Oxford Illustrators, Oxford 112 (bottom) (by courtesy of Prof. G. Gullini, Turin), 140–148
Picturepoint, London 49, 105 (top), 107 (top), 111 (center), 123
Radio Times Hulton Picture Library, London 51
R. V. Schoder, SJ, Chicago 55
Schwitter Library, Lieli, Switzerland 40
Tate Gallery, London 27
Ian Todd 86
U.S. Geological Survey 13
University of Newcastle upon Tyne, by courtesy of Professor R. M. Harrison 50
University Museum, Philadelphia 53 (bottom), 127, 130 (left), 130 (bottom right)
Warka Report, 1932 34 (top)

The Publishers have attempted to observe the legal requirements with respect to the rights of the suppliers of photographic materials. Nevertheless, persons who have claims are invited to apply to the Publishers.

Glossary

Aceramic Without pottery, used to refer to archaeological assemblages or settlements where pottery is not in use.

Acropolis Citadel or raised part of a Greek city, the inner fortified area in which the major temples stood.

Agglutinative languages Family of languages in which compound ideas are expressed by the combining of simple words or elements. Sumerian and Turkish are both agglutinative languages, though not otherwise related.

Akkad Northern part of what was later Babylonia, that part of Mesopotamia which lies south of Baghdad, named for its Akkadian-speaking inhabitants. The city of Kish was the major urban center in Akkad in the earliest historical period.

Akkadian Earliest known dialect of eastern **Semitic**, spoken by some of the inhabitants of Mesopotamia at least as early as the third millennium BC. Together with the **Sumerians** who appear to have occupied the southernmost parts of the region, Akkadian-speaking peoples constituted a major element in the population of southern Mesopotamia from the time of the earliest written records, and possibly very much earlier.

Alabaster Hard compact form of either the carbonate or the sulphate of lime, a white or creamy stone much prized in the ancient world, especially for the manufacture of vases, statues etc.

Ali Kosh phase Aceramic phase following the **Bus Mordeh phase** at Ali Kosh, to be dated in the latter part of the seventh millennium BC.

Alluvium Soil consisting of silt deposits left by flood waters; most of southern Mesopotamia and much of the land in river valleys elsewhere consist of alluvial silt.

Anu Originally the most important of the Sumerian gods, the god of heaven, the "sky."

Appliqué Applied decoration.

Archaic painted ware Very distinctive type of painted ware associated with early levels of settlement at Hassuna on which either a lustrous red paint is employed, or the paint, or the body of the pot, or both, are burnished.

Seeder-plow, as depicted on a second-millennium BC seal

Ard "Scratch plow" which breaks the surface of the soil without turning it.

Assyria Northern part of Mesopotamia, in historical times the home of the Semitic-speaking Assyrians. Ashur, Nineveh, Nimrud and Khorsabad were at various times the capitals of Assyria.

Azurite Deep blue basic carbonate of copper, occurring in copper deposits. It was used both as an ore of copper and as a pigment.

Babylonian Later "classical" form of **Akkadian**, written in **cuneiform** script, and associated primarily with Hammurabi and the First Dynasty of Babylon (early second millennium BC). Babylonian was the *lingua franca* (common or diplomatic language) of the entire Middle East throughout most of the second millennium.

Basilica Building with a nave, apse and lateral aisles; originally used in Roman towns for the transaction of public business, its plan was early adopted for the Christian church.

Bedouin Desert-dwelling nomads of the Near East, who now account for about a tenth of the area's population. Their chief means of livelihood are their herds of goats and sheep and, in modern times, camels. They live in tents and follow a regular pattern of movement throughout the year, camping where water and grazing for their animals are available. The existence of tribes pursuing such a way of life is attested in the earliest written documents from Mesopotamia.

Bell, Gertrude Margaret Lowthian (1868–1926). Orientalist and traveler, political officer in Baghdad during World War I, Oriental Secretary to the High Commissioner in Baghdad (1920–26). She alone was largely responsible under the British Mandate for the establishment of the Iraq Antiquities Department and the Iraq Museum. Her accounts of her Near Eastern journeys and records of ancient monuments from 1892 onwards place her among the greatest and most readable of British travelers.

Beveled-rim bowl Mass-produced, mold-made crude pottery vessel characteristic of the Uruk period, particularly in its later phases. Such vessels have a very wide distribution in western Asia and are possibly to be interpreted as ration measures.

Botta, Paul-Émile (1802–70). Professional member of the French consular service, first consular agent in Mosul (1842). In 1843 he began excavations at Khorsabad, capital of the Assyrian Empire under Sargon II (722–705 BC). The magnificent stone reliefs from Sargon's palace, which Botta shipped to the Louvre (1846), provided the European public with their first view of the treasures that were to be found in ancient Assyria and created an enormous enthusiasm for further archaeological work in Mesopotamia.

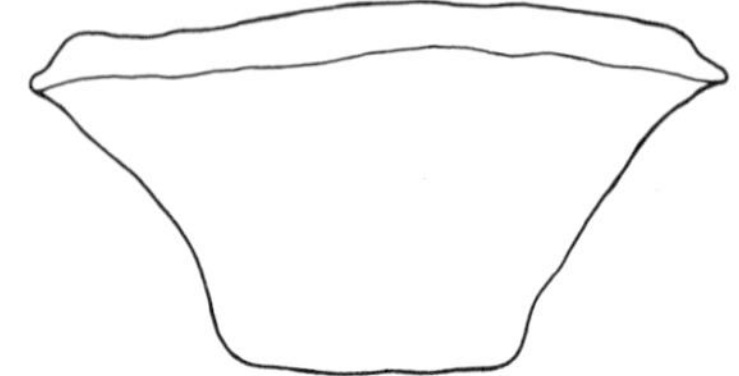

Beveled-rim bowl

Braidwood, Robert J. (1907–). Distinguished American prehistorian, Professor of Anthropology and Old World Prehistory in the University of Chicago (1954–74). Best known for his work in Kurdistan where he undertook for the Oriental Institute (Chicago) the first scientific investigation of the origins of agriculture (1948–55). His pioneer work at Jarmo, which was part of this project, is now being extended by his excavations in collaboration with the well-known Turkish archaeologist, Professor Halet Çambel, at the earlier site of Çayönü in southern Turkey (1964–). Braidwood has also excavated a number of important prehistoric sites in Iran and Syria.

Bread wheat A cultivated **hexaploid wheat** (*Triticum aestivum*), found on western Asiatic sites from the late seventh millennium onwards (Can Hasan III).

Buckingham, James Silk (1786–1855). English traveler, journalist, member of Parliament, author of a number of travel books on the Near East.

Budge, Sir Wallis (1857–1934). Keeper of Egyptian and Assyrian Antiquities in the British Museum (1893–1924). He traveled widely in the Near East purchasing cuneiform tablets and other antiquities for the British Museum. *By Nile and Tigris* (1920) provides an interesting if sometimes pompous account of his travels and experiences in Mesopotamia and Egypt (1886–1913).

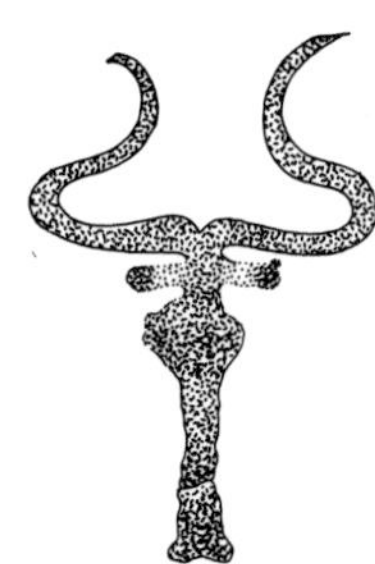

Bukranium motif from a Halaf sherd

Bukranium Greek word meaning the head of a cow, used with reference to the ancient Near East to describe the bull's head motif on **Halaf** pottery and the horned skulls installed in shrines at Çatal Hüyük and other sites.

Burnish To polish; to rub pottery while in the leather-hard or partly dry stage with a small tool or pebble in order to produce a polished surface.

Bus Mordeh phase Earliest, aceramic phase at the farming site of Ali Kosh in Khuzistan, probably to be dated early in the seventh millennium BC.

Caprid Specifically, referring to goats, but more generally to both sheep and goats, members of the sub-family Caprinae. Fragmentary bones of sheep and goats found on archaeological sites are often difficult to distinguish.

Carination Angle or ridge where the profile of a vessel wall sharply changes direction.

Celt Chisel-edged implement.

Chert Form of quartz that resembles flint but is of inferior quality.

Childe, Vere Gordon (1892–1957). Undoubtedly the most distinguished prehistorian of this century. Born in Sydney, New South Wales, he came to Oxford in 1914; in 1925 *The Dawn of European Civilization*, the first of a series of major books, was published, and in 1927 he was appointed to a newly founded chair of prehistory in Edinburgh; from 1945 to 1956 he was both Professor in and Director of the Institute of Archaeology in the University of London. Childe's major contribution lay in the more theoretical aspects of archaeology; his knowledge of the evidence was vast and he wrote with great clarity. His *The Most Ancient East* (1928) and *New Light on the Most Ancient East* (1934) represent the first important attempt at a synthesis of the prehistoric Near East evidence; his mastery of the material both in the Near East and in Europe was incredible in one individual and is unlikely, with the increasing complexity of the subject, to be equalled again.

Club wheat A **hexaploid wheat** closely related to **bread wheat**.

Cone mosaic Elaborate form of temple ornament employed in the Late Uruk period. Geometric patterns were formed by the use of different-colored clay or stone cones which were set into the wall facade or, in some cases, free-standing columns. The buildings at Uruk (Warka) provide the finest example of the use of this technique.

Cuneiform See **pictographic script**.

Cylinder seal Seal shaped like a small cylinder and bored through its long axis. Like **stamp seals** cylinder seals were used to mark property and, in later times, as "signatures," but they were rolled rather than stamped onto the clay. The pattern carved onto the seal would then emerge as a frieze-like impression on the tablet or clay sealing.

Impression of an Uruk cylinder seal

de Morgan, Jacques (1857–1924), French Director-General of Antiquities in Egypt who, on an exploratory mission in Persia in 1889–91, visited the site of Susa and immediately recognized its archaeological importance. He was instrumental in persuading the French Government not only to purchase from the shah the sole right to dig for antiquities in Persian soil but also set up the Délégation Française en Perse to exploit this concession. Under de Morgan's direction the Délégation began work at Susa in 1897 and his successors are there to this day. The finds from Susa were spectacular, among them the early painted pottery (Susa A) which remains artistically the finest prehistoric pottery ever discovered.

Dentalium Type of sea shell often used for ornamental purposes. The name derives from its long tooth-like shape.

Desiccation Drying up, used with reference to increasing aridity of climate.

Eanna Ceremonial precinct of **Inanna** at Warka.

Early Dynastic period Archaeological period covering approximately the first half of the third millennium BC during which time the first really informative written documents are found and the first genuinely historical figures emerge.

É-gal Sumerian word meaning "great household," translated "palace," the residence of the **lugal**. The terms *lugal* and *é-gal* first appear on texts of the First Early Dynastic period from Ur.

Einkorn A primitive wheat of which both the wild form (*Triticum boeotium*) and the domesticated form (*Triticum monococcum*) have diploid chromosome numbers. Einkorn has a wide distribution in the Near East and is the first cereal for which there exists possible evidence for cultivation, although still of the wild form (Mureybet, before 8000 BC).

Elamite A "suffixing" language, possibly though not certainly **agglutinative**. It was spoken in Khuzistan and perhaps further east in Iran at least as early as the late fourth millennium BC. Originally written in a **pictographic script** with Sumerian analogies, it was subsequently transcribed in an apparently unconnected linear script. Later in the third millennium it began to be written in Akkadian cuneiform in which it gradually developed a special syllabary of its own. A dialect of Elamite continued in use in Khuzistan until the 10th century AD, if not later. Its linguistic affiliation is unknown although there is a possibility that it is related to the Dravidian tongues of southern India.

Electrum Natural alloy of silver and gold.

Emmer A tetraploid form of primitive wheat of which the wild type (*Triticum dicoccoides*) is native to Palestine, in particular the Upper Jordan Valley, and to southern Turkey and northern Iraq. Wild emmer has so far been found on ancient sites only at Jarmo and Çayönü while the domesticated form (*Triticum dicoccum*) is the most common cultivated cereal found on early farming sites in the Near East from the late eighth millennium BC onwards.

En Sumerian word meaning "lord," later a political title, originally held by the spiritual head of the temple who could be either male or female depending on the sex of the principal deity of the city. In cities like Uruk where the chief deity was female (**Inanna**) the *en* attained, because of the economic responsibilities of his office, a position of major political importance as "ruler." In cities like Ur, where the *en* was female, this did not happen, and political power came to be associated with the secular office of **lugal**.

Engaged column Half-round pillar projecting from the face of a wall used singly or in a series as a form of decoration.

Enki "Lord Earth," god of the sweet waters under the earth, one of the chief deities in the Mesopotamian pantheon, in historical times the city-god of Eridu.

Eridu ware Elaborately decorated monochrome painted pottery characteristic of the earliest al 'Ubaid 1 or "Eridu" phase in southern Mesopotamia. Its known distribution is limited to a very small area roughly between Warka and Eridu; to be dated sometime around 5000 BC.

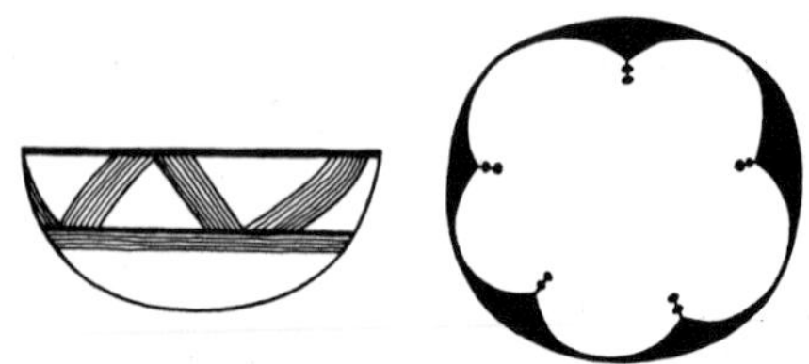

Painted 'Ubaid 1 or "Eridu" bowl

Face-pot Pottery jar ornamented with the representation of a human face, often with applied clay eyes, ears etc. First found on sites of the Samarra phase in Mesopotamia. Undoubtedly the most elaborate ones are those associated with the latest phase of occupation at Hacılar in southern Turkey.

Fertile Crescent Crescent-shaped cultivable borderland between the highland zone and the desert in western Asia. The term was first suggested in a school history, *Ancient Times* (1916) by James Henry Breasted (1865–1935), first Director of the famous Oriental Institute in Chicago (1919) and the man largely responsible for the extensive program of excavation and research carried out by the Oriental Institute in the Near East in the 1930s.

Fire-pit Any pit in which a fire has been built, but used here specifically for a type common c. 8000 BC (Mureybet, Ganj Dareh) in which it is thought that roasting or parching of food, especially grain, may have taken place. These pits contain ashes and burned stones and are sometimes surrounded by stone slabs set on edge, but there is no direct evidence as to their purpose.

Flotation Technique of isolating carbonized seeds and other plant material from the soil from an archaeological deposit by adding water (or carbon tetrachloride under laboratory conditions) and stirring gently to allow the plant material to "float" to the top. Various mechanical devices have now been devised to facilitate large-scale retrieval of such specimens.

Garrod, Dorothy Annie Elizabeth (1892–1968). Distinguished prehistorian whose work on cave sites in the Near East, in particular at Zarzi in Kurdistan and on Mt Carmel, is basic to our understanding of the early prehistory of the area. In 1939, never having held any previous academic post, she was elected to the Disney Chair of Archaeology in Cambridge, becoming the first woman professor in either Cambridge or Oxford.

Garstang, John (1876–1956). Most widely known for his excavations at Jericho (1930–36), and his work on the Hittites in Turkey. In 1929 he became Director of the British School of Archaeology in Jerusalem and first Director of Antiquities, creating the Department of Antiquities for the British Mandate government. In 1937–39 and again in 1946 he excavated the site of Yümük Tepe near Mersin in southern Turkey, investigating some 10 meters of Neolithic deposits. He was the first Director of the British Institute of Archaeology at Ankara in Turkey (1948).

Glume Husk of grain.

Groats Coarsely ground grain which can be cooked into a mush or gruel but is unsuitable for bread-making.

Haematite Iron oxide, an ore of iron; varies from a red earthy powder, sometimes known as red **ocher**, to a dark shiny material.

Hajji Muhammad ware Pottery characteristic of the second, al 'Ubaid 2 phase in southern Iraq, but found also throughout the succeeding 'Ubaid 3 levels. Distribution: from Mandali, east of Baghdad, to Ain Qannas near Hofuf in Saudi Arabia; to be dated in the first half of the fifth millennium BC. Particularly characteristic is the use of large areas of solid dark paint and "reserve" decoration.

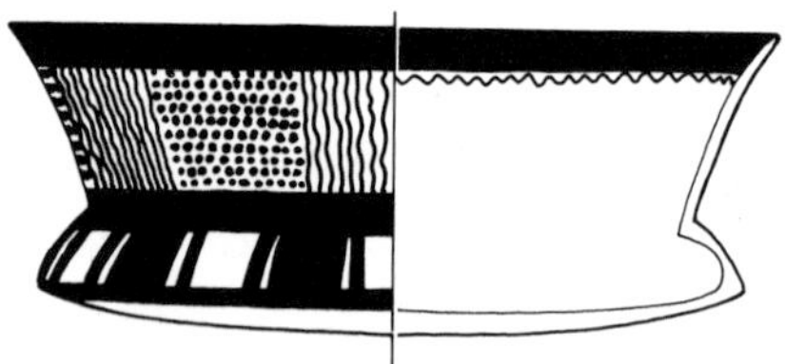

Halaf bowl from Arpachiyah

Halaf ware Elaborately ornamented, sometimes polychrome painted prehistoric pottery named after the site of Tell Halaf in northern Syria where it was first discovered by Baron Max von Oppenheim. Better known from the excavations at Arpachiyah and now Yarim Tepe II, Halaf ware has a very wide distribution on sites of the late sixth to mid-fifth millennium BC, from the Mediterranean through northern Syria and Iraq northwards to Lake Van and even into the Caucasus.

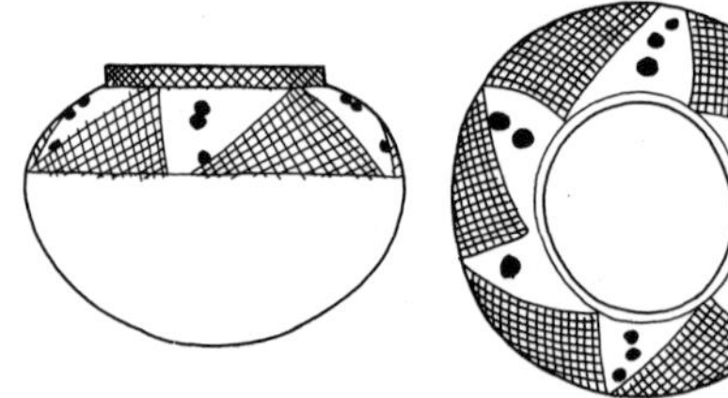

Hassuna standard painted ware

Hassuna period Earliest phase (sixth millennium BC) of farming settlement so far identified in the northern plain of Mesopotamia. Hassuna material would appear to be restricted to this area. Evidence for the earliest Hassuna phase so far known comes from Umm Dabaghiyah and Tell es-Sotto, and perhaps also Telul eth-Thalathat near Tell Afar.

Herodotus Greek historian whose works earned him the title "Father of History." Born at Halicarnassus in southwestern Turkey c. 485 BC, he died in Italy in 425 BC. As a young man he traveled widely in the Near East, and his comments on countries in the Persian Empire and their history are of great interest to modern scholars. His description of the city of Babylon is especially well known, though it is unlikely that he ever visited it.

Hexaploid wheat Polyploid mutant containing 42 (6×7) chromosomes. **Bread wheat** (*Triticum aestivum*) would appear to be the earliest hexaploid wheat found in western Asia; it contains two sets of chromosomes present in the tetraploid (4×7 chromosomes) emmer-durum wheats plus a third set found in the diploid (2×7 chromosomes) wild goat-face grass (*Ae. squarrosa*). Since no wild hexaploid wheat occurs in nature, it is assumed that the hexaploid bread wheat developed only after the advent of wheat agriculture through a crossing of the wild goat-face grass with cultivated tetraploid wheat (**emmer**).

Hilprecht, H. V. German-American Assyriologist who took part in the first American expedition to Nippur (1888). His book *Exploration in Bible Lands during the Nineteenth Century* (1903) provides a contemporary though often critical account of the work of his predecessors in Mesopotamia.

Holocene Most recent geological period, in which we are still living. Most authorities date its beginning in Europe to about 8300 BC, after the end of the Last Ice Age. The **Pleistocene**-Holocene boundary in the Near East is much less clear.

Ice Age Term commonly applied to the last great period in the earth's geological history known as the **Pleistocene**. The Pleistocene began perhaps some three million years ago and was a time of great climatic change. It is known as the Ice Age because on at least three or four occasions large parts of the earth's surface were covered with glaciers.

Inanna (correctly Innin) Sumerian goddess, queen of heaven, daughter of **Anu**, deity primarily responsible for fertility, the Semitic goddess Ishtar. Inanna was the goddess honored in the **Eanna** precinct at Warka and was also tutelary deity of another important early city, Kish.

Incised ware Pottery ornamented with a pattern cut or scratched into the clay. Incised ware occurs as part of both the Hassuna and Samarra assemblages.

Isohyet Line drawn on a map connecting places with equal rainfall.

Jamdat Nasr Site near Kish excavated by Langdon (1925–26) and Watelin (1928), at which was first found the attractive polychrome pottery (plum red and black paint) that is characteristic at some sites of the latest phase of the Uruk period (Uruk III). Clay tablets of this phase have been found here, at 'Uqair and at Warka.

Kenyon, Dame Kathleen Renowned for her excavations at Jericho (1952–58) and Jerusalem (1961–67). Formerly lecturer in Palestinian archaeology at the Institute of Archaeology, University of London; Principal of St Hugh's College, Oxford (1962–73).

Kilim Type of thin woven woolen rug, worked like a tapestry but by a method that creates two equal surfaces on the right and reverse sides of the fabric. Kilims are still made in tribal areas of the Near East and are commonly decorated with elaborate geometric ornament.

King-List List written in Sumerian of the earliest cities exercising "kingship" and their rulers, compiled from a number of legendary and historical sources, probably at the time of Utu-hegal of Uruk (2123–2113 BC). The King-List begins with a preamble enumerating five cities "before the Flood" after which "kingship" reappears in Kish. The first known royal inscription is of the penultimate king of this first dynasty of Kish, Enmebaragesi (or Mebarasi), c. 2600 BC.

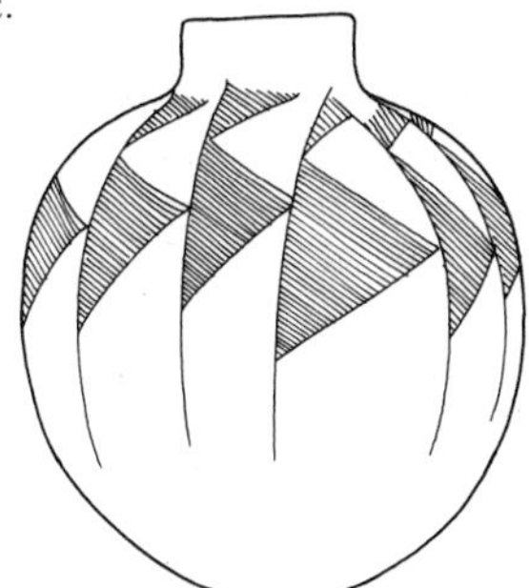

Hassuna incised ware

Koldewey, Robert (1855–1925). Distinguished German archaeologist who excavated Babylon on behalf of the *Deutsche Orient-Gesellschaft* (1899–1914).

Kurd Inhabitant of the mountainous northeastern region of Iraq known as Kurdistan and of adjacent areas of Turkey, Iran and Syria; the language spoken by the Kurds is a dialect of Farsi (modern Persian).

Lapis lazuli Semiprecious stone, a rich deep blue in color, often flecked with gold. It is a relatively rare stone, and its only source in the Near East is Badakshan, deep in the mountains of modern Afghanistan. Lapis lazuli was a highly prized commodity in ancient times, and was imported into ancient Mesopotamia at least as early as the end of the al 'Ubaid period.

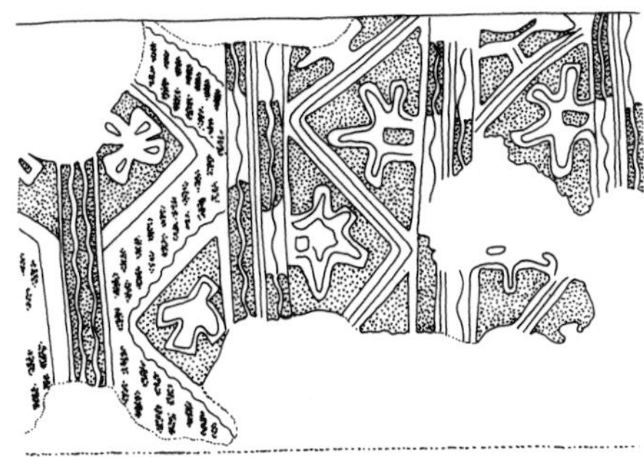

Kilim pattern from a wall painting, Çatal Hüyük

Lawrence, Thomas Edward (1888–1935). "Lawrence of Arabia." Famous as a leader of irregular troops and adviser to the Emir Faisal during the Arab Revolt, about which he wrote in *Seven Pillars of Wisdom* (1926). He began his career as an archaeologist with Hogarth and later with Campbell **Thompson** and **Woolley** at Carchemish on the Turkish-Syrian frontier (1911–14). Unlike his colleagues in the Arab bureau in Cairo, he never returned to archaeology after the war; he became Aircraftman Shaw of the R.A.F., a role he assumed when he failed to achieve all he had hoped for the Arab cause after the war, and was killed in a motorcycle accident in 1935.

Layard, Sir Austen Henry (1817–94). One of the most brilliant and controversial figures of Victorian England – pioneer archaeologist, member of Parliament and government minister, diplomat and ambassador, art-historian and author. In two enduringly readable books, *Nineveh and its Remains* (1849) and *Nineveh and Babylon* (1853), he recounted the pioneer excavations he conducted in Mesopotamia between 1845 and 1852 that made him world famous. At Nimrud and Nineveh he explored the palaces of the great Assyrian kings with their monumental sculptured reliefs, carved ivory furniture inlays and richly varied metalwork. There and in southern Iraq he discovered many inscribed tablets giving valuable impetus to the currently developing science of Assyriology. Nothing in his ensuing stormy political and diplomatic career was ever to match this achievement, which revealed his great energy, enterprise and sense of adventure as well as an unusual talent for writing about his work.

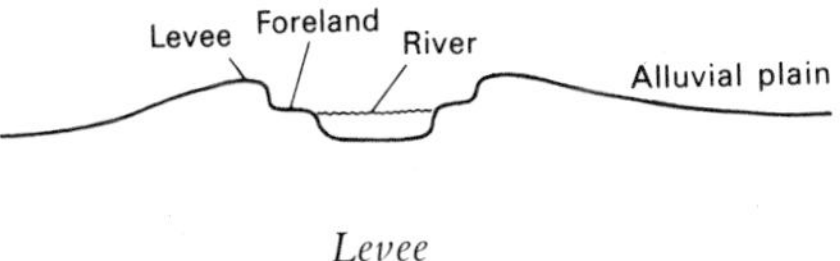

Levee

Lenzen, Heinrich J. Distinguished German archaeologist who was a member of the German expedition at Warka 1931–39. After World War II he returned to Baghdad as Director of the German Institute and reopened the excavations both at Warka and at Babylon where work had also been carried out by the *Deutsche Orient-Gesellschaft* before World War I. Lenzen is particularly noted for his meticulous excavation of the important Late Uruk levels at Warka.

Levee Natural raised bank formed along a river by the deposition of flood sediment.

Linseed Seed of the flax plant, cultivated on prehistoric sites in the Near East, in particular those where irrigation was practiced. The wild form is found at Çayönü c. 7000 BC while domesticated linseed occurs at Ramad before 6000 BC (dry farming). It is uncertain whether flax was first cultivated for its oily seeds or the fibers of its stem; the seeds were certainly a common source of oil in later periods.

Lloyd, Seton Howard Frederick (1902–). One of the most distinguished of English archaeologists working in the Near East. He began his career as an architect, first with the Egypt Exploration Society and then with the Oriental Institute (Chicago) in the Diyala and at Khorsabad. As adviser to the Directorate-General of Antiquities in Baghdad (1939–49) his work at Hassuna, Tell 'Uqair and Eridu, in collaboration with Professor Fuad Safar and Sayid Mohammed Ali Mustafa, laid the foundations for the study of Mesopotamian prehistory. From 1949 to 1961 he was Director of the British Institute of Archaeology in Ankara, and from 1962 to 1969 Professor of Western Asiatic Archaeology at the Institute of Archaeology, University of London.

Lug On pottery, a projecting piece applied to the body of the pot: lugs are often attached to cooking pots to facilitate lifting.

Lugal Sumerian word meaning "great man," in historical periods translated "king." In contrast to the **en**, the lugal was from the beginning a purely secular leader. His residence, the **é-gal**, was merely his own large private manor house, which, because of his office, came to take on the public aspects of a "palace."

Lyell, Sir Charles (1797–1875). Scottish geologist whose *Principles of Geology* (1830–33) may be ranked next after Darwin's *Origin of Species* among the books which exercised the most powerful influence on scientific thought in the 19th century and helped lead, ultimately, to a general acceptance of the real antiquity of prehistoric man.

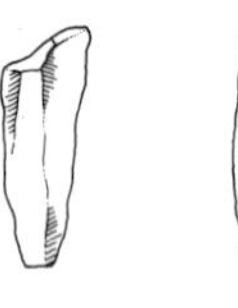

Microlithic stone tools

Malachite Copper carbonate, an ore of copper; a green mineral that takes a high polish.

Mallowan, Sir Max (1904–). Distinguished English archaeologist who began his career with **Woolley** at Ur (1925–30) and Campbell **Thompson** at Nineveh (1931–32), where he was responsible for the deep sounding that revealed for the first time the prehistoric pottery later known as Hassuna. In 1933 he excavated Arpachiyah and from 1934 until the war carried out surveys along the tributaries of the Euphrates in northeast Syria and worked at Brak and Chagar Bazar. After the war he returned to Nimrud where he launched a highly successful expedition, of which the most spectacular discoveries were many thousands of beautifully carved ivories. Sir Max was Professor of Western Asiatic Archaeology at the Institute of Archaeology, London (1949–58) and Director of the British School of Archaeology in Iraq (1947–61).

Marsh Arab Inhabitant of the marsh areas of southern Iraq.

Megaron Greek word for "hall," used to describe a type of house plan found on early Greek and Aegean sites with a long room and an entrance porch at one end.

Mellaart, James (1925–). Noted British archaeologist, since 1964 lecturer in Anatolian archaeology at the Institute of Archaeology, University of London. Has made many contributions to Anatolian prehistory, in particular in his excavations at Çatal Hüyük and Hacılar.

Mesolithic "Middle Stone Age," a period between the **Palaeolithic** and the **Neolithic** which in Europe is marked by climatic change after the Last Ice Age and significant changes in subsistence pattern. In the Near East, where there were not the major changes of climate that took place in Europe, the period is short and poorly differentiated. In both areas, however, the extensive use of bone implements and **microlithic** stone tools is characteristic.

Microliths Very small chipped stone tools, usually set in handles or shafts to make composite tools.

Mollusc shells Shells of snails, mussels etc.

Muhammad Jaffar phase Latest phase of occupation so far excavated at Ali Kosh in Khuzistan, following the **Ali Kosh phase** and probably to be dated to the first half of the sixth millennium BC. The earliest pottery so far found in Khuzistan comes from the Muhammad Jaffar phase.

Naked barley Mutant form in which the husk or glume can be freed easily by threshing, in contrast to the primitive tough-glumed forms.

Natufian Name used to describe the archaeological period in Palestine which follows the latest Upper **Palaeolithic** phase and in which the first evidence for settled villages is found. Characterized by microlithic stone tools and the extensive use of bone implements. Named for the cave site in the Wadi al-Natuf where it was first identified by Dorothy **Garrod** in 1928.

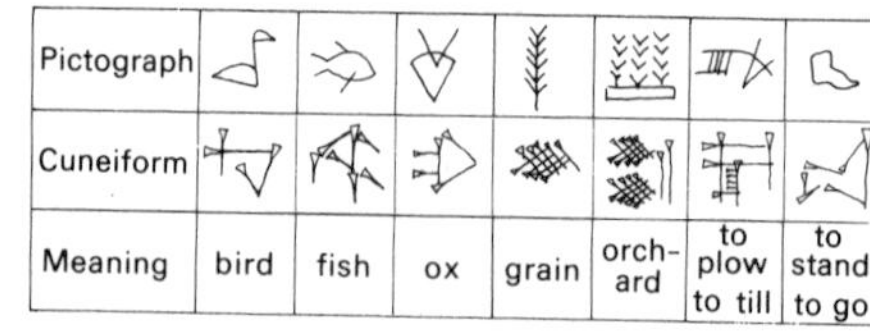

Pictograph							
Cuneiform							
Meaning	bird	fish	ox	grain	orchard	to plow to till	to stand to go

Pictographic symbols and their cuneiform equivalents

Neolithic "New Stone Age." The archaeological stage following the **Mesolithic** in which, theoretically, farming villages are found, and pottery and ground stone tools are widely used while metal is not. This term now has little meaning in the Near East where settled villages occur before agriculture; and at some sites there is evidence of the use of metal before pottery.

Nephrite Hard, green stone, a variety of jade.

Neutron activation Method of analysis to determine the proportions of various elements present in an object. The specimen is bombarded with neutrons, becomes weakly radioactive and emits gamma rays. Analysis of the gamma ray spectrum shows even minute quantities of chemical elements.

Nomad See **Bedouin**.

Oasis Small area, well supplied with water in an otherwise desert environment.

Obsidian Natural, usually black, glass formed by volcanic activity. When available it was preferred to flint for making chipped stone tools, since a much sharper cutting edge could be made. There are a number of obsidian sources in volcanic areas of Turkey. Material from each source has a distinctive composition.

Ocher Kinds of native earth consisting of clay and an oxide of iron, used as pigments varying from light yellow to brown (see **haematite**).

Onager Type of wild ass (*Equus hemionus*), once commonly found in areas of treeless steppe in western Asia and hunted both in prehistoric and later times.

Oryx Variety of antelope that has been hunted to extinction in its native Saudi Arabia.

Palaeobotany Study of plant remains from archaeological sites, usually carbonized seeds or seed impressions.

Palaeolithic "Old Stone Age." The period during which tools were made predominantly of chipped stone and when neither polished stone nor metal was in use. The Palaeolithic begins with the emergence of early forms of man and ends with the close of the **Pleistocene** Ice Age. The Upper Palaeolithic begins around 40,000 BC with the advent of Homo sapiens (the modern form of man) and improved forms of too

Petrie, Sir Flinders (1853–1942). One of the greatest of the 19th-century archaeologists whose work in Egypt and Palestine not only provided the foundation for modern studies of ancient Egypt but laid the basis of "artifact analysis" in archaeology and the principles of seriation – comparative dating on typological grounds – in a system which he named "sequence dating."

Pictographic script Type of writing using pictures for words. The earliest writing in Mesopotamia is pictographic. It later developed into the more schematic system known as cuneiform, named for the "wedge-shaped" strokes formed in writing with a stylus on tablets made of clay. In later periods the cuneiform sign, while retaining its original pictographic meaning, acquired phonetic or syllabic readings as well.

Place, Victor (1818–75). **Botta**'s successor in Mosul (1852), a French architect who reopened the excavations at Khorsabad and completed the plans of Sargon's palace and other buildings on the summit of the mound.

Pleistocene Geological period corresponding to the last great Ice Age. Estimates based on potassium-argon dating place the beginning of this period between 3·5 and 1·3 million years ago; it ended with the retreat of the last glaciers in Europe c. 8300 BC.

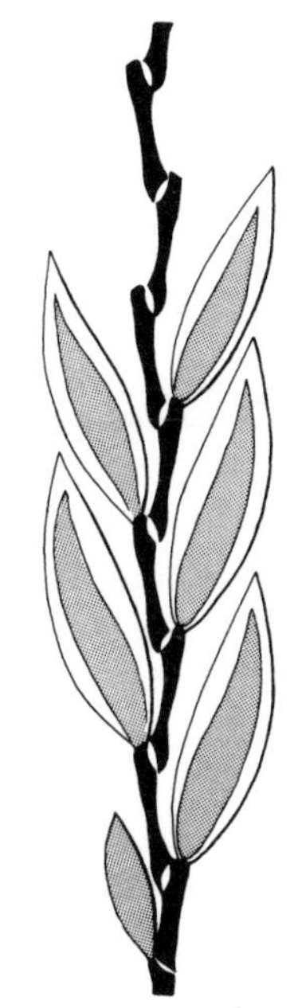

Schematic diagram of a cereal spike

Pollen core Stratified core taken by boring through soil or sediments, normally lake sediments or peat bogs in which plant pollen is well preserved. Pollen from the different layers is analyzed to give information about the contemporary climate.

Porter, Sir Robert Ker (1775–1842). English painter and traveler. In 1804 he was appointed historical painter to the Tsar of Russia. In 1811 he married a Russian princess. In 1817 he traveled to the Near East where he made many valuable drawings and transcribed a number of cuneiform inscriptions. A book describing these travels was published in 1821. Knighted in Swedish, German and English courts, his wide popularity together with his paintings did much to stimulate interest in the newly found antiquities of Assyria and Babylonia.

PPN-A Pre-Pottery Neolithic A. An archaeological phase known largely from the site of Jericho and dated to the eighth millennium BC.

PPN-B Pre-Pottery Neolithic B. A phase in the Levant following PPN-A and dated to the seventh millennium BC. As the name suggests, pottery is not yet found, although its use was known on contemporary sites in the Zagros. There is, however, evidence for farming and herding at both Jericho and Beidha.

Proto-Neolithic Term which has been invented to circumvent the unsatisfactory **Mesolithic-Neolithic** terminology. Used in particular at Jericho to describe a phase of settlement without architecture, falling between the "Mesolithic" shrine and the "Neolithic" though not necessarily farming villages of "Pre-Pottery Neolithic A."

Quern Large flat stone on which grain is ground by rubbing with another smaller hand stone. Prehistoric querns are often "saddle-shaped."

Rachis Stem of grasses, including cereals. Wild cereals have what is known as a brittle rachis which shatters easily and constitutes an important part of natural seed dispersal. In domesticated cereals the rachis or axis is "tough" and does not shatter, thus enabling more efficient harvesting by man. In the diagram the black, composite column is the rachis or axis. Its component parts, the internodes, are separated by white interstices denoting the points at which, in the wild cereal, the rachis comes apart in sections or units consisting of the internode with attached spikelet. These disintegration points may become solid by mutation; then the axis does not fall apart but remains one tough column. This toughness of the spike is the most significant property in domestication. The spikelet consists of two glumes or husks (the dotted area) enclosing one or more florets (white area) which develop into the fruit or grain.

Radiocarbon dating Method of dating organic material by measuring its carbon 14 content. Living matter contains a known percentage of the radioactive isotope of carbon (C-14). At the time of death radioactive decay begins to take place, the carbon 14 returning to nitrogen 14 and emitting a beta particle in the process which can be "counted." After 5,730 years half of the original C-14 content will have disappeared; this figure is said to represent the "half-life" of C-14. In the computation of radiocarbon dates a previous less accurate half-life of 5,568 years is used to avoid the confusion that would result from changing the basis on which the dates are calculated. Thus the dates quoted in this book, on the old half-life, are consistently too young. In the chart on p. 138 each date is quoted with a "standard deviation." It must be understood that owing to the random nature of radioactive decay the true date of any sample is no more likely to be the mean or average date than a date at the limits of the deviation. Other factors affect the general reliability of dates, especially in the period c. 5000–2000 BC. There now exist calibration curves based on tree rings of known age from which radiocarbon samples have been tested. These enable approximations to calendar years to be made, but there is still disagreement over the curves themselves and their general applicability. Near Eastern archaeologists tend not to "calibrate" their dates as most prehistoric dates in this region lie considerably earlier than the earliest dendrochronological (tree-ring) samples. The earliest published calibrated date is radiocarbon 4760 BC/calendar 5350 BC. Charcoal and charred grain, both likely to be contemporary with the archaeological level in which they are found, give the most dependable dates; bone and shell are less reliable, and large timbers that are often reused from earlier buildings can give very misleading results.

Rawlinson, Sir Henry Creswicke (1810–95). English soldier, scholar, diplomat, member of Parliament, a man of extraordinary personality, Rawlinson is best remembered as a pioneer Assyriologist. It was he who obtained, at considerable personal risk, the full copy of the famous trilingual inscription of Darius at Behistun. His translation of this text, published in 1846, was as important for the decipherment of cuneiform as was the translation of the Rosetta Stone to that of ancient Egyptian. Rawlinson's many learned contributions to ancient history included the publication of a number of cuneiform texts, the *Outline of the History of Assyria* (1852), which was drawn up "in great haste, amid torrents of rain, in a little tent upon the mound of Nineveh, without any aids beyond a pocket Bible, a notebook of inscriptions, and a tolerably retentive memory," and many important geographical notes on his travels published by the Royal Geographical Society.

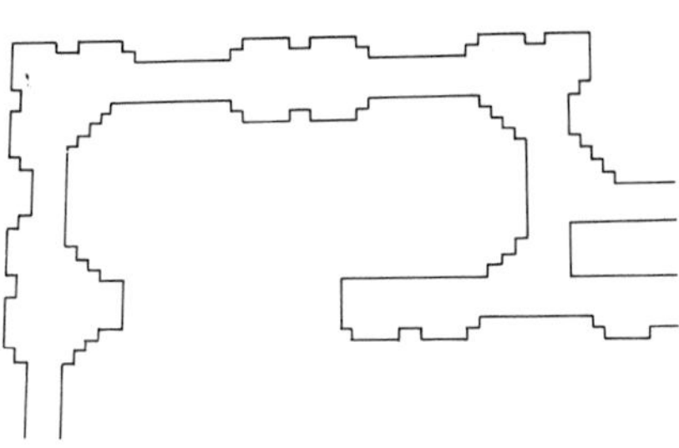

Rebated pilasters, Tepe Gawra

Rebated pilaster Regular projection from a wall face with its outer corners stepped back.

Revetment Retaining wall or facing.

Rich, Claudius James (1787–1820). One of the most brilliant and linguistically gifted of 19th-century English travelers and writers in the Middle East. Rich was the first Resident of the East India Company in Baghdad and devoted much time to the investigation of the archaeology of the country. In 1820 ill health forced him to the less taxing climate of Kurdistan, and his travels there form the subject of his most important book, *Narrative of a Residence in Koordistan*. He died of cholera in Shiraz in 1820, at the premature age of 33.

Rift valley Long steep-sided valley formed by subsidence of the earth's crust. The Jordan valley is an example.

Salination Process of becoming increasingly salt. Owing to lack of drainage the salt content of flood water in Mesopotamia tends to become concentrated in the soil. As soil salinity increases, fertility is reduced until eventually the land has to be abandoned as totally unproductive.

Interior decoration on a Samarra bowl

Samarra ware Type of elaborately decorated prehistoric pottery first found by the German traveler and archaeologist E. Herzfeld in a prehistoric cemetery beneath the 9th-century AD Islamic capital, Samarra, which he was excavating (1912–14). For many years this prehistoric Samarra ware was thought to be only a luxury product associated with the Hassuna culture, but recent excavations at Sawwan and Choga Mami clearly show that it is characteristic of a separate archaeological assemblage found across north-central Mesopotamia, between Baghouz and Choga Mami, south of the lands occupied by the people of the Hassuna villages. These Samarran settlements lie south of the zone where rain-fed agriculture is possible and represent the first extensive exploitation of irrigation agriculture.

Sanga Administrative head of a temple whose original duties appear to have been those of an accountant.

Sargon See **Botta**.

Scapula Shoulder-blade.

Schliemann, Heinrich (1822–90). German merchant who retired at the age of 46 to pursue a life-long fascination with archaeology, and in particular to devote himself to discovering the remains of Troy. This he accomplished in four seasons of excavation at the site of Hissarlik in northwestern Turkey. He was one of the first to recognize the problems of excavating stratified **tells**. His work at Troy aroused tremendous interest and together with that at Mycenae in Greece proved for the first time the existence of prehistory in the Aegean.

Semitic languages Sub-group of the Hamito-Semitic language family which includes among its modern forms Hebrew and Arabic. An early form of an eastern dialect of Semitic, **Akkadian**, was spoken by some of the earliest inhabitants of southern Mesopotamia, particularly in the northern part later known as Akkad. In later times a number of Semitic-speaking groups are known to have had their origins in Saudi Arabia.

Shaft grave Grave in which the burial chamber is approached by a vertical shaft.

Sherd Piece of broken pottery. Archaeologists use such broken pieces to identify and date archaeological sites and the levels within them.

Six-row barley Form of barley which has six fertile kernel rows as opposed to the two found in **two-row barley**. It is uncertain whether the six-row form has a wild ancestor, or is a mutant of the two-row form.

Slag Fused refuse left after smelting.

Spatula Broad-bladed instrument for working pigments etc.

Speiser, Ephraim Avigdor (1902–65). Distinguished American Orientalist who was responsible for, and the first director of, the excavations at Tepe Gawra (1927, 1931–32, 1936–37) and Tell Billah (1930–32). Born in Galicia, he emigrated to America in 1920 and settled in Philadelphia where at the University of Pennsylvania he was to have a brilliant career as a philologist and historian. His excavations at Gawra were of the greatest importance for Mesopotamian prehistory.

Spelt A hulled **hexaploid wheat** apparently not found in the Near East, with the possible exception of Yarim Tepe. It is common later in prehistoric Europe.

Stamp seal from Tepe Gawra

Stamp seal Small object, usually made of stone and often button-shaped, with a pattern cut into the face for impression on clay. Stamp seals are found as early as the sixth millennium BC, especially on sites with Halaf and Samarra material, and come into common use towards the end of the 'Ubaid period. They are used to mark portable property to which a piece of clay bearing the impression of the seal is "tied."

Standard painted ware Monochrome painted pottery of the **Hassuna period**; the term is used to distinguish the later matt-surface ceramic (standard ware) from the earlier burnished or lustrous-painted pottery (**archaic painted ware**). The standard Hassuna wares also include pottery decorated with **incised** ornament and some that is both painted and incised.

Stele Upright stone slab, decorated with carvings, inscriptions or both.

Steppe Level plain devoid of forest.

Sumer Southernmost part of Mesopotamia, inhabited in the fourth millennium BC and almost certainly earlier by people speaking the Sumerian language. The sites of Ur, Eridu and Warka are in Sumer.

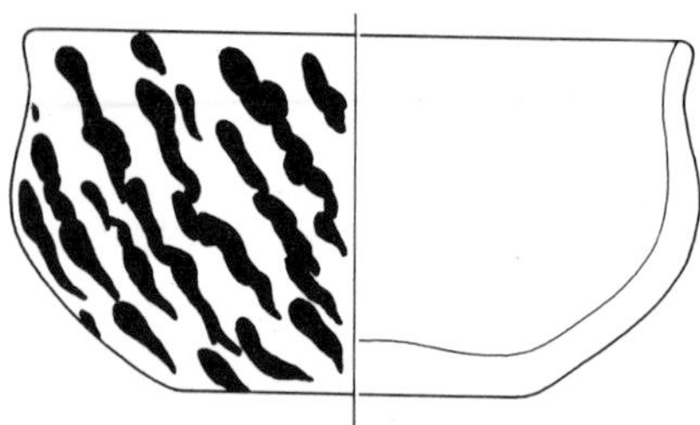

Tadpole-painted bowl from Jarmo

Sumerian language Language spoken by a large proportion of the inhabitants of **Sumer** in the **Early Dynastic** and almost certainly much earlier periods. It had died out as a spoken language by the end of the third millennium BC but continued in use as the preferred language for religious and literary composition well into the second millennium, if not later. In structure Sumerian is an **agglutinative** language, that is one in which elements are combined together to express compound ideas; it is a language with no known relatives.

Tadpole ware Name coined by **Braidwood** for the painted pottery found at early Zagros farming settlements. The name derives from the irregular tadpole-shaped pattern.

Tauf Arabic word for packed mud walling. The mud is mixed with straw to prevent cracking and is simply piled by hand in "courses" which are allowed to dry before the next higher course is added.

Tell Arabic word used for an artificial mound created by the gradual accumulation of occupation debris resulting from long periods of occupation on the same site and the associated rebuilding or replacement of houses and other structures. The use of mud-brick as a building material is largely responsible for the rapid growth of such mounds in the Near East.

Theocracy State or government ruled by gods, directly or indirectly through a priestly class.

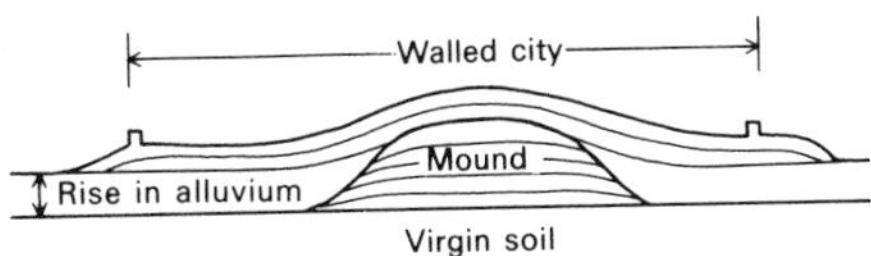

Section through a Mesopotamian tell

Tholos Circular domed structure, a term originally applied by archaeologists to Mycenaean tombs.

Thompson, Reginald Campbell (1876–1941). Noted English Assyriologist. Excavated on behalf of the British Museum at Carchemish (1911), Nineveh (1927–31) and at Eridu (1918).

Thomsen, Christian Jurgenson (1788–1865). First curator of the National Museum in Copenhagen. Thomsen arranged his collections by classifying them into three ages of Stone, Bronze and Iron, representing three chronologically successive stages in man's history. Although the idea itself was not entirely new, it was Thomsen who developed it, emphasizing the need for accurate description and classification of antiquities, thus laying the basis for the future discipline of prehistoric archaeology.

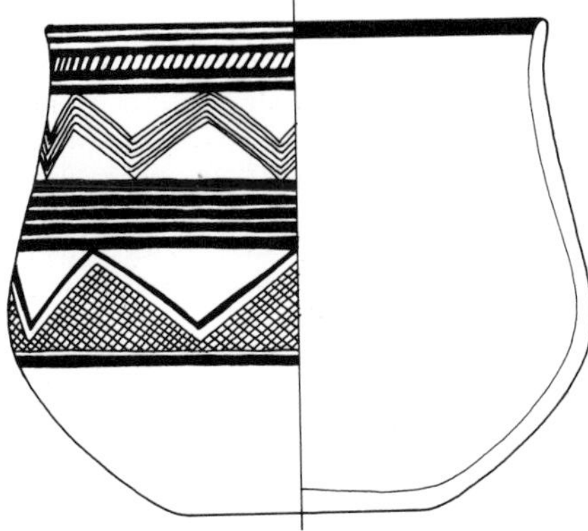

A "Transitional" vessel in the Samarran style

Transhumant Referring to a form of subsistence in which part but not all of a settled farming community follows a pattern of nomadic herding for part of the year. In western Asia flocks and herds are often taken over considerable distances for summer grazing.

Transitional Word often used to describe an archaeological phase in which traits characteristic of both the preceding and succeeding phases appear. Used specifically of a type of post-Samarran pottery found at Choga Mami (c. 5000 BC) and sites in Khuzistan which combines elements of the Samarran style with those of **Eridu** and **Hajji Muhammad**.

Tripartite building Very distinctive building plan common to early Mesopotamian temples and houses of the 'Ubaid and Uruk periods; such buildings have a long central chamber with symmetrically disposed side rooms.

Tundra Treeless Arctic steppe or plain.

Two-row barley *Hordeum spontaneum*, the wild barley found on sites in western Asia, and its domesticated form (*H. distichum*) have two fertile kernel rows; **six-row barley**, possibly a mutant of the two-row form, is also found.

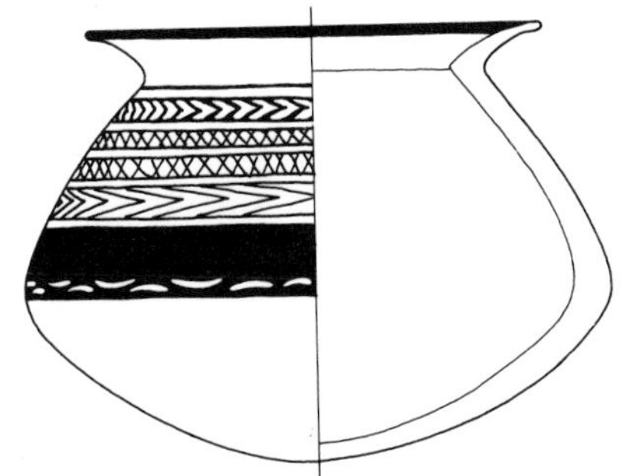

Painted 'Ubaid jar, Arpachiyah

'Ubaid ware Named for the site of Tell al 'Ubaid near Ur, where it was first discovered, this monochrome-decorated, buff or green pottery is found on fifth-millennium sites in Mesopotamia. Slight changes in style of painting together with changes in other artifacts enable archaeologists to differentiate four chronological phases of the archaeological period associated with the use of 'Ubaid ware. The earliest, 'Ubaid 1 or "**Eridu**," is confined to **Sumer**, but by the beginning of 'Ubaid 3 (c. 4500 BC) pottery of this very distinctive style is found in quantity not only in Mesopotamia but also in adjacent areas of Iran, Syria and Saudi Arabia.

Unken Sumerian word for "assembly" which, like the title **en**, appears on the earliest **pictographic** texts.

Uruk ware Named for the site of Warka, where the only sequence for the archaeological phase identified by this pottery has been excavated. Uruk pottery is wheel-made, mass-produced and for the most part undecorated. Especially characteristic, particularly in the latter part of the period, are tall jars with drooping spouts, **beveled-rim bowls** and the use of twisted handles and reserved slip decoration. The Uruk period occupies most of the fourth millennium BC; material of this phase is found throughout Mesopotamia and in northern Syria.

Uruk ware

Ussher, Archbishop (1581–1656). Learned and distinguished scholar, born in Dublin, later Archbishop of Armagh. Of his numerous writings the best known is the *Annales Veteris et Novi Testamenti* (1650–54) which produced a long-accepted chronology of the Scriptures, the Creation being fixed at 4004 BC.

Woolley, Sir (Charles) Leonard (1880–1960). Perhaps the best known of British Near Eastern archaeologists, noted particularly for his work at Ur (1922–34). Here he excavated a great sequence of settlement going back to the al 'Ubaid period in the fifth millennium BC, establishing for the first time the true chronological position of this prehistoric culture. His most startling discoveries, however, were made in the famous Royal Cemetery which yielded incomparable treasures of early Sumerian civilization, now housed in the Iraq, University of Pennsylvania and British Museums. He began his life as a field archaeologist in Egypt, but in 1912 succeeded Campbell **Thompson** as director of the excavations at Carchemish (1912–14, 1919). In his later years he dug at al Mina and Alalakh in northern Syria. Not only was he a highly successful excavator, but he was a delightful raconteur and a fluent writer who did much to popularize his subject.

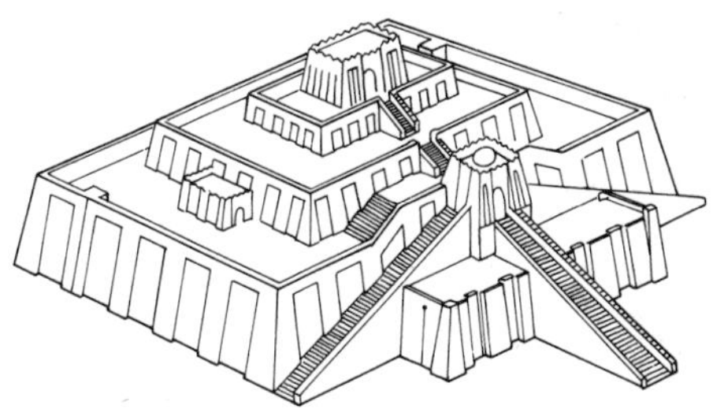

Reconstruction of the Ur ziggurrat

Ziggurrat High tower built in "stepped" stages, with a shrine at the top. The first true ziggurrats are found in the late third millennium but it is likely that they developed from the high temple terraces of late prehistoric times. Perhaps the best-known ziggurrat is the one at Babylon, the so-called Tower of Babel, described by **Herodotus**. The best-preserved one is at Ur, illustrated here.

Index

Page numbers in *italics* refer to illustrations or their captions.